Praise for Selling with Noble Purpose

"McLeod combines a wealth of field experience with unique insights to drive revenue."

Marshall Goldsmith
*#1 Leadership Thinker in the World (Thinkers50—*Harvard Business Review*)*

"If you sell based on a deep mission and purpose, revenue will follow. As Lisa Earle McLeod explains in this remarkable book, you have to start with how to change another life ... then work back from that purpose."

Tom Rath
Author of StrengthsFinder 2.0

"Lisa McLeod is the expert in sales leadership. McLeod has coached top-tier sales teams at Apple, Kimberly-Clark, and Procter & Gamble, where we both began our careers. She shows you what it takes to drive growth."

Jim Stengel
Former Chief Global Marketing Officer, Procter & Gamble
Author of Grow

"Selling with Noble Purpose is eminently practical. I strongly recommend it for any leader or salesperson. McLeod is right about the big picture and gets down to the nitty-gritty of how to make it happen."

Steve Denning
Forbes

"Follow McLeod's teaching and—not only will you be hugely more financially successful—you'll LOVE what you're doing even more!"

Bob Burg
Author of The Go-Giver *and* Endless Referrals

selling
with
noble
purpose

selling *with* noble purpose

How to
Drive Revenue *and* Do Work That Makes You Proud

Lisa Earle McLeod
with Elizabeth Lotardo

2nd Edition

WILEY

Published by John Wiley & Sons, Inc., Hoboken, New Jersey.
Published simultaneously in Canada.

For general information on our other products and services or for technical support, please contact our Customer Care Department within the United States at (800) 762-2974, outside the United States at (317) 572-3993 or fax (317) 572-4002.

Wiley publishes in a variety of print and electronic formats and by print-on-demand. Some material included with standard print versions of this book may not be included in e-books or in print-on-demand. If this book refers to media such as a CD or DVD that is not included in the version you purchased, you may download this material at http://booksupport.wiley.com. For more information about Wiley products, visit www.wiley.com.

Library of Congress Cataloging-in-Publication Data is Available.

ISBN 9781119700883 (Hardcover)
ISBN 9781119700920 (ePDF)
ISBN 9781119700890 (ePub)

Cover Design: Wiley
Author Photo Credit: Jon Rizzo Photography

Printed in the United States of America

SKY10032812_012822

For Jay Earle:
a man who believed work should
be meaningful and fun!

"If you want to build a ship, don't drum up people to collect wood and don't assign them tasks and work, but rather teach them to long for the endless immensity of the sea."

—Antoine de Saint-Exupéry

Contents

Contents

Introduction

What Is Selling with Noble Purpose?

Hearts are the strongest when they beat in response to noble ideals.
—Ralph Bunche, winner of the 1950 Nobel Peace Prize

"The words *selling* and *noble* are rarely seen together. Most people believe that money is the primary motivator for top salespeople and that doing good by the world runs a distant second. That belief is wrong."

When I first wrote those words in 2012, I had no way of knowing the first edition of *Selling with Noble Purpose* would upend traditional beliefs about sales and spur a global movement. At the time, the notion that you could galvanize a sales force around something more meaningful than money was a new, and not always welcome, idea. Thankfully, times have changed. At least in part.

We started writing this new edition of *Selling with Noble Purpose* before the COVID crisis began. By the time we were finishing this book, the weight of the crisis was upon us. Markets had become volatile, businesses were closing, and people all over the world were afraid. They were afraid for their health, afraid for their livelihood, and afraid of what the future might hold.

We are experiencing a reset like never before. Business norms are being challenged, and teams are being called upon to innovate, reinventing what they sell and how they sell on a daily basis. A growing chorus of customers are asking: Is your sales team here to help me? Or are they just trying to close me?

Here's what we know to be true: amid disruption, one thing that can keep a salesforce motivated and committed to delivering the highest results is a sense of purpose.

The teams you'll read about in this book use their purpose as a North Star to guide them during times of uncertainty and unrest. Purpose enables them to make quick decisions and to put their highest ideals into action.

Over the last five years, purpose has become a hot topic in business. Organizations proudly announce their purpose across social media. Leaders talk about their purpose during the annual meeting. Yet what the COVID crisis has revealed with stark clarity is that purpose must be more than a mantra or management technique: during disruption, purpose is a lifeline to your customers and your team.

The core idea of this book is that sales teams with a noble purpose bigger than money—whose aim is to improve life for customers—outsell transactional teams who focus on internal targets and quotas. During a crisis, the contrast between transactional sellers and noble purpose sellers is on display.

It's long been assumed that sales teams are primarily driven by economic incentives alone—when in fact, nothing could be further from the truth.

We stand in a place and time where the role of business in the world is being questioned. The pressure for short-term profit is a constant, yet there is equally forceful pressure to do right by our people and customers and make the workplace more meaningful for all. Sales is where money and meaning come together. It's time for us to harness the fierce urgency of now to transform the way we conduct business and restore nobility to the sales profession.

The Curbside Conversation Where Selling with Noble Purpose Was Born

A decade ago, I was part of a consulting team asked by a major biotech firm to conduct a six-month double-blind study of its sales force. The purpose of the study was to determine what behaviors separated top salespeople from average ones. The study revealed something no one expected: the top performers all had a far more pronounced sense of purpose than their average counterparts.

The salespeople who sold with Noble Purpose—who truly wanted to make a difference to customers—consistently outsold the salespeople who were focused on sales goals and money.

It was a startling discovery that I might have missed, had it not been for a curbside conversation at the Phoenix airport.

I was finishing a two-day ride-along with a sales rep. As she dropped me off at the airport, I asked her a question I hadn't asked the other reps: "What do you think about when you go on sales calls? What's going on in your head?"

"I don't tell this to many people," she confessed, looking around the car as though someone was going to hear her secret. "When I go on sales calls, I always think about this particular patient who came up to me one day during a call on a doctor's office.

"I was standing in the hallway, talking to one of the doctors. I was wearing my company name badge, so I stood out. All of a sudden, this elderly woman taps me on the shoulder."

"'Excuse me, Miss,' she said. 'Are you from the company that makes this drug?' pointing to a pamphlet on the counter.

"'Yes, ma'am,' I replied.

"'I just want to thank you,' she said. 'Before my doctor prescribed your drug, I barely had enough energy to leave the house. But now I can visit my grandkids; I can get down on the floor to play with them. I can travel. So thank you. You gave me back my life.'"

The sales rep told me, "I think about that woman every day. If it's 4:30 on a rainy Friday afternoon, other sales reps go home. I don't. I make the extra sales call because I know I'm not just pitching a product. I'm giving people their life back. That grandmother is my higher purpose."

Sitting in that blistering Phoenix heat, I realized she had said something incredibly important. I thought about that conversation during my entire flight back to Atlanta. I kept turning it over and over in my head.

Our consulting team had spent months shadowing salespeople all over the country. We'd conducted in-depth interviews and analyzed every aspect of the sales calls. But this was the first time anyone had opened their heart and spoken in an authentic, emotional way about what truly moved them. While others had spoken in corporate platitudes, here was a salesperson speaking the language of the soul.

Was this what spelled the difference between average performers and top performers—this seemingly esoteric construct; this thing called *purpose*?

Keep in mind: this was 10 years ago. At that time, the conversation about meaning and purpose at work was the realm of ministers and non-profits. Yet here I was in a corporate setting, and I knew I had spotted something important. I went back to the transcripts of the interviews, looking for purpose. I didn't see it at first. Then I looked closer—and there it was, in the rep who said, "My dad was a doctor. Doctors have an even harder job than most people realize. I want to make it easier for them."

It was there in the rep who was thrilled to be discussing the science, and who practically glowed when he said, "Isn't it amazing the way that we're able to do these things?" There were other reps who spoke about the impact they had on nurses and patients. Although none of these people actually used the word *purpose*, the essence was there.

At the end of the project, the client asked us to look across all the reps and identify who we thought were the top performers. It was a double-blind study, so the other consultants and I didn't know who was at the top and who was just average.

I had found five representatives who conveyed a sense of purpose in the interviews. I told the client, "I think these five are top-performing salespeople."

Every single one was correct. And the rep in Phoenix who went on sales calls thinking about the grandmother? She was the number-one salesperson in the country three years running.

Imagine the scene: a science-based firm with commercial endeavors around the globe. The leadership team is largely doctors, scientists, and MBAs. They've gathered around an impressive marble conference table to hear the results of the extensive sales study. I have now just seemingly magically identified the top sales performers without knowing any of their sales numbers. Of course, the next question is pretty obvious.

"How did you know?" they asked, looking at me as if I was some kind of wizard.

The answer I came up with left something to be desired. The best way I could describe it at the time was to say, "The top performers have a different story in their hearts." It sounded fuzzy.

It *was* fuzzy. I could tell it wasn't resonating. I (painfully) elaborated, "It's like they're being guided by something more noble." Still blank stares.

The senior leadership team was looking for something more concrete. I knew I was seeing *something*, something that went beyond the traditional business approach. It was deeper, and it was real. I remember thinking to myself, if we can bottle this, we can create magic.

That initial study revealed what larger research projects would later validate: The top performers weren't driven solely by money. They were driven by purpose.

Ironic, isn't it? The salespeople who cared about something more than just money wound up selling more than the salespeople who were focused only on quota. Years of client work and several research studies later, the findings leave no doubt: a Noble Sales Purpose (NSP) is the difference between a sales force that is merely adequate and one that's truly outstanding.

It took the better part of a decade to decode and bottle the magic I had observed in that first study. As it turns out, my initial assessment was actually accurate: the top performers *do* carry a different story in their hearts. What took a bit longer to figure out was how the story got there, what the story meant, and how to scale it across an organization.

And here's the most exciting part. While selling with Noble Purpose is innate to top performers, it is not limited to top performers. It can be activated in almost everyone. Noble Purpose is a philosophy and strategy that can scale across even the largest of organizations. The result is a differentiated sales team who show up in a much more powerful way for customers. But it's even bigger than that. Noble Purpose drives exponential business results, and it also helps us become better human beings. It connects us and advances our relationships and our society in a way that we need now more than ever.

How Noble Purpose Plays Out

Imagine two salespeople. They're both waiting in the lobby to meet with a customer. One salesperson has been told by his boss, "Your purpose is to close deals." The other salesperson believes her Noble Purpose is to improve the customer's business.

Which salesperson is going to ask better questions and uncover more customer intelligence: the seller focused on the deal, or the seller focused on the customer? Which rep is going to be more innovative and engaging: the seller focused on the single transaction, or the seller focused on improving the client's business?

Now let's put you into this scenario. Imagine you're the customer. Which salesperson would you rather have calling on you: the one sitting in the lobby thinking about his deal? Or the one sitting in the lobby thinking about helping you?

The answer is obvious. Customers would rather buy from a salesperson whose purpose is to help them than a salesperson who is only trying to close them.

Organizations have tried for decades to get sales teams to be more consultative and customer-oriented. They try sales training and they adopt customer-centric strategies, yet progress is often only incremental at best. The reason is that the cadence of daily business is still focused on internal numbers. We need look no further than the auto industry to see what happens when salespeople lack a Noble Sales Purpose.

Who would you rather do business with?

The automotive industry has powerful brands. They have innovative engineers and do extensive research to identify exactly what we might want or need in a car. Their marketing people create compelling campaigns building brand value. Dealerships tout their service. But what happens when you start talking with a salesperson? The first thing they want to find out is, "How much can you spend?"

Years of work, thousands of hours, millions of dollars building a brand, and it can all fall apart on the showroom floor if you encounter a transactional salesperson.

As anyone who has done it can attest, buying a car can be an absolutely soul-sucking experience. Most car salespeople don't care about making a difference in your life. All they care about is closing the deal—*because closing the deal is the only thing their sales manager has told them to care about.* Closing the deal is at the center of their sales training. It's what their CRM system and comp plan point them toward. And it's what their manager's boss emphasizes on a daily basis. The entire sales ecosystem is focused on the close instead of the customer.

This plays out in very obvious ways in the auto industry, but the same thing happens to teams who sell million-dollar software systems, health care equipment, banking services, and everything in between.

The internal conversation becomes the external conversation. If your internal conversation is only about targets and quotas, with little or no mention of customer impact and value, that's the way the sales team will approach customers.

Salespeople whose Noble Purpose is to *improve* the customer outperform salespeople whose purpose is to *close* the customer.

Lest you have any doubts about the power of purpose, the research tells us:

- **Organizations with a purpose bigger than money outperform their competitors.** A 10-year growth study of more than 50,000 brands around the world shows that companies who put improving people's lives at the center of all they do outperform the market by a huge margin.[1] The study, done by an independent consulting group in partnership with my colleague, former Procter & Gamble chief marketing officer (CMO) Jim Stengel, reveals that "Those who center their business on improving people's lives have a growth rate triple that of their competitors, and they outperform the market by a huge margin."

- **The economics of self-interest are not sustainable or even accurate.** The traditional business model based on the assumption that the workforce is self-interested—motivated only by money, prestige, and promotion—has proven ineffective. In their book *The Economics of Higher Purpose*, distinguished scholars Robert E. Quinn and Anjan V. Thakor cite research about employees who are "positive energizers" who are not risk-averse or effort-averse, and who are motivated by intrinsic rewards. The authors, who have extensive expertise in economics, describe purpose as a valuable "off-balance sheet resource" that can unleash these positive energizers.

- **Noble Purpose sales teams have a competitive advantage over quota-focused teams.** In our work with over 200 firms, we tracked the behavioral differences between teams with a Noble Sales Purpose and those with a conventional economic mindset. Purpose-driven sellers consistently have a better understanding of customer issues, gather more robust customer intelligence, create more client-focused presentations and proposals, get to more senior levels within client companies, and are less likely to experience pushback on pricing.

- **Salespeople with a sense of purpose put forth more effort and are more adaptable than quota-focused reps.** In her study "Understanding and Leveraging Intrinsic Motivation In Salespeople," Dr. Valerie Good from Michigan State University asserted, "A sense of purpose—the belief one is making a contribution to a cause greater and more enduring than oneself—is an important contributor to sales

---

[1] Millward Brown Optimor, "Stengel Study of Business Growth."

success. Yet one that has rarely been studied." Dr. Good was inspired to conduct her research because of her father-in-law, who sold truck wheels. He'd been a top salesperson for decades, driven by his belief that the right wheels on an 18-wheeler saves people lives.

Good's study revealed, "Intrinsic motivation—inherent enjoyment, satisfaction, and purpose—is more positively associated with increased salesperson effort and adaptability than a desire for money over time." The internal drive to make a difference that she observed in her father-in-law proved to be the underpinning behind long-term sales success.

The data is clear, and it confirms what we already know in our hearts to be true: a Noble Purpose engages people's passion in a way that spreadsheets don't.

The Changing Face of Business

Business is changing because customers and employees are changing. People are no longer willing to settle for a transactional work life—or even a transactional sale. They want more.

Making a living and making a difference are not incompatible goals. The traditional business model tends to separate money and meaning. Making money becomes the organizing element of the organization, while making a difference is relegated to an optional byproduct. Improving lives is nice; we'll try to do it if and when we make enough money.

Yet a growing body of evidence tells us this model is wrong. In fact, it's completely backward. When targets and quotas become the primary organizing element of your business, the result is mediocrity at best. Instead of making more money, you wind up making less money. Profit is crucial, of course. But it's not the best starting point for driving sales revenue.

It doesn't have to be this way. As you'll discover in this book, there's a widespread, unspoken problem in sales. It's the startling gap between what organizations want salespeople to do when they're with customers versus what most organizations really reinforce on a daily basis.

Let's be clear: wanting to make money for your family or to buy yourself nice things or build wealth is not immoral. Noble Purpose does not conflict with economic motivation; it adds another dimension. Noble Purpose unleashes a largely untapped source of motivation, and it creates an organizing framework that differentiates you from a traditional, economic incentive-based organizational mindset.

When the Business Roundtable, a group of America's most prominent CEOs, announced that the shareholder primacy model—dictating that organizations must maximize profits for shareholders above all else—was no longer working or appropriate, they gave an official voice to what many leaders were experiencing.

The traditional "shareholder primacy, profit-at-all-costs" model creates a transactional relationship, with employees and customers who (correctly) discern that numbers matter more than they do. It's not surprising that during the decades when shareholder primacy rose, employee engagement tanked. In an age of internet-forced transparency, organizations who are primarily self-focused are quickly revealed.

Yet as an increasing number of firms embrace the value of higher purpose, many organizations still struggle to bring purpose to life with their sales team.

The message from the top is, "We have a purpose." But the daily sales cadence of "close the deal" drowns out the purpose conversation. It's a costly missed opportunity.

Sales is where purpose can come alive or wither and die. As the center of a commercial model, sales can deliver outsized returns on purpose, emotionally and financially. When you activate a sense of Noble Purpose in sales, it drives engagement, innovation, differentiation, and ultimately revenue.

For the last decade, this is what I've been studying, researching, and speaking and writing about. I'll share what we've learned from implementing selling with Noble Purpose with over 200 organizations. I've had the privilege of working with teams at organizations like Google, Salesforce, Dave & Busters, and Roche, helping them enhance their culture and drive sales performance. But Noble Purpose is not just for a few sexy high-profile organizations. We've also worked with less-well-known firms who have achieved even more dramatic results.

In this book, you'll meet a concrete company whose blue-collar team is redefining an entire industry; a commercial bank that went from malaise to winning awards; and a team of travel salespeople who bring so much passion and purpose into their client interactions that customers from around the world ask them for sales calls.

These seemingly everyday companies harness the power of purpose to break sales records and become leaders in their spaces.

In this new, updated edition of *Selling with Noble Purpose*, I'll cover the dramatic changes in the business landscape and in customer and employee attitudes that have made Noble Purpose a business imperative. I'll also share:

- The direct impact of purpose on profitability (it's more than originally anticipated)
- Why so many purpose-driven organizations struggle to activate their purpose in sales, and how to overcome this challenge
- Examples of firms who experienced exponential financial payoffs from Noble Purpose, and how they did it
- Examples from firms whose purpose programs failed, and a breakdown of what went wrong
- Strategies for turning managers into belief-builders for your organization
- Why most sales ecosystems can have a chilling effect on customer engagement, and how to align your sales ecosystem toward customer impact
- Innovative training techniques for activating purpose in frontline salespeople

We've deepened our study of *Selling with Noble Purpose*, yet one thing remains the same:

When you tap into someone's desire to make a difference, you unleash a force more powerful than anything found in a traditional business model.

When you cultivate a Noble Purpose through your sales team, you create a tribe of true believers: a team who can beat even the most formidable of competitors.

It's called a Noble Sales Purpose because it is:

- **Noble:** In the service of others
- **Sales:** Based on what you sell
- **Purpose:** Your reason for being

You don't have to create world peace. Your Noble Sales Purpose can be about making your customers more successful or about improving your industry.

This book is about getting your entire sales organization aligned, empowered, and excited about making a difference to customers. When you are clear and specific about how you want to help customers, and you activate your Noble Sales Purpose across your entire sales organization, you create an unstoppable team.

A friend of mine who was burned out from two decades of working in politics once told me, "In every office, there's always a TB."

"What's a TB?" I asked her.

"A true believer," she said. "That starry-eyed optimist who still believes they can make a difference. But here's the thing all the jaded staffers don't tell you—everyone else in the office is secretly jealous of the true believer."

I've come to understand the reason everyone is jealous of the true believer: we all have a secret true believer inside us, just waiting for permission to come out.

Selling with Noble Purpose is about igniting the true believer that lurks in the heart of every salesperson. Because as much as salespeople want to make money, they also want to make a difference.

selling
with
noble
purpose

1

Sales: A Noble Profession?

In the end, it is impossible to have a great life unless it is a meaningful life. And it is very difficult to have a meaningful life without meaningful work.
— Jim Collins, author of *Good to Great*

Making a living and making a difference are not incompatible. As a leader, you can do both. You must do both.

In Part 1, you'll learn how a Noble Sales Purpose (NSP) can reframe your sales narrative to create more competitive differentiation and emotional engagement. And you'll learn why an NSP is crucial during times of uncertainty and volatility. We'll explore what an NSP is and what it's not—and why it matters to you and your sales force.

We'll look at some surprising information about why overemphasizing profit has an alarmingly negative effect on salespeople and customers and how you can reframe the profit question inside your company. You'll learn the brain science behind NSP and where it fits within the structure of your larger organization.

You'll also learn why passion, despite its high value, is not enough to sustain performance. Finally, we'll address the leadership question that changes everything, and how you can use it to jump-start your team.

If you're thinking, "We're just an average (accounting, software, landscape, furniture, fill-in-the-blank) firm. I'm not sure our work is noble," we'll tell you right now: if your customers are buying from you, then you are adding some value. You do have a Noble Purpose, and it's time for us to find it.

1

The Great Sales Disconnect

I stayed the course ... from beginning to the end, because I believed in something inside of me.

—Tina Turner, entertainer

S uppose you wrote the following goal on your office whiteboard: "I want to make as much money as possible." Now suppose your clients saw it. How would they feel? How would you feel knowing that they'd seen it? Would you be proud or embarrassed?

What if you went over your prospect list, and the only thing written next to each prospect's name was a dollar figure and a projected close date? Would your prospects be happy if they saw that? Would they want to do business with you? Probably not; it reduces them to nothing more than a number. Yet that's exactly how most organizations talk about their customers on a daily basis.

Imagine a salesperson walking into a customer's office and opening the sales call by plopping a revenue forecast down on the customer's desk announcing, "I have you projected for $50,000 this month. Give me an order now!"

That rep would be thrown out in a second. Yet that's the kind of language most organizations use when they talk about their customers internally. It's like two different worlds.

Think about the typical conversation a sales manager has with his or her sales rep. It usually goes something like this:

"When are you going to close this? How much revenue will it be? Are all the key decision-makers involved? Who's the competition? What do you need to close this deal?"

All the questions are about when and how we're going to collect revenue from the customer. These questions matter, but they aren't enough to create any kind of differentiated conversation (internally or externally).

Very few managers ask about the impact the sale will have on the customer's business or life.

We expect salespeople to focus on customers' needs and goals when they're in front of customers, but the majority of internal conversations are about the organization's own revenue quotas.

Although it's an unintended disconnect, it's a fatal one.

Unfortunately, the current sales narrative of most organizations is flawed, fatally out of sync with what really matters to salespeople and customers. Salesforce CEO Marc Benioff articulates the transactional mindset that so many sales teams used to embody, describing it this way: "If you were meeting with a customer, your singular goal was to leave the room with a signed contract—in as short a time as possible."

Benioff points out the flaw in this approach, writing in his book *Trailblazer*: "It didn't incentivize anyone to consider whether the customers on the other side of these transactions really needed the software or whether it helped them make progress on their business goals."

In a traditional sales organization, the entire ecosystem surrounding the sales team—the customer relationship management (CRM) system, weekly sales meetings, conversations with managers, recognition, and everything else that influences seller behavior—are all pointed toward targets.

It's assumed that sellers will focus on customers when they're interacting with customers. But are we surprised when they don't? Everything in the ecosystem is driving them toward thinking about nothing but their own quota.

Most organizations want to have a positive impact on their customers' lives. It makes good business sense, and it appeals to our more noble instincts.

Yet when managers are caught up inside the pressure cooker of daily business, their desire to improve the customer's life is eclipsed by quotas, quarterly numbers, and daily sales reports.

This results in salespeople who don't have any sense of a higher purpose other than "making the numbers." It sounds fine enough in theory, but customers can tell the difference between the salespeople who care about them and those who care only about their bonuses. Sales targets are important, but they don't create a compelling narrative.

The great disconnect between what we want salespeople to do when they're in the field (focus on the customer) versus what we emphasize and reinforce internally (our own targets and quotas) results in mediocre sales performance.

What Lack of Purpose Costs a Sales Force

When the customer becomes nothing more than a number to you, you become nothing more than a number to the customer—and your entire organization suffers.

When you overemphasize financial goals at the expense of how you make a difference to customers, you make it extremely difficult for your salespeople to differentiate themselves from the competition. And the problem doesn't stop there. It has a ripple effect, causing salespeople who:

- Think only about the short term
- Fail to understand the customer's environment
- Cannot connect the dots between your products and customers' goals
- Cannot gain access to senior levels within the customer

Then the problem escalates:

- Customers view you as a commodity.
- You have little or no collaboration with them.

- Customers place undue emphasis on minor problems.
- Contracts are constantly in jeopardy over small dollar amounts.
- Salespeople's default response is to lower the price.
- Sales has a negative perception in the rest of the organization.
- Top performers become mid-level performers.
- Salespeople view their fellow salespeople as the competition.
- Customer churn increases.
- Salespeople try to game the comp plan.
- Sales force morale declines.

It's not a pretty picture. When the internal conversation is all about money, the external conversation becomes all about money. And all of a sudden, that's the last thing you're making.

Companies have tried a variety of methods to solve this problem. Organizations spend millions on sales training programs teaching salespeople how to ask better questions and engage the customers. They spend even more millions on CRM systems to capture critical customer information. They host off-site retreats to create mission and vision statements. They hire expensive consultants to craft lengthy slide decks articulating their value proposition.

The results are short-lived at best. Salespeople abandon the training the minute a high-stakes deal is on the table. No one updates the customer intel in CRM. The mission and vision are put on a meaningless placard in the lobby. And the value story is reduced to a bunch of pretty slides that sound just like everyone else's.

The reason these solutions don't deliver sustained improvement is because they address only the symptoms. They don't tackle the root cause: the lack of purpose.

Peter Drucker, widely considered the most influential management thinker in the second half of the twentieth century, famously said, "Profit is not the purpose of a business but rather the test of its validity."

I'll take that a step further: **Driving revenue is not the purpose of a sales force; it's the test of its effectiveness.**

If you want to create a differentiated sales team, you have to point them toward a different target. Instead of pointing your team toward a number, which is likely what your competition is doing, point your team toward a Noble Sales Purpose (NSP).

A Noble Sales Purpose is a definitive statement about how you make a difference in the lives of your customers. It speaks to why you're in business in the first place. Used correctly, your NSP drives every decision you make and every action you take. It becomes the underpinning for all your sales activities.

For example, one of our clients provides IT services for small businesses. Their NSP is simply, "We help small businesses be more successful." It's not elaborate or sexy or poetic. Instead, it's clear and effective. It drives everything they do. Every decision, large or small, must pass through that filter: "Will this help us make small businesses more successful?" If the answer is no, they don't do it. Every new product and service they create—every sales call—is focused on how they can make their customers' small businesses more successful. You'll read more about how this team used their NSP to drive a decade worth of growth later in the book.

For now, notice how this simple statement goes beyond the standard value proposition or product description. It doesn't include "and our community" or "through our values like integrity and hard work" or anything like that. It's simple. And clear. That's why it works.

Their NSP describes the impact they aim to have on customers. It serves as the North Star for the organization.

The leadership team first began implementing their NSP in 2009, during the height of the recession. In a tough economy, when customers were cutting back on outside IT services, the NSP approach helped the company post double-digit sales growth. While other firms were descending into transactional sales to get business, they stayed true to their NSP and won clients away from competitors. As the economy improved, their NSP drove even more growth. Their reputation grew, and their customers became their best sales ambassadors.

Profits are the result of your work, not the sole purpose of your efforts.

The evidence tells us that purpose is the secret to driving more revenue. As one of my favorite purpose colleagues, Roy Spence—who has worked in the purpose space for decades—says, "Purpose is your reason for being; [it] goes beyond making money, and it almost always results in making more money than you ever thought possible."

An NSP approach can be counterintuitive for leaders schooled in a "managing to the money" style. For some, it's almost heresy. Yet the results speak for themselves.

Our client Doug Williams, the CEO of Atlantic Capital Bank, articulated it best when he said, "I've realized I need to manage to the numbers, but I need to lead to the Noble Purpose." Later in the book, you'll read about how Williams and his team used their NSP—"We fuel prosperity"—to transform their organization, grow income from continuing operations by 81%, and be voted a Best Place to Work based on anonymous employee surveys. Eighteen months after they began their Noble Purpose journey, Williams was on the cover of *American Banker Magazine* as one of the top bankers in America for his team's remarkable turnaround.

An NSP drives more revenue than financial goals alone because an NSP taps into a human instinct even more powerful than our desire for money.

Reframing the Sales Profession

As the famous saying goes, nothing happens until somebody sells something. Salespeople are linchpins; they're the ones who bring in the revenue that keeps everything else running. If you want to create a prosperous organization, you need to sell. Personally, I believe a role in sales is one of the highest callings you can have in an organization.

Unfortunately, not everyone feels this way. There are two widespread misperceptions about sales:

1. Sales is sleazy.
2. Sales is easy.

Scott Jensen, a former sales coach at Deloitte, tells a story about being a young sales manager with another company. Upon walking into an internal departmental company meeting, he heard one of the other department heads say, "Here comes the commission whore." The rest of the group laughed at the joke.

This story makes my head spin. How can an organization create differentiation and pride if they believe their sales team is only self-interested? The simple answer is, you can't. Differentiation and pride come from a deep-seated belief that your work is actually helping people. That's where you come in: your job as a leader is to build that belief across your organization.

What's Gained from Approaching Sales with Purpose

Your Noble Sales Purpose points you in a nobler and, ultimately, more profitable direction. It's the starting point for a series of changes that can dramatically improve your sales force and the bottom line.

An NSP:

- Brings the customer voice to the front and center of the conversation
- Provides an organizing framework for planning and decision-making
- Improves the quality of your existing sales training
- Helps mid-level performers set more ambitious goals
- Helps top performers stay focused on delivering value
- Differentiates your conversations with customers in a way products and specs cannot
- Acts as a reset button during times of challenge and change

This book is written for sales leaders because you set the tone for your organization. Whether you're the Chief Revenue Officer, a sales manager, an aspiring sales leader, or a CEO who wants to change the way your team approaches customers, your mindset, language, and strategy are where everything starts.

An NSP is not a tactic. It's a strategic shift in the way you approach your business. It's more than a simple sales technique; it's a sales leadership philosophy that turbocharges all other techniques. It's the missing ingredient a sales force needs to take their performance to the next level.

You gain the following from approaching sales with an NSP mindset:

- Your sales team becomes more resourceful since they're always looking for ways to help customers' businesses.
- Clients take you to the higher-level people in their organizations because they see you as a resource and not someone in it only for their own quota.
- You shorten the sales cycle. You ask more robust and second-tier questions, delving into critical customer business issues and creating urgency.
- You bring the customer's voice into your organization, which helps you create better products, services, and marketing.

- You create proposals and presentations that are more compelling and persuasive because they're organized around the client's goals, not focused on your product's or service's features and benefits.

- You don't have to "act like" you care about your customers, because you really do care.

- You love your job because you have a more noble purpose than just "selling stuff to make money."

- You're more likely to talk about your job in social situations, and when you do, people are more likely to be interested in hearing about it—since making a difference in people's lives is exciting.

- Sales coaching improves because leaders speak in depth about client situations and goals.

- You're better able to manage obstacles because you don't get defensive and take them personally. You see them for what they are: simple requests for help.

- Your NSP becomes your North Star: a way of resetting yourself during tough times.

Why Selling with Noble Purpose Becomes Self-Reinforcing

Unpack the inner drivers of most salespeople, and you'll find that money occupies a substantial part of their mental real estate. But people are complex; we have multiple motivations.

When we did a deep dive into the internal motivation of salespeople, we found the top performers do care about money. They're not complete altruistic do-gooders. Many (myself included) initially got into sales because they wanted to make good money.

But here was the notable difference. Over time, the top performers added a layer of purpose. It often developed as a result of seeing their positive impact on customers. Because they were more attuned to it, they saw it more readily; it stuck and then became self-reinforcing. It became their default.

For top performers, their internal talk track, the narrative in their heads that drives their daily behavior, is about the impact they have on customers. It doesn't matter what's going on inside their organization; their internal compass always resets back to the customer.

Mid-level performers, on the other hand, tend to mirror the prevailing organizational story, whatever that may be. If the organization emphasizes a financial carrot-and-stick mentality, that's where their brains will go. If the organization has a narrative of a higher purpose, that's where their brains will go. The organizational talk track becomes their internal talk track.

When we do deep dives with salespeople who aren't top performers, we usually find that they too have a secret desire for purpose and meaning. They simply haven't reflected on it or spoken about it because nothing in their organization prompts them to think that way. It's not their default setting.

Their potential Noble Purpose is there, but it has yet to be activated. It's like a switch in the off position that needs someone else to turn it on. This book is about flipping that switch to on.

In his book *Drive: The Surprising Secret About What Motivates Us*, Daniel Pink writes, "The science shows that the secret to high performance isn't our biological drive or our reward-and-punishment drive, but our third drive—our deep-seated desire to direct our own lives, to expand and extend our abilities, and to live a life of purpose." Pink goes on to say, "Humans, by their nature, seek purpose—a cause greater and more enduring than themselves."

The discord between what social science knows (humans crave purpose) and business does (the carrot and stick) creates a transactional relationship with both employees and customers.

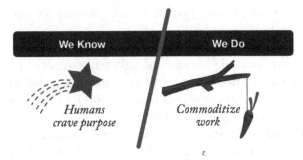

Nowhere is this dissension greater than in sales, where organizations continue to dangle incentive programs, bonuses, and trips in front of salespeople, hoping that it will motivate them. Yet time and again, the incentive programs produce short-term spikes in performance from a small percentage of people. In most organizations, the top performers remain the same year after year, while the rest of the sales force stays stuck in the mediocre middle.

What's ironic is that many organizations do make a difference to their customers, serving a larger purpose. They just don't talk about it with the salespeople.

We once worked with a security firm that was literally saving people's lives. The executive leaders made a regular practice of describing the meaningful impact their services had on customers to the tech team, the customer service group, and even the accountants.

Yet it was like they developed a sudden case of amnesia when they interacted with the sales department. All the discussions in sales meetings and coaching sessions were about quotas and revenue or product features and roll-out plans. They almost never talked about the impact the services had on actual human beings.

This was a huge mistake.

The very people who should be on fire for making the difference to the customers—the sales force—almost never heard the purpose-driven narrative. Talk about a mismatch.

Is it any wonder that their sales force struggled to maintain margins and was often treated like a commodity by their customers? If all you talk about is money and margin when you're inside the organization, it's only natural that's where things go in customer conversations.

Is it any surprise the company had high turnover in sales and their best people left for a competitor? The salespeople felt very little affiliation for their company, the leadership, or even the customers. It was never about anything but numbers, so when another company started offering the reps the promise of better numbers, they jumped at it.

Purpose drives higher sales numbers and strengthens your team's commitment to your firm and your customers. When your entire organization is focused on making a difference to customers, people are engaged more deeply. They're more likely to innovate because they know they're part of something important, something bigger than themselves.

An NSP solves the great sales disconnect. It combines making money with making a difference. It bridges the gap between internal conversation and external conversation.

What This Book Can Do For You

I want to make this extremely clear: this is not a book about marketing. This is a book about sales. Your NSP is not a tagline. It's a philosophy and methodology that leaders can use at every level of their operation to grow revenue and do work that makes everyone in the organization proud.

The strategic framework, the case studies, and the techniques you'll learn in this book are drawn from 20 years of research and the thousands of hours my colleagues and I have spent studying, coaching, training, and observing salespeople and sales managers.

In addition to observing their behavior, we've conducted in-depth interviews to uncover their mindsets, attitudes, and beliefs. We draw from our experience and the latest neuroscience and organizational research to create models and processes to activate your NSP and keep it alive in the cadence of daily business. We've spent the last decade testing and refining the NSP methodology with over 200 organizations.

We've worked with some of the best sales organizations in the world like Google, Kimberly-Clark, and Procter & Gamble, We've also implemented Noble Purpose with lots of not-so-sexy firms: people you might not be familiar with, like midsize banks, startups, entrepreneurs, franchise organizations, non-profits, healthcare teams, and a host of others. Whether you work for a global giant or a small firm that's just getting started, the ideas in this book can be applied immediately.

This book is meant to be practical. I want you and your team to be able to show up in a bigger, better, bolder way tomorrow, not next week. As such, at the end of each chapter, you'll find a quick summary box including "Do One Thing"—a single idea you can implement immediately.

As a sales leader, you have the power to change the culture around you. It may sometimes seem as though your customers, your team, your industry, and perhaps even your boss are working against you. But I promise you this: you will begin to see a shift in the people around you when you start operating from a place of purpose. It almost always happens faster than you expect.

I want to say a word here about naysayers. You're probably hearing a few of their voices in your ear right now. You know, the people who are reluctant to change. People who think this fluffy stuff is just that: too fluffy to matter. Perhaps you're one of those people yourself. If you have some of those doubting voices in your own head, or in your team, take heart. The research proves this works. But you know what else proves this works? The flicker of hope and enthusiasm you'll get when you start talking about it with your team.

I'm going to let you in on a secret: Your life is about much more than just making money. It's about the impact you have on other people. You already make a difference, and I want to help you make an even bigger difference. When you know that your job matters, you perform at a higher level and enjoy it more.

When you love your job, your whole life lights up—and so does everyone around you.

You deserve that. We all do. Are you ready to get started?

Chapter 1: The Great Sales Disconnect

Salespeople who sell with a Noble Sales Purpose (NSP), who truly want to make a difference in the lives of their customers, outsell salespeople focused on internal targets and quotas.

Transactional sellers	Noble Purpose sellers
Think short-term	Think about long-term customer impact
Fail to connect the dots between product and customers' goals	View product as an opportunity to positively impact customers' goals
Have a default response to lower the price	Sell at a high margin because they enable the customer to see the value

In traditional sales organizations, the sales ecosystem surrounding the sales team (CRM, recognition, manager interactions, etc.) points toward internal targets instead of customer impact. When targets and quotas are the primary organizing element of a business, the result is mediocrity at best. Instead of making more money, you make less.

Aligning a sales force around a Noble Sales Purpose (NSP):

- Brings the customer's voice to the front and center of the conversation

- Provides an organizing framework for planning and decision-making

- Improves the quality of your existing sales training

- Differentiates you from the competition in a way that product features cannot

- Improves emotional engagement
- Gives you a North Star during times of stress and change

When your entire organization is focused on making a difference to customers, people engage more deeply, they care more, and customers respond, and you win the market.

Do one thing: Look at the ecosystem surrounding your sellers, and ask yourself: are they pointed toward customers, or toward internal targets? Identify one area you can infuse the customer's voice into the conversation.

2

How a Noble Sales Purpose (NSP) Changes Your Brain

Great minds have purpose, others have wishes.
—Washington Irving, short-story writer

Imagine you're at a neighborhood party or standing on the sidelines of a kid's soccer game. You engage in a conversation with the person next to you, and he asks the age-old question: "What do you do for a living?"

How do you answer? You've likely been asked the question a hundred times, so you probably have a standard job description-type answer. If you're alone right now, say it out loud. If you're reading this book on a plane or in a coffee shop, just mumble your answer under your breath.

Pay attention to how you feel saying those words.

If you're like most people, you probably give a fairly rote response that doesn't require much thinking: something along the lines of, "I sell software" or "I'm regional manager for XYZ Company." If you work for an impressive firm or you have an impressive title, you may have said, "I run a sales team for Google" or "I'm the VP of Sales at Clorox." But it's usually still a pretty standard answer.

Again, remember how it feels to say those words out loud. This is your baseline.

Now, to give you an understanding of what Noble Purpose does to your mind, we're going to go a bit deeper.

I'd like you to think about a time when you made a difference to another person at work. Perhaps you helped someone on your team, did something great for a customer, or lent an ear when a colleague needed to talk. It may have happened in your current job, or it may have been in a past job. Either one is fine.

- What was the situation?
- How did you make a difference?
- What did the other person say?
- How did he or she look?
- How did you feel afterward?

Imagine yourself telling this story out loud. In fact, if you have a colleague or friend nearby, tell them your story.

Compare how you felt in the first scenario, when you described what you did for a living, with how you felt in the second scenario, where you told a story about making a difference.

What do you notice?

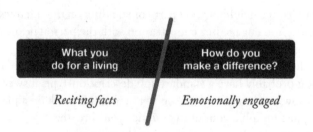

How was the second time different from the first time? Which one did you enjoy talking about more? Which one was more engaging? Which one makes you prouder? And here's the key question: which story would you rather listen to if you were on the other end?

Most people experience a pretty dramatic shift when they move from function-based conversation to a more purposeful "make a difference" conversation.

When I pose these questions in keynotes, I ask people: "Tell the person next to you what you do for a living." The room is a low-level buzz. Then, when you ask people to describe a time you made a difference to another person at work, the whole room lights up. The physical and emotional difference between the two scenarios is startling. When I ask groups to compare them, I hear things like:

> "The first time was a no-brainer, but the second time I was totally into it."

> "The first time was boring; the second time was more emotional."

> "I was on autopilot the first time, but the second time it was like I was reliving the experience again."

> "The first time I thought it; the second time I felt it."

That's a fairly accurate description of what happens to your brain. The first time—when you describe your job—you're using your brain at a very basic level, almost on autopilot. The second time, when you describe making a difference, you ignite your frontal lobe. This is the part of the brain associated with reasoning, planning, problem-solving, language, and higher-level emotions such as empathy and altruism.

Describing the meaningful impact you had on another person engages a higher-level part of your brain than when you describe your job function. Here's what I observe when people do this exercise: When people talk about what their basic job function, they:

- Smile politely
- Use rote language, such as *reseller, provider, end-to-end solutions, implement*, and so on
- Sit relatively still

And their listeners nod nicely.

When people describe making a difference, they:

- Smile with their whole faces
- Use colorful details, such as describing the look on someone's face or the setting

- Become much more animated and describe the impact they had on someone

And their listeners lean in and ask questions.

People share the two experiences—what they do for a living versus making a difference—within five minutes of each other. When you stand on the stage, watching people respond, you'd think it was a completely different day. They look like an entirely different group of people.

The first time, it's just a regular crowd of businesspeople politely speaking to one another in low voices. The second time, volume cranks up. The people get engaged. They start laughing. Some people even stand up when they tell the second story. They can't help themselves.

There's more energy and enthusiasm in the air. When you watch them the second time, you'd think they'd just won the lottery or heard some great news. And in a way, they did. By describing how they made a difference to someone, they got the best payoff a human being can have: they were reminded of just how much their life matters.

These are the kind of powerful emotions that selling with Noble Purpose can ignite.

Customer Centricity Is Not Enough

A lot of organizations prioritize customer centricity. It sounds good in theory. Let's rally our organization around customer needs. Go team! But customer centricity as it's typically implemented is missing a crucial element: impact.

Meeting the customer's needs is certainly better than ignoring your customer's needs. But it can put your team in a reactive position, one that is no different from any of your competitors. If customers are telling you their needs, they're also telling your competition. Most customer-centric strategies as they're practiced today rely on the unspoken assumption that the customer has the best and most accurate understanding of their needs. In many cases, this isn't true. As Henry Ford famously said, "If I had asked people what they wanted, they would have said faster horses."

It's not that sellers should be arrogant and ignore customers' needs. But they should have expertise that the customer does not. Exceptional sellers have insights into how customers can achieve their goals: insights customers may not have thought about.

Telling your team to simply focus on the customer could mean anything from helping the customer achieve their goals, to giving the customer a lower price. Without clarity about the impact the organization wants to have on customers, people can wind up feeling like indentured servants. Consider the difference between an organization that says, "Our goal is to meet our customer's every need," versus an organization whose stated purpose is "We improve the way our customers do business." Which organization feels more empowered? Trying to please the customer is nice, but it's hardly galvanizing, and it's rarely differentiated. When you have clarity about how you want to improve the customer, you create a more innovative organization.

Selling with Noble Purpose goes beyond pleasing customers; it's about improving customers.

When your people understand that *we are here to improve our customer's lives and businesses in ways they may not have even known were possible,* your team has a clear North Star. The customer is at the center of the business, but instead of merely reacting to customers, the team is proactive about helping customers get to an even better place.

The stakes become higher, and the role of everyone on the team becomes more important.

The Two Big Human Needs: Belonging and Significance

Once you get beyond basic needs like food and shelter, human beings have two core emotional needs: belonging and significance. We want to be connected to other people, and we want to know that what we're doing matters to someone. The need for belonging and significance transcends age, culture, sex, race, and socioeconomic status.

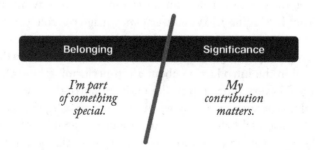

> *Our deepest desire is to make a difference in the world,*
> *and our darkest fear is that we don't.*

We don't just want to make a difference in our personal lives or through philanthropic activities. **We want to make a difference at work**. We spend the better part of our waking hours at work. Those hours ought to mean something. When you know that your job matters to people, you come alive. Your frontal lobes light up, and you have greater access to problem solving, language, and empathy.

Yet for some reason, many teams seem to operate as though some bizarre memo went out years ago saying, "Please don't bring any emotions to work." This mentality is entirely unhelpful. When was the last time you heard a CEO say, "I wish my people weren't so motivated and excited"? Any good leader knows, achieving peak performance requires emotional buy-in. The reasons people resist addressing emotion at work is because:

- **Emotions are messy and hard to understand.** When you bring in the good emotions, you're also going to have to deal with negatives. This can feel like Pandora's box; people resist opening it.
- **People aren't skilled at dealing with other people's emotions.** Even the silent, stoic boss is generating an emotional response from his or her team. It may not be acknowledged, but it's there. It feels safer to back away from other people's emotions rather than owning the role you may play in creating them.
- **We delude ourselves into believing our business decisions are logical.** One look inside any merger or acquisition will tell you that emotion plays a role in every business decision. Logic makes you think; emotion makes you act.

Ignoring the emotional element doesn't make it go away; it simply prevents you from leveraging it. When we acknowledge the role emotions play, we can learn to tap into them for good. If you want to create a highly engaged team, you can start by strengthening their emotional connection to their work.

You read in the introduction about a top-performing biotech salesperson who outsold every other rep in the entire country three years running. She achieved this because every day when she went on calls, she remembered a grandmother she had helped. Thinking about the grandmother did more than just motivate this sales rep to make extra sales calls on a rainy Friday afternoon. It ignited her frontal lobe, which made her a better problem-solver and strategic planner, more skilled with language, and more empathetic with her customers.

Is it any wonder that she was the number-one rep three years running? Her peers and competitors were likely conducting sales calls with the basic parts of their brain, going through the motions mechanically without igniting any kind of purpose in themselves or their customers.

But because the top rep was thinking about the person she had helped—the grandmother who, because of her product, could now play with her grandkids—she was leveraging both her intellect and her emotions to their fullest extent.

A Noble Sales Purpose ignites that type of higher-level thinking with everyone on your team. It serves as an organizing element for your sales force and keeps you focused on the big picture. It's your version of the grandmother.

Sellers who carry a clear picture of the impact they want to have on customers in sales calls are more powerful. They're more creative, they're higher energy, and they're more resilient in the face of setbacks. Your job as a leader is to proactively help them generate that mental picture and keep it alive on a daily basis.

An NSP answers three questions for your team:

- What impact do you and your company have on customers?
- How are you different from the competition?
- On your best day, what do you love about your job?

An NSP is not "We're going to be the number one provider of end-to-end solutions." That's your goal, but it doesn't speak to how you make a difference in clients' lives. An NSP isn't about your desired position in the market. It's about how you impact your clients today.

A 10-Degree Shift Can Change Your Direction

Imagine you're sitting in a jet parked on a runway. If you alter your direction 10 degrees north, you wind up at a totally different destination. This is how just a small shift at the start of the journey puts you on an entirely new trajectory.

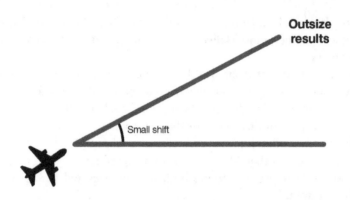

Establishing your NSP is the seemingly small shift on the runway that takes you to a more exciting destination. You may already have a clear purpose statement, or your NSP may be found inside your existing mission and vision. Or you may be starting from scratch. Whatever the case, as you read this section, notice how these organizations use their NSP as a starting point to create competitive differentiation, ignite emotional engagement, and drive revenue growth.

The following are examples of organizations driving exceptional results by using an NSP. Keep in mind as you read these examples that crafting your NSP is the start of the process.

Atlantic Capital Bank: From Transactional Banking to Fueling Prosperity

Atlantic Capital Bank (ACB) is an Atlanta-based commercial bank founded in 2007 with approximately $3 billion in assets. CEO Doug Williams and his team founded ACB to create an exceptional bank. In an industry mired in negative press, they wanted to establish themselves as honest bankers who truly care about customers. Yet after a decade of solid growth, they found themselves becoming just like other banks.

In the day-to-day drumbeat of the financial industry, it's challenging to keep the focus on client impact. With pressure to hit financial metrics, the numbers can often become the only story anyone talks about. But Williams knew a numbers-only story is a recipe for a transactional relationship with clients and becoming a commoditized brand. He wanted to differentiate.

When we interviewed teammates, managers, customers, and the executive team to uncover ACB's points of competitive differentiation, we discovered that others shared Williams' sentiment. Working with the executive team, we crafted ACB's Noble Purpose: *We fuel prosperity*.

In an industry where other banks talk about building personal wealth, ACB chose prosperity because they wanted to communicate a shared commitment to a more holistic ideal.

The executive leadership team got specific about how their purpose drives strategy. We created purpose maps articulating ACB's Noble Purpose, target customers, points of differentiation, and leading indicators of success. For every employee, the story was clear: we are the team who fuels prosperity.

The activation plan included personal messages from Williams, leadership coaching, and integrating ACB's Noble Purpose into recruiting, hiring, onboarding, marketing, and sales behavior. A critical element of the rollout was training the sales team and the sales managers. Instead of the traditional product-focused approach, the team learned how to connect with clients in a deeper, more meaningful way. ACB cofounder and Executive VP Kurt Shreiner says, "We changed the way our people think. You focus on the client and helping them achieve their dreams, versus I'm going to sell another product. Our internal and external conversations are entirely different."

In a matter of months, the culture shifted. The team became more engaged. Fueling prosperity was at the core of customer conversations, decision-making, and daily operations.

A year after launching their Noble Purpose initiative, ACB's year-over-year continued operations before-tax income increased by 81%. Williams and his team say there's a new energy in the air. Clarity about ACB's purpose enabled the executive team to make a smart divesture without belaboring the process. Backstage teams are more customer-oriented, and bankers are proactively pursuing new clients.

> Atlantic Capital Bank
> *We fuel prosperity*
> 81% increase in continued operations income
> Voted Best Place to Work

In 2019 ACB was voted a Best Place to Work in Atlanta, based on anonymous employee surveys. They were also chosen as one of the Best Banks in America by *American Banker Magazine*. As mentioned earlier, Williams was featured on the cover of *American Banker* with a story describing his team's dramatic transformation.

Supportworks: Redefining the Home Contracting Industry

Attracting and keeping top talent is a business imperative. It's even more challenging when you're hiring blue-collar workers, in the middle of Nebraska, to muck out people's basements.

Supportworks (and their sister company, Thrasher) is an Omaha-based concrete and foundation repair firm that wanted to establish competitive differentiation for their brand in a bigger, bolder way. Their products aren't sexy, but they're the best in the business. The leadership team needed to help their national network of dealers break out of the price trap that is so common in the home service industry.

In our first session, the leadership team talked about how the contracting industry had a bad reputation. When you call a contractor, you never know whether they're going to show up or not. Pricing is often sketchy. Contracting firms are also notoriously poor employers.

Supportworks wanted to change that. They wanted to redefine the home contracting industry for the better. They wanted to set a new standard for how customers are treated in the industry. We landed on their Noble Purpose: *We redefine our industry*.

Supportworks decided they were going to be the company that changed the frame for what customers expect, and the company wanted to become a destination employer in the process.

Because they sell through dealers, Supportworks couldn't mandate a top-down approach. They had to get their dealers excited about implementing the Noble Purpose with their own teams. We created a plan to help dealers link each employee's job to the greater purpose of the business, and gave them tools to establish differentiation in their markets.

Convincing a rough and tough crew of predominately male leaders to talk about purpose and praise their teams was no small task. We knew the connection between purpose and recognition had to be accessible, be easy, and not require a long speech. Supportworks created Purpose Citations: peel-off pads for managers in the field to give quick positive feedback about how employees were living their purpose. Managers could check off things like "enviable smarts" or "contagious do-goodery."

As of this writing, Supportworks' purpose training is lauded as some of the most differentiated training in the contracting world.

Supportworks has also become a destination employer. They've been voted a Best Place to Work multiple times. Employee engagement has soared. Revenue has exploded as they've added dealers across the country who want to become part of their movement. Their team will tell you, Supportworks is unstoppable.

Supportworks
  We redefine our industry
  Record dealer expansion
  Voted Best Place to Work

CMIT Solutions: From Techies to Trusted Advisors

CMIT Solutions is a franchise organization that provides managed IT services for small businesses. When CEO Jeff Connally took over the business in 2006, he began to shift the team from hourly billing to a managed services, fixed-fee model.

Most of CMIT's franchisees have a technical background. They were used to being on call and billing their time for client requests. Few of them had any sales experience.

When asked to describe themselves, they typically say, "We provide IT service." Yet our interviews with their most successful franchisees revealed that CMIT does much more than simply provide IT services. The best franchisees were advisors to their clients; advisors who alleviate and prevent some of the biggest headaches in business: system problems. Their team landed on an NSP that reflected their aspirations for their customers: *We help make small businesses more successful.*

Connally says, "When we went from 'We sell IT services' to 'We help make small businesses more successful,' it changed everything. That seemingly simple reframe pointed our team in an entirely new direction. Now our guys feel like the white knights of the IT world. They're going after new business with a zeal they never had before."

CMIT launched their Noble Purpose during the recession. Despite a tough economy where clients were cutting back on outside vendors, they grew sales by 35% the first year. Changing their focus from the services they provide to the impact they have on clients created a shift in the way their team approaches customers. Connally says, "Our people are technical, so their tendency is to jump right into the tech stuff. Now, instead of [taking that approach], we take a step back and address the situation from a business perspective."

He continues, "We pulled our NSP to the front and center of everything we do. It helped move our franchisees from simply being IT providers into a trusted advisor/partnership role."

Post-recession, CMIT held fast to their NSP, using it to drive exponential revenue growth. In a world where organizations aspire to increase earnings by 10x, CMIT's earnings have increased by a multiple of 36x. They're driving outsize earning because they're attracting and holding on to the right franchisees.

CMIT's franchise churn rate has gone from 39% when they launched their NSP to below 4%—an almost unheard-of number in the franchise world, where anything below 12% is considered very good. The team went from selling franchises to awarding them. They've now become the largest managed services provider in the mid-market space.

CMIT

We help make small businesses more successful
Earnings increased 36x
Franchise churn down 35%

G Adventures: Igniting Passion and Purpose in Resellers

Make no mistake, G Adventures *is* a sexy company (no offense, banking, basements, and IT). As the global leader in adventure travel, they take people everywhere from African safaris to cycling in Tuscany to trekking the Inca Trail. Their team is committed to changing lives through travel. The company had experienced 20% year-over-year sales growth for over two decades.

Yet as exciting as G Adventures is, they needed to translate their passion to their resellers: travel agents who book trips for their clients. The sales team knew their trips were life-changing, but the travel agents often saw G Adventures as just another vendor.

To help you understand the business model, many travelers still turn to travel agents for advice about where to go and for help with complex trips. Agents direct a large number of travel decisions and dollars. Because of this, every tour company, hotel, and travel vendor on the planet wants agents to love them. The agents themselves typically join the industry because they are passionate about travel. Yet as they progress in their careers, agents often find themselves booking dream trips for others while they sit at their desks.

The sales team at G Adventures wanted to do more than sell trips: they wanted to help their agents rediscover their own sense of purpose. They landed on their NSP: *We help people discover more passion, purpose, and happiness.*

In this case, "people" extended to agents. This required transforming the sales process. Instead of showing agents photos and videos of trips, the team created interactive sales experiences. They used everything from inspirational card decks and music to an actual magic trick to help their agents, people sitting at their desks, reconnect to the power of changing lives through travel.

The sales team even went so far as to change their job titles from account executives to Global Purpose Specialist, or GPS for short. They wanted to make it clear that their job is to help agents discover more passion, purpose, and happiness in their jobs, so they can help people discover more passion, purpose, and happiness on trips.

G Adventures' impressive year-over-year 20% sales growth has now become 35% growth. Their annual event, the Change Makers Summit—held for the agents who change the most lives—has garnered international recognition as one of the most innovative events in the industry.

G Adventures
We help people discover more passion, purpose, and happiness
20% sales growth → 35% sales growth
Industry leadership

Orange County Court: Simple Elegance

Many companies tend to try to "kitchen sink" their NSP—that is, to throw in every single thing you could possibly do for customers. It's important to fight the temptation to overdescribe; a simple statement is much more powerful.

One of my favorite examples of simple elegance comes from California's Orange County Court system. Their NSP is: *We unclog the wheels of justice.*

You might not think of a court system as having customers, but the Orange County Court believes they do. They consider the plaintiffs, the defendants, the jurors, and the lawyers all their customers. Their NSP speaks to their desire to make a difference in people's lives during times of conflict and stress. They strive to implement the principles of our country in a just, fair, and efficient way for all parties involved.

Interestingly, Orange County's NSP didn't come down from the executive team. It came from a single person. During a leadership program, the 60 top managers, divided among 8 tables, discussed how Orange County makes a difference to customers. When the teams reported back their results, one of the in-house attorneys stared at the lists on the flip charts and said, "You know what we do? We unclog the wheels of justice."

You could have heard a pin drop in that room after she said it. Sixty people sat taller in their chairs, smiling because they knew their jobs mattered. I swear that I even saw some of them start to get misty-eyed.

These words spoke to the highest aspirations of everyone in the room. That single powerful statement contained what Jim Collins refers to in his book *Good to Great* as "the quiet ping of truth like a single, clear, perfectly struck note hanging in the air in the hushed silence of a full auditorium at the end of a quiet movement of a Mozart piano concerto."

An ideal NSP is not full of bravado or bluster; it's not something you hope to do. It's something you can do right now. It's fully within your grasp, and every person in the room knows it. It doesn't require explaining or defending, because it taps into what you're already doing and what you want to do more of. Your NSP names who you are on your best day as an organization.

You Don't Have to Create World Peace

You'll notice that none of the preceding examples include discovering lifesaving new drugs or creating world peace. They come from five very different organizations in industries whose products (commercial banking, foundation repair, IT support, travel, and court services) don't always scream "Noble Purpose."

I intentionally chose these organizations to demonstrate how seemingly ordinary companies are harnessing the power of purpose. These examples demonstrate that no matter what you sell, you can always find your NSP.

If the guys at a concrete company can find their NSP, so can you.

You might also notice that when we talk about these firms, we don't use impersonal pronouns. Instead of saying "The company uses its NSP to differentiate," we say "The company uses *their* NSP to differentiate." Our words create worlds. Referring to your company as an "it" is as impersonal as referring to customers as its. The best teams don't talk about the company and the customers; they talk about *our* company and *our* customers.

Why Mission and Vision Aren't Enough

Mission and vision statements can be compelling. But more often than not, they're internally focused. In *Grow: How Ideals Power Growth and Profit at the World's Great Companies*, former Procter & Gamble (P&G) CMO Jim Stengel writes, "When you strip away the platitudes from those documents, what's left typically boils down to: 'We want our current business model to make or keep us the leader of our current pack of competitors in current and immediately foreseeable market conditions.'"

In today's more socially aware times, mission and vision have expanded to include other stakeholders. Yet many don't amount to much more than: we want to serve our customers, our employees, and our communities, make as much money as possible, and be nice people while we're doing it.

This is the *blah blah blah* formula for mediocrity.

Even the largest organizations benefit from a succinct purpose. I was a sales manager for P&G early in my career. During my tenure, I saw our stock rise and split, delivering a 199% return. But by 2000, P&G was in trouble. The company lost $85 billion in market capitalization in only six months. Jim Stengel says, "P&G's core businesses were stagnating and its people were demoralized."

Great brands weren't enough. P&G's people needed a purpose.

A.G. Lafley, then the CEO, asked Stengel to take on the role of global marketing officer to help transform the culture of the company to one wherein "the consumer is boss."

Stengel says, "To hit these big targets, we needed an even bigger goal: identifying and activating a distinctive ideal, a purpose. Improving people's lives would be the explicit goal of every business in the P&G portfolio."

Stengel writes, "A.G. Lafley and I—along with the rest of the senior management team—expected each business leader to articulate how each brand's individual identity furthered P&G's overarching mantra of improving people's lives. We also had to model the ideal ourselves. And we had to measure all our activities and people in terms of the ideals of our brands and the company as a whole. The success of that effort brought P&G's extraordinary growth from 2001 on."

Notice, each one of the brands had to clarify its alignment toward the purpose. Identifying a larger purpose put P&G back on course. The 175-year-old consumer giant remains one of the most admired companies in the world. The company's story demonstrates that no matter how big you are or how long you've been in business, you can always reclaim your Noble Purpose.

Southwest Airlines is another commonly cited example of a company founded on a Noble Purpose. Since you've already seen how Noble Purpose is being used by several less-high-profile firms, I'll use Southwest here to illustrate the difference between mission, vision, and purpose. Roy Spence, who worked with Southwest on their purpose in the early days, explains in his book, *It's Not What You Sell, It's What You Stand For*:

- **Purpose** is the difference you're trying to make.
- **Mission** is how you do it.
- **Vision** is how you see the world after you've done your purpose and mission.

He illustrates how it works at Southwest:

- **Purpose:** "Southwest Airlines is democratizing the skies."
- **Mission:** "We democratize the skies by keeping our fares low and spirits high."
- **Vision:** "I see a world in which everyone in America has the chance to go and see and do things they've never dreamed of—where everyone has the ability to fly."

Their purpose, *democratize the skies*, trumps everything. It doesn't make Southwest immune from market pressure or potential hazards in the high-stakes, high-risk game of air travel. What their purpose does do is point their team and act as a lens for decision-making. If your mission and vision are vague, or you don't have them, don't worry. The right purpose is the most important thing for pointing your team.

Spence tells a famous story from several years ago. Consultants came into Southwest and said that if they started charging for bags, they would immediately add $350 million to the bottom line. "All the other airlines are doing it," the consultants said. Southwest could make a fast profit if they did the same.

Senior leaders Dave Ridley, Gary Kelly, and others said, "No, that violates the purpose of our company," and instructed the team to "go find the money." Charging for bags wouldn't give more people the chance to fly; in fact, it would make the skies less accessible.

"But you'll make more money," said the consultants and finance team. The answer was still, "No. It doesn't serve our purpose." Ultimately, Southwest's refusal to stray from their purpose made them money instead of costing them money. Southwest launched an ad campaign called "Bags fly free." Nine months later, the financial team reported the results. By running the ad campaign and sticking to their purpose, Southwest drove $1 billion in new revenue, taking additional share from their competitors.

Your NSP keeps you focused on what matters: the customer.

Preventing Your Personal Wells Fargo

The primary purpose of an NSP is to create competitive differentiation and emotional engagement, and to give you a North Star during times of challenge and uncertainty. Having said that, an NSP can also keep you safe from costly mistakes and ethical lapses. Your NSP keeps your team from going down a rabbit hole of unethical behavior simply to hit their numbers.

The *Harvard Business Review* 2019 issue's lead article, "Are Metrics Undermining Your Business?," describes a problem the authors refer to as *strategy surrogation*. Surrogation occurs when the metric of a strategy replaces the strategy itself.

Using Well Fargo to illustrate, authors Michael Harris and Bill Taylor describe how employees at Wells Fargo opened 3.5 million deposit and credit card accounts without customers' consent in an effort to implement its now-famous cross-selling strategy. CEO John Stumpf frequently told his team, and the press, *cross-selling is the centerpiece of Wells Fargo's strategy.*

To be fair, sometimes Stumpf added that cross-selling was the result of serving customers well. But Wells Fargo didn't spotlight daily measurements of how well they served customers. Instead, they measured and rewarded cross-selling. In effect, the metric became the strategy. And we all know how that turned out.

The HBR piece says, "The costs from that debacle were enormous and the bank has yet to see the end of the financial carnage. In addition to paying fines ($85 million) reimbursing customers for fees ($6.1 million) and eventually settling a class action lawsuit to cover damages as far back as 2002 ($142 million)." The authors note, "Wells Fargo faces strong headwinds in attracting new customers." The reputational damage will follow the company for at least a decade, and probably closer to a generation.

Surrogation: When the Metric of the Strategy Takes the Place of the Strategy

While Wells Fargo may be the current poster child for bad behavior, they're hardly the first firm to focus on the metric instead of the strategy or to look inward, at objectives, versus outward, at customer impact. That's why you want to make your NSP—the impact you have on clients—as clear and present as you do your sales targets.

Surrogation occurs in even the most well-intentioned organizations because client impact is harder to codify than sales numbers. Leadership authentically proclaims, "We want to be customer-driven." But when they try to find a way to measure the success of their strategy, it's easier to double down on a single indicator, like cross-selling.

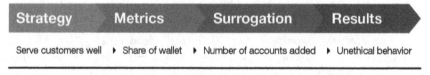

Strategy	Metrics	Surrogation	Results
Serve customers well ▸	Share of wallet ▸	Number of accounts added ▸	Unethical behavior

How to erode customer trust and destroy your brand

Organizations driven by a Noble Purpose measure cross-selling and other typical revenue-driven metrics. But they use a multitude of additional metrics. They assess leading indicators—which tend to be more qualitative—rather than relying solely on sales numbers, which are more quantitative lagging indicators.

For example, Atlantic Capital Bank, which you read about earlier, measures the number of referrals they get from clients. Rich Oglesby, President of the Atlanta division, says, "It's an imperfect number, but it tells us how well we're delivering on our Noble Purpose—we fuel prosperity." The team does not get individual bonuses on the number, so there's no incentive to cheat or say you got a referral when you didn't or steal someone else's referrals. Instead, the team tracks referrals and celebrates them as a metric of how they're performing in live time as a team.

Revenue is a lagging indicator: it tells you how well you did in the past. Client referrals are a more leading indicator. They tell you what clients are experiencing with your organization right now. When they love doing business with you, your clients become your best ambassadors. Part of a purpose-driven strategy is to identify the leading indicators that tell you how you're doing with clients today. These vary by industry and organization. Once you're clear about your NSP—the impact you want to have on customers—it's easier to find the metrics that will measure your progress.

Business is a series of qualitative behaviors and beliefs that produce quantitative results.

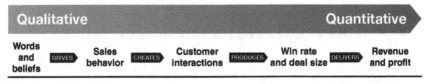

Leading indicators   *Lagging indicators*

The leadership opportunity is at the *beginning* of the process to shape the language and beliefs of the organization. Those are 100% within leadership's control. If you focus on the lagging quantitative indicators, the team will scurry around to hit them, but often at the expense of customer trust. As Doug Williams of ACB said earlier, while you may *manage* the back-end numbers, you want to *lead* to the purpose, which is more qualitative.

Imagine if Wells Fargo had a NSP similar to Atlantic Capital Bank's. Picture their CEO telling the team, "Our purpose is fueling prosperity for our clients and our communities." Envision a division leader saying, "If you're a banker, our purpose should be your North Star. All of our products should be designed with client prosperity in mind. When you speak with clients, find out what prosperity means to them, and then use our solutions to help them get there."

If Wells Fargo leadership had articulated a Noble Purpose like that, and they had cascaded down through management, it's unlikely the company would have experienced the widespread problems it did. If an individual banker did create fake accounts, their colleagues probably would have reported it, because it was out of alignment with the stated organizational purpose.

John Stumpf initially claimed the Wells Fargo employees creating fake accounts were outliers. He tried to lay the blame on a few overly aggressive managers. But it didn't ring true. It didn't ring true for the market, or employees, or customers. Stumpf's much-repeated directives about cross-selling and his reputation for pressuring sales teams made it obvious that he may not have committed the crime, but his language and strategy laid the foundation for it to occur.

Your Noble Purpose decreases the likelihood of unethical behavior and increases the likelihood of employees stopping it if they see it happening.

How NSP Drives Shareholder Value

Picture two firms in the software space. One is the leader in the employment market. The other is a software company that serves schools, foundations, and non-profits.

The firm in the talent space was founded for the purpose of helping people find great jobs. They've driven exponential sales growth for over 20 years. They're a top-performing tech stock, and their client engagement is high. Their new CEO has big plans to take the firm to an even higher level.

The other firm, which helps non-profits connect with donors and improve contributions, is also the leader in their space. But unlike the first firm, they're not growing. Several of their flagship products have stagnated, and their team is having trouble differentiating themselves. Top performers are leaving, and morale in the sales team is low. This company also has a new CEO, who they hope will reinvigorate the team.

Which company do you think is most likely to improve stock price? The organization with highly engaged clients, who is clear about their purpose? Or the organization with lagging products and low engagement?

Both of these firms actually exist. The first firm is Monster.com, based in Boston. In the early 2000s, Monster was the top-performing tech stock of the year and the market leader in the employment space. Monster was founded on the belief that everyone deserves a great job. The team was on fire to help people find better jobs. Then, after several years of stellar growth, the original founder and several of the early days' employees went on to new ventures. The new CEO, Sal Iannuzzi, arrived in 2007, and his challenge was to take the business to the next level. When you track the language in their public town halls and Iannuzzi's earnings calls, you can see a clear change.

The leadership team stopped talking about helping people find better jobs. Instead, their focus was on scaling and driving stock price. They went from a business focused on customer success to a business focused on itself. With no conversations about clients, innovation failed, and clients disengaged. After years of being the industry leader, Monster lost their mojo. Their revenue fell, earnings declined, the stock price tanked, the CEO was fired, and a company once worth billions was sold for pennies on the dollar. Ouch.

The other firm is Blackbaud, based in Charleston, SC. In 2014, when their products and stock price were lagging, they brought in Mike Gianoni as their new CEO. Gianoni came out of the financial services industry; he understood the product challenges and the business financials. But instead of focusing exclusively on the numbers, Gianoni did something different. He focused on the impact Blackbaud had on customers, who were schools, non-profits, and foundations. He says, "When I first started at Blackbaud leaders would stand on stage and in a 1-hour meeting they would spend 45 minutes on financials." Gianoni flipped the model. He now spends only 5 minutes on financials. His new format is "What's our purpose, how does our work impact clients, are we being effective in serving them, and are we doing OK financially?"

President and General Manager of Blackbaud's Nonprofit Division Patrick Hodges says, "Most software companies want mercenaries, people who will just sell the heck out of your stuff. Instead, we continue to pull on our Noble Purpose." The Blackbaud sales teams were trained to bring their purpose to the center of their sales efforts, and when they did, it was like unleashing the power of a thousand suns. Hodges, who was the VP of Sales for General Markets at the time, led the charge to amplify the purpose.

Since embracing their Noble Purpose in 2014, Blackbaud's customer base has grown 55%; recurring revenue has more than doubled and now comprises 90% of total revenues; the addressable market has increased by over $4 billion through acquisition and organic product builds; and the company has risen to one of the top 30 largest cloud software companies in the world. As of this writing, Blackbaud's stock price has more than doubled. Blackbaud was voted a best place to work. Gianoni was named one of the top 50 SaaS CEOs and named to *Forbes'* 2019 list of America's Most Innovative CEOs.

People often wonder if a concept like Noble Purpose can drive value in a quarterly capitalism-driven stock market. The previous two stories demonstrate that not only does it drive value (Blackbaud), but the absence of a Noble Purpose also erodes value (Monster).

These two stories are not isolated incidences. They're a side-by-side comparison of what happens when leadership focuses on the money story versus the meaning story.

Noble Purpose is hardly the only thing Blackbaud got right. They adjusted their business model, they created new products, they hired the right people, and they made hundreds of decisions that drove their success. Their Noble Purpose served as a lens for making those decisions and became the force multiplier that propelled the company forward.

Shareholders vs. Stakeholders

Shareholders are not stakeholders. It's crucial that every leadership team recognize this. Shareholders don't make sales calls; they're not required to go the extra mile, and they don't interact with customers. Shareholders invest because they expect a return on their money. Passion is not a requirement for shareholders; it's a *must* for stakeholders. The stakeholders are the employees responsible for delivering shareholder value.

A strong NSP doesn't distract you from delivering shareholder value. In fact, as you saw with Blackbaud and other firms we discussed, it enables you to do an even better job of it.

Beyond the obvious financial benefits, having a purpose gives more meaning to your job, which, in turn, gives more meaning to your life. When you have a purpose that matters, you become more effective and productive on every level.

Selling with Noble Purpose makes you money. It also makes you happier.

Chapter 2: How a Noble Sales Purpose (NSP) Changes Your Brain

Selling with Noble Purpose goes beyond pleasing customers; it's about improving customers. Customer centricity, as it is traditionally practiced, often puts employees in a reactive role. You want a team that is proactive about customer impact.

To fully engage your team, you must address the two big human needs:

- *Belonging*: We want to be part of something bigger than ourselves.
- *Significance*: We want to know our work makes a difference.

Sellers who go into sales calls with a clear picture of the impact they want to have on customers are more powerful and more emotionally engaged.

An NSP answers three questions for your team:

- What impact do you and your company have on customers?
- How are you different from the competition?
- On your best day, what do you love about your job?

Noble Purpose is available to everyone, including companies like foundation repair, IT support, financial services, and travel.

A Noble Purpose is no guarantee you'll create a top-performing, differentiated, all-in, do-the-right-thing organization, but it's very difficult to create that kind of organization without one.

Do one thing: Ask yourself and your team, "When did I (we) make a difference to a customer?" Notice how you feel. Sharing these stories is how you start reframing the sales narrative of your organization.

CHAPTER

3

Why Profit Is Not a Purpose

To have no set purpose in one's life is the harlotry of the will.
—Stephen MacKenna, journalist, linguist, and writer

In 2007, Volkswagen's new CEO, Martin Winterkorn, embarked on the *Strategie 2018* with the stated goal to bypass General Motors and Toyota by the year 2018. He succeeded. Sort of.

Volkswagen passed Toyota in sales in 2015 to become the world's largest automaker three years ahead of Winterkorn's target. The year 2015 was also when Winterkorn was forced to resign after it was revealed that his team programmed millions of vehicles to provide false readings during emissions testing.

Yikes.

Headlines chronicling bad behavior abound. From Purdue Pharma and Theranos misleading patients to Goldman Sachs calling their clients Muppets on internal e-mails, corporate scandals are not new. During the COVID crisis, it was quickly apparent which firms prioritized their employees and customers, and which firms took a more transactional approach, prioritizing their profit above all else.

In Chapter 2, you read about the high cost of Wells Fargo's ethical issues. It would be easy to paint the employees of Wells Fargo and the other transactional firms with the broad brush of greed and self-interest. I'm going to take a counter-stance and suggest that the majority of these firms are staffed with well-intentioned people who are simply trying to provide for their families and do their jobs to the best of their abilities. Their leadership pointed them in the wrong direction. When your North Star is earnings, you align your entire organization around what we now know is an ineffective model. Employees follow accordingly.

Why Leaders (Unintentionally) Overemphasize Profit

When leaders believe their sole purpose is to produce profit, it creates a cascading system that dehumanizes customers. Instead of seeing customers and employees as individual people who deserve help and respect, these real humans begin to be viewed as anonymous targets whose sole purpose is to help the company make money. They become "its."

The way leaders talk about customers matters.

When you describe customers as "its," people become numb to the impact their work has on real live human beings.

When you unpack each one of these high-profile scandals, you can see multiple instances where the language used to talk about customers eroded any affinity the team may have had for helping them.

Good leaders don't make a practice of using disparaging names for customers, but talking about customers as anonymous targets and prospects, while perhaps not intentionally malicious, isn't much better in terms of results.

When leaders talk about customers solely as a means to achieve their own goals, it radiates out to every single person in the organization. That kind of language creates a culture that says, "We don't exist to do something for our customers; customers exist to do something for us." People no longer care about helping customers; they just want to make money off of them. And it's only a matter of time before the customers start to feel it. It creates a coarse transactional culture, where both employees and customers alike feel less valuable.

Being intentional about the way you discuss customers changes the conversation. Once you start doing that, it becomes increasingly obvious that most traditional organizations are built on a flawed model. The majority of organizational language and decision-making is rooted in an implicit model that puts profit at the center. In extreme examples, this can cause ethical lapses. For some organizations, putting profit at the center of the model doesn't create immoral behavior. But it doesn't create differentiation, either. In a Noble Purpose organization, you reorient the strategic center.

The 6 Ps: Putting Profit into Perspective

Effective organizations set objectives for themselves in five key areas:

- *Profit*: Financial goals and measurements
- *Process*: Internal productivity standards and measures
- *Products*: Innovation and product development goals
- *Promotion*: Sales, marketing, and public relations goals and strategy
- *People*: Employee development metrics and goals

To be successful, a business should measure all five areas.

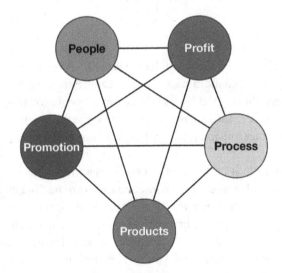

There's a natural tension between the circles. Profit goals affect the goals for processes, products, people, and promotion. Product goals affect profit, process, people, and promotion, and so forth. They're all interconnected. When one pulls, the others feel a tug. The challenge is managing the natural tension between the five areas. The public debacles at Wells Fargo and other companies reveals what happens when you overemphasize profit: it pulls all the other areas out of whack. Overemphasizing profit puts people, products, promotion, and process goals at risk.

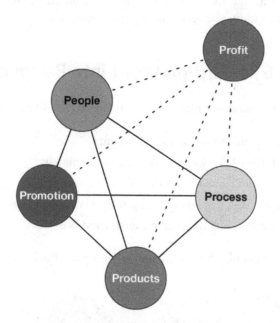

A strong NSP solves this problem because it serves as the central hub. In the following figure, client impact becomes the strategic organizing principle of your business. Putting the NSP at the center prevents you from focusing too heavily on one area at the expense of the others. Everything is viewed through the lens of customer impact. Instead of each area standing alone, each supports your NSP.

Without an NSP at the center, people treat individual or departmental goals as their end game. The consequences can be disastrous. Viewing the other functions through the lens of profit alone limits your thinking. Concentrating solely on profit removes your focus from the customer, it stifles innovation, and distorts the entire system. Instead, think of profit as a measurement of how well you're performing against your NSP. It's critical, which is why it's one of the key areas where you set goals and targets. However, it's not the center.

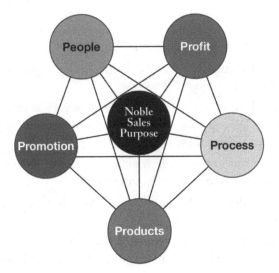

How NSP Drives Innovation

When you overemphasize profit, you limit yourself to questions such as these:

- How can we make our processes faster and cheaper?
- Which products are the most profitable? How can we make them more profitable?
- How much do our people cost? How can we generate more revenue with fewer people? How can we get each person to generate more revenue?
- What's our promotion expense? How much does our sales and marketing cost? How can we cut them? How can we get sales to produce more revenue?
- How can we make our process leaner and more profitable? How can we get them to reduce expenses?

These are not bad questions. However, they don't prompt the kind of innovative, customer-oriented mindset you need to differentiate your sales force or give you a competitive advantage.

Having an NSP at the center drives you to be more innovative by asking these types of questions:

- How do our processes affect our customers? How might we improve our processes to benefit our customers?
- What are our customers' goals? What kinds of products would help them achieve those goals?
- What problems do our customers encounter? How can we help them solve these? What products, services, delivery systems, or programs can we create to address these issues?
- How can our promotions reach more customers? How could we tailor our promotions to better serve our customers?
- How is our sales force helping our customers be more successful? How can they get better at that?
- Are some customers more profitable than others? Why is that? Are we serving them better? If so, how can we duplicate that with other customers?
- Why are some customers less profitable? Are we doing too much or too little for those customers?

The first set of questions—those centered on profit—is internally focused. These questions ask about your business: "How can we make more profit off what we're already doing now?" They view the other four Ps through the lens of profit alone.

The second set of questions—the NSP questions—is about improving the customer's condition. These questions ask how we can become more effective in each of these five areas so that we can better activate our NSP.

Profit questions have a narrow internal focus; NSP questions open the door to a bigger, more customer-driven conversation.

Consider the well-known story of manufacturing conglomerate 3M. 3M's purpose is to solve problems. In fact, one of the company's engineers was so determined to solve a customer's problem that he invented a new form of tape, which he later developed into Scotch Tape. Another engineer who was having trouble finding his place in his hymnal solved that problem by inventing Post-it Notes.

It's doubtful that either of these highly profitable products would have come to market if 3M's purpose had been profit alone. 3M's clearly stated purpose—"solve problems"—prompts their people to start asking different questions and looking in different places for answers.

3M leverages purpose in recruiting. The company's site tells potentiation candidates, "At 3M, our 93,000 employees do work that matters, applying our science in ways that make a positive impact on people's lives around the globe." If you're a young person embarking on your career or an older person looking for a change, 3M's call to action sounds a lot more exciting than "come join our team of metric-focused clock punchers."

The 6 P model is powerful when applied to sales. Sales leaders who put NSP at the center of their sales organization create a team constantly looking for new ways to add value for customers. They discover new opportunities. They find gaps that the competitors aren't meeting. They identify new pockets of business.

Financial goals rarely touch the human heart or move the human spirit. Use the NSP questions in your next leadership meeting to start a new dialogue. You don't have to ask them all at once; just pick two or three as a jumping-off point. If you're a salesperson, ask them of yourself or your peers.

You may not have control over the products your company creates, but asking these questions about your own customers will ignite a different line of thinking that will compel you to come up with innovative ideas.

NSP doesn't keep you from having the profit conversation; it adds additional high-gain elements to the mix.

Numbers Provide False Certainty

An overemphasis on profit is our default model largely because it's how most people are trained to assess business. When you look at a P&L or revenue report, the numbers are self-evident. They're concrete and easy to understand. Cut expense here, add more revenue there, tweak this, move that, and voilà—the profit number at the bottom changes.

Human beings love certainty. A numbers conversation focuses on what's easy to see. An NSP conversation is more abstract: it's less cut-and-dried. It's more qualitative. It tends to go around in a few circles before you land on a solution. Many people are uncomfortable wading outside the sea of numbers, and this is exactly why you need to do it.

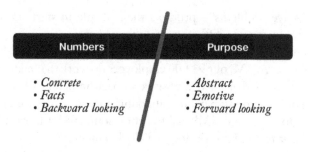

Sales isn't just about numbers. It's about real live human beings. It's about customers, salespeople, and everyone who surrounds them. The way they think and feel about one another will determine your organization's success or failure. Good leaders do more than assess and measure yesterday's numbers. They look forward toward the ideas and behaviors that will drive tomorrow's numbers.

Focusing too intently on short-term profit is the most common reason organizations lose their sense of purpose. But it's hardly the only one. Overemphasizing other areas such as process improvement, promotions, or even misplaced energy on products and people can cause an organization to lose sight of its NSP. Purpose may seem conceptual or fuzzy when compared with easier-to-measure things like shareholder value, turnaround time, and cost per unit. That's why you, as the sales leader, need to be proactive about bringing your NSP to the front of every discussion.

When your sales force knows that making a difference to the customers is their primary purpose, you begin to imagine an innovative, passionate, and profitable business environment—and then bring it to life.

Chapter 3: Why Profit Is Not a Purpose

Organizations default to financial metrics because they're concrete and easy to understand. But these lagging indicators will not drive innovation, creativity, or customer loyalty. Overemphasis on financial goals puts everything else in the organization at risk, particularly your relationship with customers.

Putting your NSP at the center points everything and everyone in your organization toward customer impact.

Financial goals do not touch the human heart or move the human spirit. We gravitate to these backward-looking, seemingly concrete metrics because we crave certainty.

A sales team that internalizes their NSP has the moral fortitude to sit with the uncertainty required for creativity and innovation.

If you want to create a tribe of true believers, put your NSP at the center of your model.

Do one thing: Use the 6 P model to frame the discussion at your next meeting.

4

Where Passion Falls Short

Purpose is the reason for your journey; passion is the fire that lights the way.
—Unknown

The words *passion* and *purpose* are often used somewhat interchangeably. I've used both in this book. Now it's time to do a deeper dive. Passion and purpose are actually two distinctly different things. And one is significantly more effective than the other for driving revenue and engagement.

Let's start by clarifying the differences. Passion is when you feel excited about your work. Purpose is when you believe your work is contributing to others.

Is his groundbreaking five-year study of more than 5,000 employees and managers, Berkeley Professor Morten Hansen explored the distinction between passion and purpose to determine which has a greater impact on job performance.

In his book *Great at Work: How Top Performers Do Less, Work Better, and Achieve More*, Hansen reveals the links between passion, purpose, and performance. In Hansen's study, people who were low on both passion and purpose were in the bottom 10% of performers. It's hardly surprising. When you're not excited about your job and you don't feel it has any meaning, you're not likely to be an overachiever. It's also not surprising to discover that people who had both passion and purpose, those who were excited about their job and felt it had meaning, were in the top 80th percentile of performers.

Here's where things get interesting. What do you think happens when you isolate the two elements? It might surprise you to learn:

- Employees who were passionate—who expressed excitement about their jobs—were still poor performers if they lacked purpose.
- Employees who did not feel passion, yet had a strong sense of purpose, were much better performers, scoring in the 64th percentile of performers.

The lesson here is clear: purpose beats passion. This is great news for leaders. Here's why: passion is personal—it's about you, and what excites and pleases you. Purpose, on the other hand, is the impact you have on others; it's more likely to be shared.

The Power of Being Steadfast

Think about someone you know who is passionate about something (perhaps it's you). How do they describe their passion? When most people describe their passion, they look inward and think about the impact their passion has on them. But passions can be fleeting. Anyone who has ever been passionate about something—be it writing a novel, remodeling a home, or even being a parent—knows passion does not always hold up in the face of setbacks. It waxes and wanes.

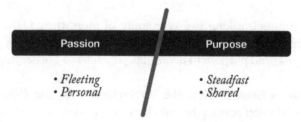

A sense of purpose is more steadfast; it stems from a belief that your work or cause matters to others. Purpose looks outward; you think about the impact you have on someone besides yourself. When people are counting on you, you're more likely to stick with it when things get tough. Passion is dependent on your energy level and circumstances. The pull of a purpose is as strong on the easy days as it on the hard days.

If you've ever had the challenge of managing a low-energy, low-excitement salesperson, you've probably experienced moments when you wanted to shake some passion into them. (I can't be the only one who has had this thought.) It's frustrating when people aren't as excited as you are.

You'll get a bigger payoff by pointing your team to a purpose. As Chip and Dan Heath write in their book *The Power of Moments*, "Passion is individualistic. It can energize us, but it can also isolate us because my passion isn't yours. But in contrast, purpose is something people can share. It can knit groups together."

A customer-driven purpose gives your team the fortitude to deal with the inevitable setbacks and rejection inherent in sales. A team that is passionate about your product will give a great pitch *the first time*. A team with clarity about the impact your product has on customers—the team's Noble Sales Purpose—will tailor their pitch to the customers and be more tenacious about working through the five layers of influencers required to make a big sale.

They will also be more willing to tackle the mundane aspects of the job, like updating the CRM and doing customer research. Knowing your work matters fuels you on the days when passion wanes.

Wharton business school professor Adam Grant's now-famous study of call center workers illustrates the financial impact of infusing your team with purpose. Grant studied paid employees at a public university's call center whose job was to phone potential donors and ask for money. As you might imagine, it's not a fun job. The employees don't get paid much and suffer frequent rejections from people unhappy about getting calls during dinner. It's hardly the kind of work that inspires passion. Turnover is high, and morale is often low.

In the 2007 study, Grant and a team of researchers—Elizabeth Campbell, Grace Chen, David Lapedis, and Keenan Cottone from the University of Michigan—arranged for one group of call center workers to interact with a scholarship student who benefited from their fundraising efforts. It was a quick five-minute conversation where call center workers were able to ask about the student's studies. But it had a huge impact on the team's sense of purpose. Over the course of the next month, callers who had met with a student spent more than two times as long on the phone and reeled in a donation average of $503, a 170% increase compared to the previous average of $186.

Put a few 000s on those numbers and apply them to your sales team. Managers often focus on trying to improve results by focusing on individual motivation. Yet these studies reveal that illustrating collective purpose and the impact of the work is easier to implement and produces better results.

Which begs the question: if Noble Purpose is so powerful, why aren't more organizations using it?

The short answer is fear. Fear of failure, fear of looking stupid for doing something different, fear your team won't buy in, but mostly, fear that it won't work.

In their book *The Economics of Higher Purpose*, Robert E. Quinn and Anjan V. Thakor describe why many organizations do not pursue higher purpose:

- Lack of belief and personal doubt. Leaders think their workforce is self-interested and will not respond.

- The tyranny of the here and now. Leaders don't think they have the luxury of time to pursue purpose.

- What will my financiers think? Leaders worry about what their board, creditors, and shareholders will think of pursuing high ideals when quarterly earnings are on the table.

Noble Purpose requires a level of transparency and vulnerability that makes many people uncomfortable. Researcher and author Dr. Brené Brown introduced the world to the power of vulnerability, describing it as "uncertainty, risk, and emotional exposure."

Noble Purpose calls upon leaders to be willing to step into a place of vulnerability. Brown's work resonates deeply with leaders because of the truths she exposes. Dr. Brown says, "Vulnerability is the absolute heartbeat of innovation and creativity. There can be zero innovation without vulnerability."

If all this is making your head spin, take heart: it can be challenging to move beyond the traditional models most of us were trained in. But the payoff is huge. When you set the stage with a Noble Purpose, you attract more high performers. Your business takes on a new importance. When your people believe they're part of something bigger than themselves, they're more willing to step into what previously felt uncomfortable.

Managers Are the Front Line Belief-Builders

When I first became a sales manager, I received a briefcase and a sales target. I was lucky because I also got a good bit of leadership training. But there's one thing no one talked to me about: belief.

Belief is central to creating a high-performance organization, and it's actually the reason we exist as a species. In his breakthrough book *Sapiens: A Brief History of Humankind*, historian and philosopher Yuval Noah Harari documents why homo sapiens beat out other species, many of which were physically stronger and more adept. He writes, "Homo sapiens rules the world because it is the only animal that can believe in things that exist purely in its own imagination, such as gods, states, money and human rights."

Shared belief is a more powerful force than brute strength. Shared belief in a purpose enables you to harness the energy of hundreds, thousands, even millions of people, all pointing in the same direction and working toward the same goal. Harari says, "Seventy thousand years ago, there were at least six different human species on earth. They were insignificant animals, whose ecological impact was less than that of fireflies or jellyfish. Today, there is only one human species left: Us. Homo sapiens. But we rule this planet."

Our ancestors won the evolutionary contest because of what Harari refers to as "the cognitive revolution," the moment in time when Homo sapiens prefrontal cortex advanced enough to go beyond communicating information and also create imagined worlds.

Harari explains it using a simple example. Imagine you're a part of a tribe whose brains can only communicate information. Your brain is advanced enough to tell your tribe, "The waterfall is over there; go there if you need fresh water. The pack of lions is over there; don't go that way." The smartest among you can even figure out how to deceive an enemy. You can tell your rivals that the waterfall is this way, when in fact you're leading them into a den of lions. You'll triumph over the tribes that don't have accurate information. But your brain capacity is only developed enough to communicate tangible facts.

Now imagine your brain grows, and you can communicate belief. You can create a shared story. You tell your team, "We're the Lion Tribe. We fight like lions. We roar like lions. We run like lions." Now your team knows how to behave in any situation: no matter what is happening in the moment, their belief and understanding of what it means to be a member of the Lion Tribe drives their behavior.

Shared belief is scalable; telling your team where the waterfall lies is not.

So what does this have to do with you and your business?

Harari points out, "A critical threshold in human organisations falls somewhere around the magic number of 150 human beings. Below this threshold you can maintain yourself based mainly on intimate relationships. Once the threshold of 150 individuals is crossed things can no longer work that way. You cannot run a division with thousands of soldiers the same way you run a platoon."

A group connected by shared belief can grow, fast. When members of the Lion Tribe encounter an opportunity or enemy, their shared belief provides a framework for how to respond. Other things being equal, a tribe with shared belief will outperform a tribe without shared belief. I'll go a step further to say history is filled with examples of young upstarts with shared beliefs who beat out more powerful, well-resourced teams.

Organizations that focus on behavior without building shared beliefs often find the behaviors don't stick. It's impossible to create a rule for every single situation. Without a clear shared belief about what you stand for and what your 'tribe" is trying to accomplish, behavior guidelines become meaningless lists. It's worth noting that during the COVID crisis, organizations who had built shared belief about who they are and why their work matters were able to act more quickly, more generously, and with more confidence than teams whose only belief was in their financial results.

Belief ▶ **Behavior**

Noble Purpose organizations build belief in their cause by being clear about the good they do for their customers every single day. Your NSP becomes the connective tissue that binds your organization.

You read in the introduction about the research from Dr. Valerie Good of Michigan State University, which revealed that the belief that one is making a contribution to a cause greater and more enduring than oneself is more positively associated with increased salesperson effort and adaptability than a desire for money over time. Dr. Good also observed how belief impacted her students when they entered the job market. She invites past students who are out working to come back and speak to her sales class. Dr. Good noticed that while some students were enthusiastic about their jobs and organizations, talking about the company, the benefits, and what they were learning, others were excited about the impact they were having on customers. Over time, Dr. Good noticed, the young professionals who believed they were helping customers with something important consistently reported being top salespeople, despite being relatively new in their jobs. Past students who emphasized how great their company was were more likely to be in the middle.

These "true believers" mirrored the deep belief Dr. Good observed in her father-in-law years earlier when he explained to her the importance of truck wheels. He said, "Every morning I go into my home office and get right on the phone because I know how important my sales are not just to my buyers but to society. When tractor trailers travel at high rates of speed and hit a pothole, for example, an inferior wheel will bend and even crack, causing the truck driver to lose control ... and people in the other vehicles they collide with don't walk away from those types of accidents. I work hard because I know that moms and dads are returning safely home to their families when I make sales."

His belief was so strong that he outsold his company's manufacturing capabilities. They literally could not make enough wheels to keep up with his sales. The company wound up bringing him in as a partner to expand manufacturing, and the business grew exponentially.

If you want to scale, build belief.

It's worth remembering: the story of America began in people's collective belief before it became real, as did the civil rights movement, the dream of space travel, and the idea of purpose in business. Each of these movements started and grew based on a shared belief that something new was possible.

As a leader, your Noble Purpose gives you a language and framework for creating powerful shared beliefs with your team: beliefs that will translate to customers.

Chapter 4: Where Passion Falls Short

Passion is nice, but purpose drives better results. Purpose is essential for scaling belief.

(continued)

(continued)

Passion is personal: it's about what excites you and what pleases you. It can be fleeting and does not always hold up in the face of setbacks. It waxes and wanes.

Purpose is steadfast: it stems from a belief that your work or cause matters to others. When people are counting on you, you're more likely to stick with it when things get tough.

Managers are the front-line belief builders for purpose. A leader's job is to cascade meaning.

Organizations that focus on behavior without building shared belief often find the behaviors don't stick. You need a clear shared belief about what you stand for and what your 'tribe" is trying to accomplish to keep behavior guidelines from becoming meaningless lists.

As a leader, your Noble Purpose gives you a language and framework for creating powerful shared beliefs with your team, belief that will translate to customers. Belief can scale and be translated to customers.

Do one thing: Tell your team why you believe your product/ solution matters.

5

The Leadership Question That Changes Everything

When you know better, you do better.

—Maya Angelou, poet

*H*ow *will this customer be different as a result of doing business with us?* It's the question most sales managers don't ask. The few who do ignite a chain reaction that drives outstanding sales performance.

Imagine two salespeople who are about to go on a big sales call. They're both meeting with their managers beforehand. One manager asks their seller the usual questions: When are you going to close it, how much will it be? Are you dealing with the decision-maker? Who else do we need to get involved? They're good questions; they reveal where the sales rep is in the sales process and the likelihood of closing.

Now picture the second salesperson. Their manager asks all the usual questions, but goes one step further. Their manager also asks, "How will the customer be different as a result of doing business with us?"

This question changes everything. Now, instead of only thinking about their deal, the rep is thinking about the impact on the customer. If they know the answer to this question and can articulate to their boss, it becomes the centerpiece of the story they carry forward to the customer.

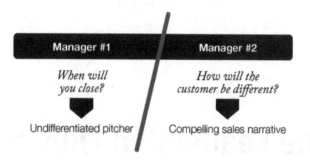

If the seller doesn't know how the customer will be different as a result of buying from them, there's a problem. A seller who can't answer that question for their boss is not prepared to articulate value for a customer.

That single question—How will the customer be different as a result of doing business with us?—*tells you as a leader everything you need to know about what's likely to happen on an upcoming sales call.*

It can be a tactical question you use with a single opportunity. It's also a larger *strategic question* that will guide product development, marketing, and sales support. The ability to answer that question, and your pursuit of improving the answer to that question, changes everything for a team. When you ask your internal teams on a regular basis, "How will the customer be different as a result of doing business with us?" you drive more innovative product development. Marketing becomes more crisp and differentiated. Sales support teams know where to focus to help customers get the most value from your solution.

I know just how powerful this redirection can be because I've experienced it myself. In my late 20s, I worked for a small sales training and consulting firm. My boss, the VP of sales, was a man named Durwood Snead. (You can't make up a name like that.)

I'd joined the small upstart firm because I believed in what they were doing. My first assignment was to grow the Southeast business. We were starting at ground zero. At that point, we were a $5 million company.

On my first day of work, I didn't get a client list. We didn't have any clients in my region. Instead, Durwood and I started our prospect list, mapping out a plan for calling on major firms in the Southeast. Then I hit the road.

During that first year, Durwood and I met weekly for a sales pipeline review. But we did it a bit differently. When I brought up a customer's name, Durwood would ask standard sales manager questions: "When are you going to close?" and "Who needs to be involved?" But then, probably because we were both so excited about what we were doing and the impact we could have on clients, we went further.

Durwood asked questions about each prospect like, "Who are they?" and "What are their goals and challenges?" These customer-focused questions framed our prospects as more than just targets; they were people we wanted to help. As my boss, Durwood pushed me to think more deeply than I might have been inclined to.

This was in the days before widespread CRM systems; pipelines weren't as automated as they are today. In hindsight, I'm glad we did these in person, old-school style. It enabled Durwood, who was a decade older than me, to build belief in a young, impressionable salesperson who was on the road trying to convince potential customers to switch over from larger more established firms and do business with us.

The part I remember most about our pipeline meetings was the discussion about what was possible for our customers. We talked about how they'd be different if they did business with us. We'd imagine how their people would be better with their customers and close more sales, and how the managers would become better coaches. We'd become positively giddy discussing the ways our programs could help these companies and the people in them.

Now, after having assessed thousands of sales conversations, I realize what a gift I was given back then. Those pipeline conversations accomplished two things:

1. Build belief in the salesperson (in this case, me).
2. Solidify a powerful sales narrative to share with customers.

Without realizing it, I was experiencing something rare in sales. That coaching enabled me to see myself and my job differently. I tapped into a creativity and tenacity I didn't even know I had before.

You probably won't be surprised to learn that we closed a lot of business that year. In a region with no clients the previous year, we brought in over $1 million in recurring revenue. Keep in mind, the entire company had done only $5 million the year before. Not only did we bring in new business, but we brought in marquee clients: big brands that moved away from other firms to do business with us.

We were on the rise. We were making a name for ourselves and growing something we believed in.

Unfortunately, shortly after that, we got a new president who wasn't as focused on clients as Durwood was. They clashed, and my much-loved boss left. I didn't realize how much our conversations were guiding me and driving me until we stopped having them.

After Durwood left, I began reporting to the new company president. I was selling the same programs, and we were using the same spreadsheets for sales pipelines, but the president never asked about our customers' lives and ambitions and how our programs might improve their businesses. I remember one conversation in particular where I found myself thinking, "When he looks at me, all he sees is a revenue number." I went from being a person who made a difference to customers to being a profit center.

I quit within a year. Looking back, I have great empathy for the president. He was under huge pressure to deliver numbers. He was simply managing the business in the traditional way he'd been taught. And if I want to be brutally honest with myself, I realize, *I could have been the one discussing client impact.* Why wasn't *I* talking about how we make a difference to customers? I was the one in front of the customers seeing it firsthand. Instead, I waited to be asked, which was a big mistake.

But I also have empathy for my twenty-something self who didn't fully understand why our story was changing and the impact it would have on our sales results.

Sometimes the universe gives you a gift in an unexpected package. I'm eternally grateful I experienced such a dramatic before-and-after example of how sales leaders can shape belief and point their teams toward client impact. While I didn't fully process it until years later, those early conversations laid down a template I've carried with me my entire life. I also saw the ugly truth of what happens when a business shifts its lens away from the customer.

How Words Create Worlds

The way managers talk to salespeople matters. It matters a lot.

The words of front-line sales managers are in the sales team's ear more often than executive town halls or sales training.

In those conversations with Durwood, we were building and reinforcing belief by reminding ourselves about the impact our programs had on customers. We were also preparing me for the conversations I'd be having with customers.

Our discussions—about how customers' lives would be different as the result of doing business with us—gave me a different perspective on my sales activity. Weekly.

What you look at focuses your mind. That then translates into your behavior, which shifts people's perception and experience of you. A whole situation can change—all because of this gossamer thing called a thought.

The sessions when Durwood and I enthusiastically described the impact our programs would have on our customers created powerful mental pictures I carried with me into every sales call. Instead of thinking about my sales number, or even our programs' bells and whistles, I went into my sales calls thinking about the customers: how could we make life better for them and drive results for their companies? This is a model every leader can use to build belief, shape behavior, and create a more powerful team.

Try this quick exercise to see how a single question affects your mindset:

1. Make a list of your top five sales opportunities.
2. Look at each and ask, "What will it take to close this opportunity?"

As you answer this for each potential customer, monitor your thoughts and feelings. Do you feel good or anxious? Are you excited or worried you won't close? Are you thinking about all the steps and obstacles along the way?

Now, looking at that same list, ask yourself a different question: "How will this customer be different as a result of doing business with us?"

Don't give a rote answer. Really think the question through for each individual customer.

Will doing business with you get your customer better results? Will the customer be more efficient? Will he or she be happier or more successful? Will it position the customer's company better in the marketplace? How will your contact's job or life improve? Will his or her job be easier? How will it affect that person's end users? How will it impact his or her organization's bottom line? Will the customer make more money? Will the company save time or resources?

Then, take note of where this client-impact line of thinking takes you. Asking "What will it take to close this sale?" prompts you to think about sales activities.

The second question—"How will this customer be different as a result of doing business with us?"—is about activating your Noble Sales Purpose (NSP).

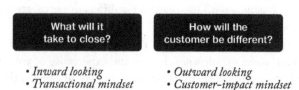

Both questions are important. But which one do you think helps sales-people do a better job in front of customers? If you said the NSP question, you're right. We've talked about how your NSP sets your strategic direction and creates competitive differentiation. Now, let's talk about how managers can use it to drive the right sales behavior.

Traditional revenue-focused pipeline questions prompt salespeople to look inward and thinking about themselves, their quota, and their tasks. The NSP question—how will this customer be different as a result of doing business with us?—prompts salespeople to look outward. It takes them away from a self-oriented, task mindset to a customer-oriented, creative, and collaborative mindset.

Moving from self-focus to client-impact, NSP focus builds confidence and pride within your team. Discussing how your work improves the customer's life gives a salesperson a powerful narrative as they enter a sales situation. A conversation about client impact reinforces two very important points in tangible and pragmatic ways:

- Our company makes a difference.
- I make a difference.

I distinctly remember the impact this shift in focus had on my own mind-set and behavior. Instead of going into sales calls worrying about how small and unknown we were, and how I was going to make the case, I approached opportunities with confidence. I was filled with ideas and constantly looking for opportunities, because I knew we could have a significant impact on the customers. I met with more people. I asked better questions. I was more persistent and assertive. I knew I wasn't selling a me-too generic solution; I was selling something that mattered. I had a purpose.

It's counterintuitive to talk about actualizing your NSP when you're concerned with revenue targets, but our experience tells us that this counterintuitive approach is the most effective way to improve sales performance.

It's challenging for salespeople to hold on to their sense of purpose in the cadence of day-to-day business. That's why you as the leader need to be proactive about bringing the NSP mindset into regular conversations with your team.

How NSP Helps You Close Bigger Deals

Front-line managers sometimes resist emphasizing the NSP when the stakes are high because they worry it will put their people at risk of becoming service people who are *too* customer-focused to close. Actually, the opposite happens.

NSP-driven salespeople are great closers. They're more assertive than quota-focused salespeople because they know that both the customer *and* their company benefit when they close a deal. They understand that their products and services make a difference to the customer, so they can't stand it for the customer *not* to have them.

During the year I worked for Durwood Snead, we unseated a much larger competitor on several national accounts. We were a small company, yet we were able to land big clients like Home Depot, Kimberly-Clark, and United Healthcare.

To say that I was a true believer is an understatement.

It wasn't conversations about our programs that made me a true believer. It was conversations about the *impact* we had on customers. It's no coincidence I left the company a year after Durwood left. Without a boss to reinforce the positive story about how we made a difference, I was merely another salesperson who sold stuff. It became just a job.

I'm sure my sales numbers would have suffered if I had stayed. And I wasn't the only one who quit. Most of the top performers left within two years of Durwood's departure, and revenues dropped. The company was eventually acquired for one-sixth the value it had been during the years we were winning business.

My personal story mirrors what happened at Monster.com and other now-bygone firms like Blockbuster, Blackberry, and Sears. When the leadership language becomes about money, differentiation and innovation die. Fortunes decline when organizations stop thinking "How will the customer be different as a result of doing business with us?"

A Sample NSP Coaching Session

Let's look at exactly how and when you can use this question: "How will the customer be different as a result of doing business with us?" One of the quickest, easiest wins is using it during pipeline reviews. When there's an opportunity on the table, simply ask your rep or team the question, and listen very carefully to their answer.

Do they know how the customer might be different? Can they describe it with specifics? Do they use language customers can relate to? Or do they give a generic answer—or worse, a blank stare?

If a rep says something like, "The customer will have the benefit of our products," dig deeper. You want your salespeople to articulate exactly how this customer will be different—not in a generic sense, but in real and concrete ways. For example, they could say, "Their systems will work faster, which will help them respond to their customers, which gives them an advantage in their marketplace." Then ask, "What impact will that have on the company, and on your buyer?"

If the rep can't explain to you how the customer will be different, how will they ever explain it to the customer?

An effective coaching conversation has two parts: revenue and NSP. As a leader, you want to discuss the revenue first, because that's what's at the top of the salesperson's mind. You want clarity about numbers before you move to the NSP portion.

You handle the NSP portion last because that's what you want the salesperson to be thinking about during the sales call. Again, it's counterintuitive, but it results in better sales calls with higher close rates. Here's a model you can implement immediately.

Coaching Conversation, Part 1: Revenue

Using whatever CRM format or tools you use, ask the rep about the total dollar value, the close date, the competitive landscape, and so forth. Make sure the rep has clear financial goals for the account and a realistic timeline for closing it.

Next, move the conversation from revenue to customer.

Coaching Conversation, Part 2: NSP

Start with that all-important NSP question: "How will this customer be different as a result of doing business with us?"

Your role as the coach is to prompt the salesperson to think deeply about the potential impact his or her solution will have on the customer. You want the rep to identify concrete ways to activate your NSP with this individual customer.

After you ask the linchpin question, go deeper by asking:

- How is our solution better than what the customer is doing right now?
- What impact would this have on the customer's revenue or profit margins?
- What effect will it have on that company's customers and employees?
- How will our solution make things more efficient, more cost-effective, safer, easier, more flexible, or more fun?
- How might this make things harder, slower, or less effective?
- What are some of the less obvious ways things will change?
- Who will be affected by this? How will their jobs be easier or harder?
- How would our competition describe the impact their products or services would have?

Don't be surprised if the reps struggle to answer these questions. Most salespeople don't naturally think this way. That's why you're coaching them.

If they don't have good answers, you'll be tempted to fill in the blanks for them. Resist this temptation, because asking questions prompts the sales reps to think. The uncomfortable moment when they don't know the answer is the exact moment their wheels start turning. You want *their* brains to explore every aspect of this. You're trying to get *them* to connect the dots between your solution and the customer's goals. You want *them* to go find that information if they don't have it. They won't learn to think this way for themselves if you describe it for them. You want your team to internalize it.

If a salesperson still can't provide you with good answers after some prodding, you usually have one of two problems:

- The salesperson hasn't internalized your NSP.
- The salesperson doesn't know enough about this individual customer to provide concrete examples of how he or she will activate your NSP.

Fortunately, both of these problems are solvable when caught early.

If a salesperson hasn't internalized your NSP, it may simply be due to a lack of understanding. The seller may not know your products and services well enough or may not have enough industry knowledge to understand the impact that your company has on customers. The salesperson simply may need more help making the link. You can do this by providing the rep with concrete examples of the impact you've had on other customers. (See Chapter 8 for more on creating compelling customer impact stories.)

A word of caution here: do not describe the impact your solution will have on the rep's specific customer. Instead, describe the impact you've had on similar customers; then ask, "How might these issues and solutions affect *your* customer?" Describing other customers provides a jumping-off point while still requiring the salesperson to think about his or her own customer in a deeper way.

The second problem—that the rep doesn't know enough about the customer to describe how that organization will be different as a result of doing business with you—is the more common scenario. The salesperson understands your NSP on a generic level but doesn't know the individual customer well enough to see how to help the customer in a meaningful way.

It's not enough for your salespeople to simply know your NSP; activating it requires the seller to develop more complex customer knowledge.

Top-performing salespeople make the NSP come alive for each customer because they know very precisely how they add value.

It's probably worth saying something here about value propositions. If you already have a compelling value proposition, great. But don't worry if you don't have one, or if yours leaves something to be desired. Peruse some of the value propositions being touted on most company websites: you'll see that most of them are vague, fairly meaningless phrases that sound exactly the same as everyone else's. Sometimes they spell out the monetary return for customers. Well-intended, yes. But focusing on the immediate monetary return can quickly lead to commoditization. It creates a transactional approach, causing your team and customers to miss the full potential impact of your solution.

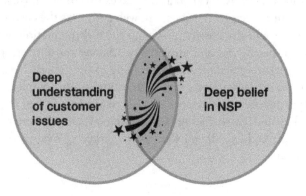

Engagement and differentiation

Average salespeople tend to use generic value statements. They can't make their recommendations more concrete because they lack in-depth customer information. Selling with Noble Purpose requires you link the customer's goals and your solution in more meaningful ways. It requires a clear articulation of the *impact* you have on the customer.

That's where you, the sales leader, come in. When you focus a salesperson on how this particular customer will be different, you open the door to a new level of understanding about that customer. This prompts the salesperson to ask better questions and make more in-depth calls. The rep establishes more meaningful connections between the customer's goals and his or her solution, which is how you articulate true value for the customer.

Salespeople learn quickly. When you make a practice of regularly asking your salespeople NSP questions, they begin to ask those same questions of their customers. When they realize that *you're* going to ask the same question every time you talk with them about a customer—"How will this customer be different as a result of doing business with us?"—they start coming prepared to answer that question.

Before we leave this topic, let's look at three strategic areas where this game-changing question can pivot your team.

Marketing

Imagine your marketing team is about to roll out new collaterals or web copy. Instead of the usual approach, the team decides that every single thing they do will focus on the question "How will the customer be different as a result of doing business with us?" When a team takes this to heart, their collaterals explore different aspects of the question; web copy asks the customer to consider their issues and the impact of solving them. Presentation decks answer the question in specific and aspirational ways. Asking and answering this question keeps a marketing team from succumbing to the generic benefits trap.

This is particularly critical in a B2B setting where complex, high-ticket sales can often degenerate into what we refer to as a *feature-fest*: endless lists of every single bell and whistle being offered, which leaves customers more confused than inspired. Instead, you want your marketing focused on the *impact* of your solution.

Product Development

In Chapter 2, you read about the team at Blackbaud who galvanized their organization around their purpose. When CEO Mike Gianoni joined Blackbaud, several of their products were becoming outdated. Gianoni challenged his product development team to think deeply about how they could improve life for customers. He spotlighted how the current products impacted customers and pushed the team to do more. The question "How will the customer be different as a result of doing business with us?" became a challenge. How can we improve their lives even more? What are some of the biggest, boldest things we can help our clients do? Not surprisingly, within 12 months, the product team had several breakthroughs.

Asking how the customer will be different as a result of doing business with us takes the product team out of their world and into the world of your customer.

Sales Engagement and Support

Sales support teams have grown as organizations recognize that recurring revenue is the most profitable, predictable revenue there is. Asking a sales support team "How will the customer be different as a result of doing business with us?" points them toward client impact. Instead of being reactive and simply answering client questions, they become proactive about helping clients experience the most value possible from the solution.

Lisa St. Germain, VP Sales Engagement for Fiserv, says, "Before we started asking this question, our demos were more generic. Now we zoom in on the impact for each specific customer. Asking this question before every demo and every support interaction was a game-changer. Our team gets clarity with our sales team about the specific client objectives. Our client gets more benefit, and they're more likely to renew."

The question "How will the customer be different as a result of doing business with us?" is what we refer to as a *tip-of-the-spear technique*. It's a linchpin that prompts a series of behavioral changes and mental shifts that have a dramatic impact on sales. It prompts salespeople to ask better questions of their customers, which then improves their business acumen, which makes them more powerful and skilled, which gives them more confidence, which takes them to higher levels, which sells bigger deals. It also prompts the departments *around* your sales team to focus on customer impact. It acts as a driving force across your entire organization.

It all starts with a single question.

Chapter 5: The Leadership Question That Changes Everything

The game-changing question "How will the customer be different as a result of doing business with us?" points your team toward customers. Asking this question early, in pipeline and deal reviews, shifts the focus from internal (when can I close it?) to external (how can I make an impact?).

When a manager asks this question in a pipeline conversation, he or she:

- Builds belief in the rep about the impact of your solution
- Solidifies a powerful sales narrative to share with customers

The language that managers use with salespeople has a huge impact on the language that salespeople use with customers. Sales managers are in the team's ear more often than the words of the CEO or any sales training.

It's challenging for salespeople to hold on to their sense of purpose in the cadence of day-to-day business. Leaders who are proactive about bringing the NSP mindset into regular conversations with your team create high-performance teams.

"How will the customer be different as a result of doing business with us?" can also be used to drive

- Marketing
- Product development
- Sales engagement and support

This question is a tip-of-the-spear technique for creating a more differentiated, impact-driven organization.

Do one thing: Start asking your team, "How will the customer be different as a result of doing business with us?"

2

Naming and Claiming Your Noble Sales Purpose

No one ever made a difference by being like everyone else.
—P.T. Barnum, businessman and founder of the Barnum & Bailey Circus

Words create worlds. The culture of your organization is defined by the language your team uses to describe themselves, their offerings, and the impact they have on customers. Choosing the right words enables you to create shared belief quickly. It's how you tell each other and the market what you stand for.

In Part 2, we'll walk you through the process of creating your NSP, and you'll discover how a few tweaks in wording can make the difference between it being effective or banal. You'll learn how to spot situations where your NSP is already happening inside your organization and turn those into emotionally engaging stories.

You'll also discover why well-intentioned people on your team often dilute your purpose, and how to avoid this trap. You'll learn how to deal with naysayers and people who don't buy in, and how to engage key players who will help infuse your NSP into the groundwater in your organization.

It all starts with the words.

6

Crafting Your Noble Sales Purpose

The secret of success is constancy to purpose.

—Benjamin Franklin

Y ou've seen how organizations and individual leaders have used a Noble Sales Purpose (NSP) to drive revenue and do work that makes them proud. Now it's time for you to name and claim your own Noble Purpose. A few things to note:

- If you're looking at your firm's existing purpose statement and you're less than thrilled with it, don't worry. You may not need to redo it. If your firm has a benign statement that does not spurn action or inspiration, or a bunch of meaningless mission/vision jargon, you can create a high-impact NSP to sit underneath it. Some call this a *nested purpose.*

- If you're thinking "We don't really make a difference; we sell hardware, software, widgets, and no-name products," I'd like to challenge your thinking. Use this exercise to think about the impact your products and solutions have on customers.

Let's walk through the three-part process for creating your NSP. Ideally, you'll land on a concise statement that describes the impact you want to have on clients. The brainstorming process is divided into three parts to get you thinking in the three key areas. We call these the *three discovery questions*.

Here are a few tips before you get started:

- **Give yourself time.** Allow yourself some creative think time. Write in the spaces, jot notes on your iPad, scribble in a journal, daydream, and think about it on a walk or drive.
- **Don't self-edit too early.** It's tempting to try to land the perfect words on the first try. Don't. This will cause you to miss your best ideas. This is a proven process. Go with the flow, and answer the questions as creatively as you can.
- **Don't worry about supporting data—yet.** Trying to use too many facts too early will stifle your creativity. There aren't any lawyers observing you go through this process. Don't worry about trying to express everything with data at this point.
- **Do it just for you.** Don't worry about sharing this with your boss or team yet. Anticipating their reactions will have a chilling effect on your own creativity. We'll cover techniques for getting others engaged in Chapter 9.

By the end of this process, you'll have a succinct statement that is both factual and inspirational. Don't try to get it there too quickly. With that in mind, let's get started.

Discovery Question #1: How Do You Make a Difference to Your Customers?

Think about the times when customers complimented you or your organization. What did they say? Not just, "You're fabulous" (although

I'm sure you are). How did they specifically describe the impact you had on their lives, businesses, or customers?

Here are some things that our clients have heard from their customers:

"You saved my sanity by recovering my data. I stopped worrying about my system."

"You helped us make our customers feel safer and happier."

"You took the headaches out of our system."

"You helped us reduce paperwork so we could focus on patients."

"You helped us reduce turnaround time."

"You gave us a competitive edge."

"You made my job easier."

So—what do your customers say about you?

If you're having trouble coming up with something, ask yourself these questions:

- How do you help customers make more money?
- How do you help customers be more efficient?
- How do you reduce their stress?
- How do you help them serve their customers?
- How do you help them be safe?
- How do you improve their lives?
- Is there an end user who benefits from what you sell?
- What impact do you have on their families?

The sky's the limit. Dig deep, and think about the ripple effect you have on people.

Discovery Question #2: How Are You Different From Competitors?

How do you provide a more robust solution? How are you faster? How do you care more? How are you more attuned to details? How are you more fun to work with?

Avoid traditional, boring, company-approved jargon. Use your own words to describe what makes you different from the rest. Think about what your customers say and why you think you're better than your competition.

You're not going to repeat this verbatim to customers. This is an exercise to get you thinking. Don't worry about citing specific data points just yet.

Discovery Question #3: On Your Best Day, What Do You Love About Your Job?

Every job has good days and bad days. Think about your own position. What do you love about it? Is it your team, your customers, your work environment? Perhaps your products are particularly exciting.

Write down the things that get you excited about your job:

1.

2.

3.

Now that you've answered the three big discovery questions—how you make a difference to customers, how you're different from your competition, and what you love about your job—you're ready to take a first pass at creating your NSP.

What themes do you see when you look at your notes? Are there any words that jump out at you? What elements are inspiring, and which are concrete? Write down the words and themes you find the most compelling:

Create Your NSP

Your ideal NSP is both compelling and concrete. It speaks to your most noble calling as a sales organization. It should also be easy to understand and repeat. It's an action-oriented statement that will inform your sales activities. Your NSP announces your intentions to the world.

This isn't an exercise in corporate messaging. Your NSP is something that's going to drive your sales behavior. Your NSP is the strategic center of your sales team. It's designed to point your team toward a deeper, more meaningful dialogue with each other and with your customers.

Here's a simple structure you can follow. Start with "We," follow it with a verb, and then state your desired impact on customers. Starting the sentence with "We" tells the team "We're all in this together; we're all responsible for delivering."

Remember, your NSP is:

- **Noble:** In the service of others
- **Sales:** Based on what you sell
- **Purpose:** Your reason for being

Here are some examples from our clients:

We help small businesses be more successful. (CMIT Solutions)

We fuel prosperity. (Atlantic Capital Bank)

We redefine our industry. (Supportworks)

We help people discover more passion, purpose, and happiness. (G Adventures)

We unclog the wheels of justice. (Superior Court of Orange County)

We help leaders drive revenue and do work that makes them proud. (McLeod & More)

We do now what patients need next. (Roche)

We champion laugh out loud fun. (Dave & Buster's)

We empower success. (Fiserv, Sales Enablement)

When looking at these sample NSPs, notice how each one addresses the impact that particular organization has on its customers. It's important to note that these are not descriptions of the firm's service; this is about their aspirations for their customers. (See Chapter 2 for more on these sample NSPs.)

Now it's time for you to create your unique NSP. If you're doing this with your team, you'll be well served to have someone else facilitate the process. This enables you, the leader, to actively participate with the team.

For the purposes of this exercise, you just want to take a first pass at it. Spend 10 minutes brainstorming five different variations before you land on one.

If you're doing this on your own, sit with these examples for a week. Practice saying them to yourself and to others. Share them with your partner or a friend. Which NSP statement garners the most powerful response? Which one rolls easily off your tongue? Which one would you be excited to share with your team? Which one would your customers nod in agreement to?

As you start to get closer to choosing one, check yourself on the following elements:

- Is it short?
- Is it easy to understand?
- Is it concrete?
- Is it exciting?
- Could you explain it to your kids?
- Would you feel proud to share it with your neighbor?
- Does it make you want to get out of bed in the morning?
- Would you be proud for your customers to read it?

When you settle on the best one, read the next chapter to test it.

Chapter 6: Crafting Your Noble Sales Purpose

Your NSP is the result of answering the three discovery questions:

- How do we make a difference?
- How do we do it differently?
- On your best day, what do you love about your job?

Your ideal NSP is both compelling and concrete. It speaks to your most noble calling as a sales organization. It should be easy to understand and repeat. It's an action-oriented statement that will inform your sales activities. Your NSP announces your intentions to the world.

Here's a simple structure:

- Start with "We." This tells the team, "We're all in this together."
- Follow it with a verb.
- End with the desired impact you want to have on customers.

You NSP is

- Noble: In the service of others
- Sales: Based on what you sell
- Purpose: Your end game

Do one thing: Create your NSP.

7

Why Specificity Is Sexy

I always wanted to be somebody, but now I see I should have been more specific.
—Lily Tomlin, comedian and actress

Have you ever been in a meeting where people are arguing over a word choice? Whether it's website copy, a marketing message, or a company e-mail, people have different opinions about which words work best. What often winds up happening is that the team includes all the words to keep everyone happy. Or they compromise, telling each other, "It's just semantics."

In the case of your NSP, the semantics matter. A lot.

The meaning attached to your NSP can make the difference between owning your market or getting left behind. A few words can make or cost you millions. Just ask the team at Mars Petcare, a company with 41 brands, some of which earn over $1 billion a year. They're outpacing longtime rival Purina. A close look at the two firms' purpose statements reveals how Mars' strategic choice of a preposition propelled a strategy that generated millions in revenue and enabled them to beat Purina in multiple markets.

The two statements are:

Purina: *Better with pets*
Mars: *A better world for pets*

What do you notice? At first look, they appear the same. But look closer: One is a call to action, while the other is more of a slogan. Can you tell the difference? Purina is telling you what they believe; Mars is telling you about the impact they intend to have. On the Mars website, Veterinary Genetics Research Manager Dr. Angela Hughes describes the company's commitment: "I would like to see humanity rise to the occasion to love our pets and ourselves the way that our pets love us."

The *Harvard Business Review* piece, "Put Purpose at the Core of Your Strategy," describes how Mars had the foresight to go into the lucrative pet health market, while rival Purina stuck with battling it out in the lower-margin, price-sensitive pet food market.

If you look at the two purpose statements, you can see why. Purina's *Better with pets* is a slogan—a mantra. It's nice, but it does not inspire action. It just tells people "We like pets." Meanwhile, when Mars tells you they are committed to *"A better world for pets,"* it galvanizes action and drives strategy. This is a seemingly nuanced but quite crucial difference.

To illustrate the dramatic differences in the way these two statements cascade to drive strategy and behavior, let's substitute children in place of pets. Imagine one organization proclaims their purpose is "better with children."

That's nice; we're all in the club. We believe the world is better with children. Or, perhaps we believe we're the company who is better with children compared to our competition. We can rally around it and feel good about ourselves. This no-action statement is certainly better than no shared belief. But if I work here, what am I supposed to do as a result of this statement? Put it on the website and have T-shirts made?

Now imagine another company who says our purpose is "A better world for children." Whoa, this is some serious stuff. This is big. We have to do something. Where do we start? We should probably identify all the things making the world bad for children. We can look at places where children are thriving for models we could scale. We're going to have to make choices: Where do we focus? How do we measure our impact? Which markets should we pursue? Which ones should we avoid?

In short, we're going to have to create a strategy to impact children.

Therein lies the difference. The semantics are everything. Pursuing those five words—*A better world for pets*—drove Mars into new products and markets. The HBR piece reports that Mars "was able to pull off a transformation because it ensured that every move it made was aligned with the same core purpose." Mars Petcare became Mars Inc.'s largest and fastest-growing division.

The difference is specificity and impact. While Purina's statement tells their team and the world what they believe, the Mars statement is a true NSP. It describes the impact they want to have. It's galvanizing. You don't even have to particularly like pets, but if you work for Mars, you know what you're supposed to do for them.

Remember in Chapter 4 when you read about why purpose drives better results than passion? Mars illustrates why. While Mars has a clear and specific purpose, Purina's statement merely describes their passion.

It's not without coincidence that in 2018, Mars Petcare President Poul Weihrauch significantly altered the composition and focus of the leadership team. The HBR piece describes how Weihrauch declared that Mars' new collective agenda "would go beyond the performance of individual businesses; it would include generating a 'multiplier effect' among the business (such as between pet food and pet health) and increasing their contribution to create a better world for pets." When you're serious about your purpose, you align your organization to achieve it.

Imagine you're a sales exec, and Mars and Purina have both offered you a job to run their sales team. Which team would you be more excited to take over? The team whose mantra is *Better with pets*? Or the team who is challenging themselves to create a better world for pets?

The right purpose engages even the cynics among us. When you're specific about the impact you want to have on the world, it creates energy. You become personally invested in the outcome.

When we work with organizations on their NSP and strategy, we tell leaders up front: your purpose drives every aspect of your business, from big strategic decisions to daily behavior. Every word counts. As the Mars vs. Purina competition reveals, it's not just semantics.

Choose a Big Enough Lane

Many organizations say they want to improve their customers' lives. The challenge is to be specific. "We make a difference" is certainly the *sentiment* you want to communicate to your team. But it's less than clear.

Your NSP must communicate *what* you intend to do and *where* you intend to do it. A good NSP is both aspirational and specific. Said another way,

---

Your NSP should articulate both your aim and your lane: the impact you aspire to have, and where you intend to do it.

For example, one of our clients is a mid-size regional bank. Their NSP is *We improve our customer's financial future*. Their lane is the client's financial future. Their aim—their aspiration—is to improve it. It's not complex.

As you look at this simple NSP, you might say that it could apply to any financial institution. You're right; it could. It could also apply to a fintech firm or a financial education center. Your NSP does not describe your product offering. The NSP in and of itself does not create the innovation or differentiation. It's the decisions you make as a result of your NSP and the way you execute that drives innovation, engagement, and differentiation. Your NSP points the way.

When Mars put a stake in the ground, deciding that their purpose was to create a better world for pets, they may not have envisioned going into pet healthcare. But it's not surprising that they expanded into that market. It's a logical strategic choice for a team who wants to create a better world for pets.

It's important to note that having an NSP does not mean you give away your services for free. Mars' choices illustrate the interplay between profit and purpose. Their NSP pointed them toward customer impact. Once you're looking in the right direction, the team can determine whether your options are financially viable or not.

Similarly, our bank client may choose to expand their portfolio. When they're making decisions about what to pursue and what not to pursue, their NSP provides a focused lens for decision making. The team can evaluate: Will this help us improve our customer's financial future? Is this the most powerful way to proceed? Is it the most efficient way? Is it the most profitable way? Improving the customer's financial future is the North Star. The other questions determine the route to get there.

The most important thing is that your NSP drives strategy and behavior.

Your NSP should point your team in a strategic direction (your lane) and provide emotional inspiration (your aim).

How to Avoid the Bookcase Problem

As you begin to introduce your purpose, you may find that people want to add to it. Do not give in to this impulse. Shorter is always better. The reason people want to add to your NSP is not because they don't like it. It's because they *do* like it.

I call this the *bookcase problem*. It's when people take something excellent and then pile mediocre stuff on top of it and ruin it.

I dubbed it the *bookcase problem* after an experience with my father. Several years ago, after my mother died, my dad decided to clean out the house and do a bit of updating. He was entering a new phase of his life. It was a phase he hadn't expected or wanted. But he determined to make the best of things, and a freshened-up home was a good place to start. You can imagine that after 25 years and four kids, there was more than a bit of "clutter" to dispose of. Carloads of stuff went to Goodwill. We said goodbye to the old bunk beds, shag carpet, and worn-out furniture. Once we cleared out the clutter, a bit of remodeling ensued.

Six months later, the result was a beautiful, clean, uncluttered space. Part of the project included installing two crisp white bookcases, right near the entry. They were visible from almost every room of the house.

I came in to help my dad arrange furniture, and one of our tasks was to decide what to put in the bookcases. My dad had boxes upon boxes of boating books, nautical decor, and Navy memorabilia. He also had photographs of the family scuba diving trips. It took lots of editing, but I was able to convince my dad to let go of some items and store others.

By the end, we had two beautiful bookcases showcasing his love for boating, reading, and his pride in the Navy and his family. One look at those bookcases, and you knew exactly who my dad was and what he stood for.

There was plenty of "white space" around the important pieces to draw attention to them. My father loved it. The next week, he had friends over, they loved it too. Everyone said, "Jay, those bookcases are so you." It was the same stuff he'd always had, but instead of it being cluttered in with a million other things, it was edited to showcase what mattered most.

When I returned the following month, my dad said, "I'm really excited for you to see the house. I loved what you did so much, I did even more!" As you might imagine, my control-freak antennae went up.

I arrived to find the beautifully edited bookcases now had at least 50% more stuff in them. Because he loved the theme so much, he'd gone out and bought more of it. Now instead of a single antique anchor, we had three. The stunning pair of large underwater photos with white space on either side of them had now been joined by seven or eight smaller photos. Everything was consistent with the original theme; only now, you didn't see any of it. More of a good thing didn't make it better: it made it less distinct and lessened the impact.

The same thing happens in organizations. You create a crisp positioning statement. Then everyone adds their favorite adjectives and adverbs, and before long, what was once clear and concise is cluttered.

It's why marketing messaging that starts out crisp gets clunky. It's why once-elegant products end up with extra drop-downs, clunky buttons, and ugly stickers all over the packaging. No one wants to edit; everyone wants to add.

Every meaningful idea is one committee meeting away from becoming mundane.

In writing, there's a popular mantra: "Sometimes you have to kill your darlings." Editing is essential. The problem is *not* that people don't like the crisp version. On the contrary, they often love it. They love it so much that they want to be part of it. That's why they want to add their take.

There's a better way to invite people to be part of your NSP. You can help your team take ownership of the crisp version by intentionally creating space for them to connect with the content.

When I asked my dad to tell me the story of each original object, he became animated and engaged. Each piece in the bookcase became even more meaningful as he rekindled his connection with it. The new things he bought didn't have that same meaning. They were like the unnecessary adverbs and adjectives people jam into a purpose statement. They're added as an enthusiastic response to the original content. But they have a chilling effect on the message.

Giving my dad an opportunity to tell the stories about why these items mattered gave him the space to own the story. He didn't need to add items to make the bookshelf his own. It was already his own; he simply needed to deepen his connection with the bookshelf.

It works the same way with teams. If you ask for feedback on your purpose statement, well-intended people will usually wind up adding words that weaken it. If you want to keep things compelling and clear, once you settle on your NSP, instead of inviting people to give you feedback, ask them to give you proof of its resonance.

> *Behind every two-paragraph mission statement is a*
> *team of well-intentioned people who fell in love with*
> *their own words and couldn't bear to part with any*
> *of them.*

Ask them to describe times when they have observed your organization doing this. Instead of eroding elegant messaging, you want to find the stories to help your team *own it*.

Here are some questions you can use to activate buy-in:

- Where are we doing this already?
- What stories can we use to illustrate that?
- What would happen if we did this in a bigger, bolder way?
- How would our customers respond if we did this consistently?
- How does your role contribute to this?
- What would it mean to you personally if you could do this on a regular basis?

The same purpose can mean different things to different people. For example, you might buy into Mars' *A better world for pets* because of your personal experience with stray cats. You might identify with it because of your passion for animals. Someone else might remember how the love of their childhood dog helped them through a rough time.

You want to get to a place where everyone on your sales team has clarity in three areas:

1. *Organization*: Why does our NSP matter to customers?
2. *Job*: How does my job contribute to our NSP?
3. *Personal*: Why does our NSP matter to me?

Asking people to think very specifically about how their role drives your purpose and what it might mean for them personally engages their frontal lobes. It makes them active participants. It helps you avoid the bookcase problem. Instead of trying to add words to your purpose, you inspire action.

Jeff Stier, who leads EY's Purpose Realized Performance Practice, says, "When you live each day committed to your personal purpose, you have greater conviction, confidence, and courage. You become the driver of your destiny." Helping your team personally connect to your purpose addresses a fundamental human longing. Stier explains, "Purpose is infused in human DNA. Ever since humans first became aware of the world around them, we've wrestled with two fundamental questions: *Where are we going?* and *How will we get there?*"

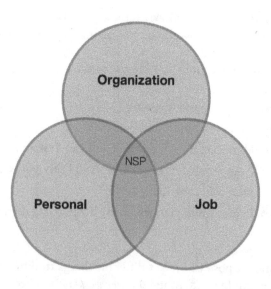

When people are clear about where you're going as an organization, how their job impacts customers, and why your NSP matters to them personally, they come fully alive. This clarity creates a rare breed of sellers, people who show up with their heart and soul and put every ounce of their effort into driving results for customers.

Being specific about your aspirations and your impact provides the specific direction and inspiration to take your team to the next level. In a world where so many people are disengaged from their jobs, this kind of specificity is sexy as hell.

Chapter 7: Why Specificity Is Sexy

Aspiration is nice; specificity is actionable. You always want to communicate both your aim and your lane.

"We make a difference" is the *sentiment*; you also need clarity about *what* you intend to do and where you intend to do it. For example: *Better with pets* is aspirational. *A better world for pets* is aspirational **and** specific.

When you introduce your NSP, people often want to add words. This is not because they don't like it; it's because they do.

Keep your NSP compelling and clear. Once you've landed on it, instead of inviting people to give you feedback, ask them to give you proof of its resonance.

To help your team internalize your NSP, ask:

- Where are we doing this already?
- What stories can we use to illustrate that?
- What would happen if we did this in a bigger, bolder way?

Everyone on your sales team should have clarity about:

- Organization: Why our NSP matters to customers
- Job: How my job contributes to our NSP
- Personal: Why our NSP matters to me

Do one thing: Ask your sales team these questions, and share the answers broadly.

CHAPTER

8

The Stories That Make Your NSP Stick

Storytelling makes the brain light up in a way no other form of communication does.
—Nancy Duarte, author, CEO, and the storyteller of Silicon Valley

The default narrative of most organizations is a money story. You've already read about why a money story doesn't win hearts and minds. If you want to accelerate competitive differentiation and emotional engagement, you need to craft a *meaning* story.

A meaning story draws from the collective shared memories and beliefs of the people who work there. It's about your journey, where you've been, what you did, who you are, what you believe, and what it means to be part of your tribe.

A 2019 PwC research project about the connection between strategic purpose and motivation revealed that a mere 39% of employees could clearly see the value they create. More than half weren't even "somewhat" motivated, passionate, or excited about their jobs. The current crisis of disengaged employees is both stunning and heartbreaking. Millions of people are showing up for work every single day and leaving their hearts at home.

Even if you're not one of the disengaged, you're affected by them. When members of a sales force are disengaged, it has a chilling effect on the entire team, not to mention your customers.

One of the core responsibilities (and great delights) of a leader is to show your team why their work matters. Knowing your work has an impact on others inspires people. You can't illustrate the deeper meaning of work with a spreadsheet or a product slick. Meaning comes through story.

The challenge is that organizations tend to sanitize their stories and boil them down to the basic facts, eliminating the emotional elements that make them compelling. In most organizations, the emotion gets stripped out in favor of generic language like *value, reliability, efficiency, flexibility,* and *superior provider of end-to-end solutions*. These words fall flat because they're the exact same words that everyone else uses.

As a leader, you can do better. You want to *accelerate* emotional engagement, not erode it. In Chapter 4, you learned why shared belief is crucial for scaling your NSP. Belief drives behavior.

Stories are the fuel of belief.

Build Belief: Create Sticky Stories

The fastest way to help your team believe in and act on your Noble Purpose is to share stories that illustrate your NSP in action. For clarity's sake, let's differentiate between *founder stories* and *customer impact stories*. Many organizations have inspiring founder stories. The tale of two geniuses tinkering in a garage or the twentysomething adventure traveler who built a global brand based on happiness is a great source of pride for the team.

You can and should share these stories often. If you want to shape sales behavior, however, you need to go one step further. You need to provide current examples of your NSP in action.

To illustrate, let's go back to the Lion Tribe from Chapter 4. Imagine you're a new member of the tribe. You hear the founder story about the three original members who wanted to form a new kind of tribe founded on the powerful principles of lions. You're inspired for sure, but do you know how to behave when you're out in the field? Maybe. Maybe not.

Now imagine your team leader tells you a second story. This one happened more recently. It's a story about one of your peers, someone just like you, who used the lion principles to save a group of children in the wild. The team leader describes exactly how the team member did it and, most importantly, the impact their actions had on the children and their parents. Now you're more than proud; you're empowered. Now *you* know how to act like a lion.

The stories you share with your team should illustrate your NSP in action. They provide proof you can deliver. We call these *customer impact stories*. They go deeper than the traditional testimonials and case studies used by most organizations.

Here's how they differ:

Testimonials: Tell people you're great: "XYZ Company was prompt and professional."

Case studies: Explain your implementation: "The customer purchased product A with the added bells and whistles of B and C. Here's how it worked for them."

Customer impact stories: Describe the impact your solution has on real live human beings. Customer or client impact stories (depending on how you refer to your buyers) include facts, and they also spell out the business and emotional impact your solution has on the real live human beings you serve. They build belief with your team and shape the team's behavior for future interactions.

Here's an example from Supportworks, the foundation repair company you read about in Chapter 2 that is redefining the contracting world. As you read these examples, imagine you're at a Supportworks sales meeting, and your boss is sharing this information. Pay attention to how you feel after each one.

Testimonial: Mr. and Mrs. Jones said, "The team at Supportworks is the best. They provided a high-quality installation on time and on budget. And they cleaned up after themselves."

If you're in the crowd at the sales meeting, you might be thinking, "I'm glad I work here. We have an excellent reputation. Our clients love us."

Case study: The foundation of the Jones family home was bowing and cracking. During the first big rain of the season, it flooded. Water was inside the home;

it was starting to create mildew and mold. We used our advanced technology to eliminate the water quickly. Then, using our patented foundation repair system, we pulled out the bows in the wall and fixed the cracks without having to jackhammer all the concrete. With the basement walls secured, we finished with a moisture barrier over the entire foundation. It was a big job. But thanks to our team, the project was done on time, with minimal disruption.

Now you might be thinking, "Our products are pretty impressive. Our team is great. We have a real competitive advantage."

Now let's take it further. Picture the leader telling ...

A Memorable Customer Impact Story

Imagine you have six-week-old twins. You arise after a mostly sleepless night to find your basement has flooded. That's what happened to the Jones family. They were just starting to get a handle on life with two new babies when they awoke to find their basement filled with six inches of dirty water. The timing could not have been worse. The mother was practically in tears when she called us.

Mrs. Jones was worried about the damage from the flood and the fast-growing mold and mildew. The last thing you want with babies is a house full of mold. They vacated the house and went to stay in Mrs. Jones's mother's basement while we worked. With both babies and all their stuff in cramped quarters, it put a lot of stress on their family.

Knowing that the Jones family was crammed into that basement with their babies, our team worked like fiends to finish. We sucked every bit of water out of the basement and used our patented products to not only fix it but, as we say, fix it forever. Because we got the parts and the team there quickly, the Jones family was back in their home within a week. They can go to sleep at night confident their basement walls will stand strong in the next big rain. They don't have to worry about mold or mildew infecting their babies. Our team was so excited about the work we did for the Jones family, they took a picture of themselves standing in the cleaned-out basement, high-fiving each other. They sent it to Mrs. Jones in a text saying, "Your clean, dry home is ready for you and your precious babies."

If you're in the crowd at the sales meeting listening, how do you feel now?

I don't even own construction gloves, and I'm ready to go muck out someone's basement! The testimonial and the case study are good. But it's the customer impact story that will make hearts beat faster. It's a sticky story, one you'll remember long after the meeting. This story tells you, "Our work matters. People are counting on us." People are counting on *you*. This is how you as a leader can build belief.

Customer impact story

- *Inspires belief*
- *Touches emotions*
- *Validates your NSP*
- *Makes hearts beat faster*

Sticky Stories Create Meaning

Customer impact stories pull you in; they ignite your frontal lobes. They help you experience the joy of making a difference to someone. Once you've heard a story like that, it sticks with you. It inspires you to want to have that kind of impact on your customers.

Logic makes you think; emotion makes you act. Instead of looking inward toward the features of your product, a customer impact story looks outward. It points the listener toward the clients and the effect your work has on them. It galvanizes a sales team because it tells them "Our NSP is real, and it matters. On our best day, this is how we behave."

Sharing stories like this one is how Supportworks transformed their organization from a traditional blue-collar contracting firm into a tribe of true believers who are redefining an entire industry. The story shows their team that *this* is how we redefine, and this is why it matters.

One of their team members was so inspired by Supportworks' NSP that he had "Redefine" tattooed on his arm. No joke. Is it any surprise their team is changing the industry?

Supportworks has plenty of client testimonials to provide social proof of their effectiveness. They also use case studies to describe how their products are used and why they're better than the competition's.

For building belief with the team, nothing wins the room like a customer impact story.

The best stories use vivid descriptions and emotional language to answer the game-changing question asked in Chapter 5: "How is this customer different as a result of doing business with us?"

Author and CEO Nancy Duarte, the preeminent storyteller of Silicon Valley, says, "Stories engage the brain at all levels: Intuitive, emotional, rational, and somatic. When we hear stories, our brains respond by making sense of information more completely."

Customer impact stories help your team make sense of your NSP. They translate the aspirational into the actual. The stories you tell around the organizational campfire—sales meetings, morning huddles, and the like—tell your tribe, "This is what we do for people."

The power of good storytelling as a leadership tool cannot be overstated. Think about your own life. What stories inspired you as a child? What were the stories your family told? How did they shape your beliefs? I grew up listening to my dad's stories. Some of my best childhood memories are of my dad telling my brother and me stories about his southern cousins.

My dad was a city boy from Washington, D.C. Every summer, he would head down to Walhalla, South Carolina, to spend a month with his southern cousins, who took great delight in teasing their "Yankee" relatives. My brother and I would beg Dad for another story about his "mean" cousins almost every night—and he was more than happy to share.

One of the most memorable was the time they told him South Carolina bees don't sting. The cousins walked through a bee-filled patch of clover in their bare feet, telling Dad, "South Carolina bees aren't like the bees up North; they don't have stingers down here."

What my dad didn't realize was that a group of boys growing up in the South in the 1950s went barefoot all summer long. The cousins' feet were so tough and calloused that the bees' stingers could barely penetrate their skin. This wasn't the case for my dad. He was stung 20 times when he took off his lace-up city-boy shoes to walk through the clover.

They also told my dad that putting manure in his shoes would make him grow taller. They swore their strapping six-foot frames had been achieved by small doses of manure in the toes of their shoes. My late-bloomer dad smelled horrible for an entire summer.

But our favorite stories were about the times my dad got back at the mean cousins.

There was the time he went out late at night and painstakingly loosened the bolts on the front wheels of all their bicycles. The next day my dad said, "Race you down the hill!" The cousins got about halfway down the hill when their front wheels started to shake and then flew off. The image of the mean cousins at the bottom of a hill in a pile of bikes as my dad rode off into the sunset never failed to get a big cheer out of my brother and me. Even though we knew how the story ended, we begged to hear it over and over again.

Any parent today would be horrified at those stories. Upon reflection, I'm kind of amazed our mother did not intervene. Perhaps she knew what those tales would come to mean for us. Listening to those stories helped shape our self-image. They told my brother and me what kind of people we are. We weren't wimpy kids. We were smart individuals who could figure things out. We were the Earle family. We wouldn't let a bunch of mean cousins get the best of us.

In telling those stories, my dad was creating the narrative of our family. He was cementing our belief in who were are and what we could accomplish. As a leader, you can do the same for your team.

Stories are the soundtrack of our lives. They shape our internal beliefs, which in turn drive much of our daily behavior. It's not without coincidence that all the great religions of the world have a book of stories. Stories remind us of who we are and who we want to be.

At first glance, your business life may not seem as colorful or dramatic as the cleaning-a-flooded-basement story from Supportworks or the mean-cousins stories I learned from my dad. But if you ask your team, you might be surprised at what you uncover.

Several years back, we were working with Graham-White, a company that makes systems that improve the safety and reliability of brakes on trains and heavy vehicles. Their NSP was *We make transportation safer, faster, and more reliable*.

We asked the sales team for examples of their NSP in action. One of the salespeople stood up and told the following story:

Locomotive engines are always in need of service. But they're running day and night, so it's a challenge to catch one stopped long enough to service the brakes. The brakes on a locomotive are crucial; lives are at stake if they fail. One of the Graham-White reps was in the middle of a field improvement program, and he didn't want to miss the moment when the locomotive came into the shop yard. He realized if he went back to the hotel and waited for the customer to call, he'd lose 30 minutes. Even though it was after midnight, he decided to wait it out.

So he slept in his car ... in the snow.

The customer called his cell phone at 3:00 am. Thirty seconds later, the salesman was standing in front of the customer's desk. The customer asked incredulously, "How did you get here so fast?" He replied, "I slept in my car." The customer couldn't believe it: "It's 30 degrees outside; are you crazy?"

The rep said, "I knew you needed me to check those brakes. I didn't want to miss it when the train came in."

The salesman thereby cemented his status as a legend: "The sales rep who sleeps in his car in the snow to keep the brakes safe."

This story was new information to most of the audience. The older sales guys knew it, but the new ones had never heard it before. Upon hearing it, they all stood a little taller, and you could tell they had even more pride in their company.

How would you feel about your organization if you heard this story on your first day of work? Would you be proud you had joined the firm? Would you repeat the story to your spouse when you went home?

If you were a customer hearing that story, would you want to do business with that firm? When Graham-White says, "We make transportation, safer, faster, and more reliable," do you believe them? I sure do.

The story cements shared belief in their NSP. It tells their team, we are the kind of people who go the extra mile to deliver on our Noble Purpose. If we have to, we will sleep in our cars, *in the snow*, to make sure we help our customers.

The Formula for Sticky Stories

You can use customer impact stories internally to scale belief and behavior. And if you haven't already figured it out, they're also one of the most powerful sales tools you can use to engage clients.

The internal story becomes the external story.

When you tell compelling customer impact stories inside the company, you prepare your team to share them with clients. The same stories work in both places: inside the company and outside the company.

Here's what makes a customer impact story compelling:

- It's true.
- It's short. You should be able to tell the story in less than two minutes, in about 300 words or less.
- It describes the impact on the customer. A good NSP story doesn't stop at the event; it describes the impact: the twins came home; the parents felt safe. You want your team to think about whom the events affected and the implications for their businesses and lives.
- It includes vivid details. Descriptions such as "six inches of water in the basement, mold, and mildew" add energy and drama to the story.
- It touches emotions. A good NSP story is about human beings whose lives were changed in some way. Emotional words such as *frustrated, angry, delighted,* and *thrilled* add energy to the story.
- Most importantly, it supports your NSP. The story's value and purpose is not to merely entertain; it is to authenticate your NSP.

If you're selling something and your customers are buying it, I guarantee you have customer impact stories. And they might be even more life-changing than you expect. That's what the team at Hootsuite discovered.

Hootsuite is the global leader in social media management. The Vancouver-based SaaS firm's platform is used by more than 17 million customers and employees at over 80% of the Fortune 1000. Founded in 2008 by Ryan Holmes, Hootsuite helps clients "unlock the power of human connection." Their platform helps organizations build lasting customer relationships at scale.

Back in 2012, Hootsuite was growing fast. They had created a new market, but competitors were quickly nipping at their heels. They needed to amp up their sales force quickly to ensure that they captured the lion's share of the growing market they had created.

Hootsuite was hiring salespeople at a rapid rate. The new salespeople needed to be compelling, and quickly. Describing themselves as a social media management platform would not create the urgency they needed to win business. Hootsuite wanted prospective clients to understand that this was more than brand building. Hootsuite's platform was a way to forge enduring relationships with constituents and customers.

Their new sales team was on fire. They were also new to the space. Many of the salespeople came out of traditional tech; some had sales experience, but many did not. The team was also competitive and wanted to win; to do so, they needed to learn how to be compelling and emotionally engaging, fast.

Hootsuite's chief revenue officer at the time, Steve Johnson, who was employee number 27, said, "A lot of our clients only buy licenses for their marketing teams; they think we're just for consumer brands. We needed to help them think bigger."

As a traditionally trained tech team, it would have been easy for the Hootsuite sales force to charge forth with a product-driven narrative. Instead, Johnson tapped into the team's competitive nature and launched the Hootsuite Story-Off.

Leaders drew on the game-changing question ("How will the customer be different?") and asked the team to look for examples of how it changed the lives of its customers. Sales managers got training to help sales reps craft the stories. They recorded client impact (the company calls their customers "clients") stories on cell phone videos during the weekly sales meeting. The teams held practice sessions where they listened to each other's stories and provided feedback. They coached each other and learned what worked best.

Then it was time to compete. Each salesperson recorded his or her story. Teams voted for the initial winners. These went on to the quarter-finals. Using the criteria I outlined earlier—true, short, client impact, vivid details, emotive, and supports the NSP—Hootsuite leaders chose the five best stories. The reps won the chance to compete on stage in a story-off during the company-wide town hall.

Imagine you're a new salesperson sitting at the Hootsuite town hall and listening to the stories. You hear about how the Mall of America uses Hootsuite to create more engaging shopping experiences. You hear about how school systems use the platform to reach out directly to busy parents. You're starting to get a sense of how your work impacts people. You're likely thinking, wow, we really do empower human connection.

Then the final salesperson takes the stage. You discover that during Hurricane Sandy, Morris County used the Hootsuite dashboard to prioritize pleas for help and send out reports about road closures and evacuation efforts.

You hear the gripping tale about neighborhoods plunged into darkness with impassable roads, trapping people in their homes. For people sitting in the dark, not knowing when or if help is coming, their phones become their lifeline. They're frantically tweeting and messaging to find help.

But they're not messaging into a dark, overcrowded void, as in so many disasters. These citizens get a response. Because thanks to Hootsuite, the Morris County social media manager has prepared for this very moment. She is collaborating with 39 municipalities to disseminate and amplify up-to-date news. In a time when it would be easy for citizens and government workers to panic, the Hootsuite dashboard prioritizes and assigns incoming messages to ensure that nothing is missed.

How do you feel when you hear this story? If you're a salesperson, do you want to repeat it to your customers? You better believe you do. That's exactly what happened. The Hootsuite sales team doubled revenue the year they held their Story-Off. After sharing their stories with each other, they started telling them to clients. As their sales grew, so did their reputation. As of this writing, Hootsuite is the world's most widely used platform for managing social media, and the company is valued at over $1 billion.

After he led the Hootsuite team to explosive growth, Steve Johnson went on to lead teams at Vidyard and Intelex. He has created over $3 billion in market value for companies he's been part of and helped lead. As someone who has successfully taken firms from startup to post-IPO, he says, "In the early days, purpose and storytelling is super important because if you don't have an overarching reason to exist, there's not enough there to motivate people. When times are tough, you need something that appeals to bigger goals and reasons."

Johnson is currently the president and COO at Berkshire Grey, a firm that combines AI and robotics to help customers change the way they handle fulfillment. He asserts that no matter what field you're in, customer impact stories are essential: "It is easy to say our product is xyz, but the definition doesn't tell the whole story. When you hear a story about achieving your purpose, then it closes the loop and makes everything much more understandable—and meaningful."

Does every sale have to save lives? No. Sometimes it's simply about helping merchants forge better relationships with their buyers, or getting on a busy parent's radar. The point is, the team knows every sale they make has an impact on someone.

If you want to scale belief, start with stories. The facts in these stories are 100% true, but it's the emotion of the client impact that enables the team to go forth with such compelling sales narrative.

It's also important to note that Hootsuite tapped into their young team's competitive nature by creating a contest. But finding the winning storyteller wasn't their only endgame. Helping the entire team become skilled storytellers and sharing those stories across the entire organization was the real point.

One person won the contest, but every single member of the sales team got to practice their own story. They also got to hear the other stories. Sharing the stories publically means, even when you don't win, you walk away knowing, wow, we help a lot of people, the work we do here matters.

Jumpstart Purpose with Customer Impact Stories

The previous chapters helped you name your NSP. Customer impact stories will help you *claim* it. They enable you to scale. The best part is, you don't need a fancy brochure or perfect web copy to get started.

At your next meeting, share a customer impact story. Simply say, "I've been thinking about the impact we have on clients." Then share the story.

Here are some places you can tell a customer impact story:

- **Team huddles.** Open with a short story to remind your team why you're there.
- **Giving praise.** Tell people the impact their actions had on the customer.
- **Town halls**. Bring in a live customer to describe the impact you have had on them.
- **Meeting with the CEO**. Use a customer impact story to add color to financial results.
- **Meetings with backstage teams.** Let non-customer-facing staff know how your organization's work impacts clients.

Whether you're sharing customer impact stories onstage in front of thousands or you're starting small, in a weekly sales meeting, the important thing is to focus on how your solution makes a difference to clients. It's not about your product or your quota; it's about the impact you have on customers.

Remember, good stories are sticky. The emotion makes them memorable. They tell your team, "This is what it means to be part of our tribe." While this book is primarily about work, sharing stories with your team members affects the way they show up for everything else in their lives. When you know your work matters, your life starts to matter more.

My dad once told me that "Every person deserves work they can believe in." He was right. Sharing stories about how you make a difference to clients elevates your team on multiple levels. It helps them be more authentic and engaging with clients. It also reminds them, "You're not a meaningless cog in a money machine; you're real live human being whose work matters to others."

Chapter 8: The Stories That Make Your NSP Stick

Stories are the most powerful way to cascade meaning and create shared belief.

Guidelines for crafting a customer impact story:

- It's true.
- It's short.
- It describes the impact on the customer.
- It includes vivid details.
- It touches emotions.
- It supports your NSP.

Places you can tell a customer impact story:

- Team huddles
- Giving praise
- Town halls
- Meeting with the CEO
- Meetings with backstage teams

Do one thing: Tell a customer impact story at your next meeting.

CHAPTER

9

Why Seemingly Sane People Resist Noble Purpose

Never compare your inside to everyone else's outside.

—Anne Lamott, writer

At this point, you may be thinking, Noble Purpose sounds great. But what about ...

- My CEO
- The board
- My boss
- Marge in accounting
- Phil in marketing
- Our purchasing department
- Our tenured sales reps

The list goes on.

Whenever I speak about Noble Purpose, someone inevitably comes up to me afterward and says, "I love this, but my company will never go for it." The person then proceeds to explain why his or her money-driven boss doesn't care about "stuff like this," or the person will say, "The people in my company are too intellectual" (or overeducated, or undereducated, or power-hungry, or disengaged) "to get into this."

The truth is, we don't know what's inside another person's heart unless they tell us.

I've seen seemingly uncaring CEOs light up at the thought that their lives and their organizations could become something more meaningful than a balance sheet. And I've watched salespeople all over the world become passionate about jobs they once thought were only about the money.

Having said that, not everyone responds positively at first.

Claiming your NSP out loud means you'll encounter questions and perhaps even some naysayers. Sometimes people are initially resistant simply because they're using the mental frames and language they've grown accustomed to. Their approach to their work is a reflection of the way they've been trained. For example, one highly analytical CFO told us, "I never knew there was another way to look at business." His rigorous financial training gave him a particular lens on the business. He prided himself on being able to strip the emotion out of financial decisions. Make no mistake; we need people like that in a CFO role. The last thing you want is someone who is squishy about the numbers.

His peers on the executive team had only ever heard him talk about money and financial controls; they didn't think he would be receptive to something more emotive. They were wrong.

After working in this space for many years, here's something I observe on a pretty regular basis: people want to step into a more powerful, purposeful, emotionally engaging space at work; their hearts are calling for it. Yet, we often doubt that others feel the same way.

If you're wondering how you can get your metric-obsessed boss on board, the first guiding principle is: meet people where they are. This applies not only to your boss, but also to your board, team, and colleagues. Just because they use different language and have different lenses on the business doesn't mean they don't care. Give people the benefit of the doubt. They may be more receptive than you think.

Part of meeting people where they are is using language they can relate to. The CFO I just described was receptive to the idea of more emotional engagement once he understood it wasn't a threat to financial performance.

Discussing the financial case for purpose was the best starting point. To paraphrase a popular book, numbers were his love language. He wound up being a purpose champion. He helped his own team identify how their work improved life for customers, and his team members started talking about it all the time. The emotional connection made their accuracy with numbers even more important.

You want to make your NSP part of the groundwater of your organization—something that flows through every aspect of the business. It should be as clear and prevalent as sales targets and product features. To help your NSP become part of your daily sales cadence, you'll want to:

- Set your boss, CEO, and other senior leaders up for success.
- Leverage the people most likely to support you.
- Prevent naysayers from taking the wind out of your sails.

Set the CEO Up for Success

First, let's discuss someone whose buy-in is crucial: your CEO. His or her words carry a lot of weight. If you are a CEO reading this book, great: consider this section your cheat sheet. There are a few key places where the words of the CEO give your purpose a huge lift.

Like it or not, people are always analyzing the leader, sometimes with more scrutiny than the leader ever imagined. Doug Williams, the CEO of Atlantic Capital Bank (ACB) whom you met in Chapter 2, discovered just how closely he was being watched after an experience with, of all things, his desk.

ACB had just moved into new offices with brand-new, beautiful, modern, ergonomic furniture. Williams's office had a standing desk as well as a seated desk. The standing desk was pretty utilitarian and relatively modest in size, while the seated desk was a large marble-top table with clean, crisp lines.

Williams, who is 6'4", said to me, "I loved the standing desk. I found myself using it all the time. I eventually realized I was avoiding the marble-top table because it was too short for me."

His office had glass walls and was near the big conference rooms where people often came and went for meetings. Employees got used to walking by his office and seeing Williams standing at his desk.

After a few months, he decided he'd actually like to sit more. He asked the facilities team to get new legs to raise the desk. Finally, he had a seated desk that was the right height. He hadn't realized how much he'd missed it.

During the first week with the newly improved seated desk, he had a number of cumbersome reports to work on, so he spent a good bit of time sitting, with all the reports sprawled across the large marble top.

At the end of the week, his admin approached him. She said, "Everyone is wondering if there's something wrong with you. Every time they walk by, they see you sitting. You used to stand. Are you sick?"

If you're a CEO or senior leader reading this right now, know that your people are watching you with the same level of analysis.

When you're trying to point your team toward purpose, people will take their cues from the leader. If you're not the CEO, your job is to make it easy for your CEO (or boss) to reinforce the message. One of the things my father told me early in my career was, "Part of your job is to help your boss be successful." It was excellent advice.

Here are six places where CEO language can dramatically elevate and reinforce your purpose. Get these right, and you can shift the narrative of the entire organization.

The Big Six CEO Moments of Purpose

Town halls. Nothing is more powerful than the CEO standing on stage, telling a client impact story (see Chapter 8). If he or she doesn't have one, find one, and brief him or her on it. When the CEO says, "Here's how we make a difference to our customers. This is why we exist," it speaks volumes.

Earnings calls. CEOs who frame their financial results around the organization's purpose signal to investors, "We're a purpose-driven firm focused on customers." When the CEO says, "Our Noble Purpose is X" it creates a public record. This is very good for your brand.

Executive team meetings. One CEO we know reads her company's NSP at the start of the monthly executive team meeting. She says, "It's like the bell at school or the gong at church; it calls people into the space and reminds us why we're here."

Strategy and budget sessions. When the boss asks, "How will this choice impact our purpose?" you change the frame. New initiatives should further your purpose, and budgeting should be done with an eye toward client impact.

One-on-one updates. When the CEO asks, "How is your team delivering on our purpose?" it helps non-customer-facing teams connect the dots.

Casual hallway conversations. It's awkward to run into the CEO. People get nervous. Make it easy and fun. One CEO we work with loves to say, "Another day of changing lives! Got any good stories for me?" His team members may roll their eyes in jest, but they sure know what's important to him.

If you feel like it's going to be challenging to get your CEO on board, remember: meet people where they are, and speak their language. Your CEO likely reports to a board and the investment community, who continually push for earnings growth. If you want him or her to buy into the idea of Noble Purpose, lead with the financial impact. From there, you can discuss the improvement in competitive differentiation (which improves margin and drives growth) and the increase in emotional engagement (which improves morale, retention, and productivity). Your CEO wants to experience meaningful work just as much as you do. You can help them.

Be Intentional with Your Early Supporters

There are three areas where alignment around your NSP is crucial.

Marketing

The right Noble Sales Purpose makes a marketer's heart sing. One CMO said, "This is what I've been trying to help the sales team articulate for years." Your NSP is your promise to your customers. Here's the caution: if marketing publicizes the *language* of your NSP before your sales team learns the *behaviors*, you might be doing yourself more harm than good.

Here's what we've observed. You create a great NSP. It goes on the website and all your presentations. The trumpets blare: "Here's our new purpose. We're Noble, and we're awesome. Yay us!" When marketing changes the messaging and collaterals, it's easy for the sales team to think the job is done.

It's not. In fact, it's just begun.

You want to ensure that your sales team understands their role in activating your NSP with customers and how their behavior needs to shift *before* you go public with it. The best marketing teams create tools and collateral to help the sales team bring the NSP to life during client interactions. Ask your marketing team to help you activate purpose in sales before they take it public. Use the examples of exceptional NSP marketing in Chapter 10 to help.

Think of it this way: internal activation before external proclamation.

Human Resources

HR has big challenges these days. The war for talent is real. At the same time, the crisis of employee disengagement is also real. Companies are fighting for the best people while trying to keep their current employees awake and alert.

Your HR team can be a powerful partner in activating your NSP. You want to ensure that your purpose is framed as a strategic initiative. It sits at the center of your commercial model to drive competitive differentiation and sales growth.

Too often, purpose is framed as just another employee engagement initiative. Sadly, this lessens the impact, especially in the eyes of most boards and executive teams. It becomes a "nice to have," lumped in with the benefits program and the foosball table. You want your organization to see how your NSP gives you a *strategic* advantage in the market. Having said that, it will help you attract and keep top talent. People want to be part of something bigger than themselves.

Your role is to make sure your purpose is more than window dressing. When you launch, your stories should *all* focus on the impact you have on customers. There's a temptation for HR to want to point your purpose toward every stakeholder. Resist this temptation. Your purpose is about making a difference to the people who buy your solution: customers.

Organizations often talk about internal customers. It sounds good in theory; the only problem is, it doesn't work. The concept of internal customers waters down urgency for actual customers. Internal customers never hold the same consequences as external customers. When everyone is a "customer," the passion, commitment, and urgency for real customers—the people who pay for and use your services—diminish.

To make your purpose powerful, ask your HR partners to help you get people engaged by identifying the impact their role has on external customers. You want every department to connect the dots to customer impact.

Social Responsibility

Often referred to as CSR (corporate social responsibility) or community affairs, this group usually lives and breathes purpose. That's why what I'm about to say may surprise you.

You don't want your NSP to be viewed as a community or social program. Here's why: if people think your NSP is about charity or simply doing good in your community, it will get sidelined. Fast.

Our team has learned this one the hard way. When your NSP is about making a difference, it's a natural thought process to think, "We should be doing this for free in communities that need help." You're right, you should. But if your team thinks your Noble Purpose is about charity, it will become marginalized, and you will lose your chance for a sales advantage. Your NSP is your sales ethos. It's the impact you have on paying customers.

Activate your purpose in sales first. When you have real traction, meaning your sales team is modeling it and you are starting to become known for it with your customers, only then should you use it as part of your philanthropy.

A strong commercial model is what enables you to create a strong philanthropic model. During the COVID-19 crisis, we saw the Noble Purpose firms mentioned in this book step into immediate philanthropic action. They were already clear about who they were and the impact they want to have on their customers, so they knew exactly what to do when the crisis hit. While other companies dithered, firms with a clear NSP doubled down on their purpose. The generosity of spirit they were already building was unleashed during a time when people needed it most.

Your purpose is meant to become the essence of everything you do. It requires support from marketing, HR, and CSR, but it doesn't sit in any of those departments. I've watched well-intended people unknowingly lessen the power of their company's NSP by handing it off to one group. Instead, use it as an opportunity to create alignment and improve the power of your brand at every level.

How to Deal with the Eeyores (If You Must)

We've covered the people who can accelerate your purpose. Now we need to talk about the negative people who may try to derail it.

We have a saying at our firm: "Noble Purpose can bring out the best and the beast in people." Here's what we've experienced. A certain (small) percentage of people have a visceral negative reaction. For whatever weird reason, they seem to be emotionally invested in making sure the workplace stays unfulfilling and transactional. If you have people on your team like this, we feel your pain.

We experienced a dose of this ourselves when our VP of Client Services and coauthor of this book, Elizabeth Lotardo, wrote a LinkedIn piece that went viral, entitled "Why Millennials Keep Dumping You: An Open Letter to Management."

In it, Elizabeth, a millennial herself, wrote, "ROI is not enough; I need something to care about today. Talk to me about how we make a difference." And "I'm desperate for you to show me that the work we do here matters, even just a little bit. I'll make copies, I'll fetch coffee, I'll do the grunt work. But I'm not doing it to help you get a new Mercedes. I'll give you everything I've got, but I need to know it makes a difference to something bigger than your bottom line."

It struck a nerve. The article has been viewed over 3 million times and counting. With over 40,000 shares and 13,000 comments, it seemed like everybody had something to say about it. Most of the comments were positive. Millennials chimed in, saying, "This is exactly how I feel." Older people said, "I'm 70, and I still want purpose at work." A few recruiters were even savvy enough to say, "You want a purpose? Come work for us."

But what truly surprised me was the number of negative comments. A solid 15% of the comments expressed downright disdain, saying things like: "The only purpose of work is to make money. The faster you understand that, the better off you'll be." And worse, some said things like, "This is why I hate to manage young people; they're delusional. You work to make your boss money. Period."

Keep in mind, when you comment on LinkedIn, it's not anonymous. There's no basementboy357. You're commenting as your professional self for all the world to see.

Thousands of professional people, many of them managers, were offended by the very idea that work could be meaningful. They weren't shy about telling the world why *work should not be fun*. I have to wonder, how's their recruiting going?

I bring this to your attention because you may encounter some of this blowback yourself. When people have a visceral emotional response to a concept like Noble Purpose, it's often because they have a framework that says work should be miserable, and they're immediately suspicious of anyone who says otherwise. The pushback is usually some version of, "I never had fulfillment in my work. Why should you expect it?" It's hard for people when their core beliefs are challenged.

If you encounter negativity like this, the first piece of advice I'll give you is, play to the top of the room. In my experience, top performers quickly get excited and see the value. When you play to the top of the room, the middle will catch up. Then the bottom of the room has a choice: get left behind, ask for help, or act like a jerk. The more time you spend activating your Noble Purpose with the top end, the less time you'll have to spend worrying about the naysayers.

This is easier said than done. I've spent many hours with leadership teams where the majority of talk time is spent figuring out how to deal with negative people. They may be only a small percent of the team, yet the rest of the team spends a disproportionate amount of time trying to please them or dealing with the fallout from their negative reactions.

You cannot let this hold you back. Do not allow anticipated negative responses to have a chilling effect on your enthusiasm. Be proactive about playing to the top of the room, physically and metaphorically. Think about who your likely champions are, tailor your message to them, and get their support first. It will strengthen your cause.

Restoring Nobility to the Sales Profession

Scaling your NSP means you're going to need to win the hearts and minds of people who aren't in sales. We've talked about the naysayers, so it's probably time for us to address the other elephant in the room. Not everyone loves the sales department. It pains me to acknowledge this, but it's true.

Sometimes it's not the concept of Noble Purpose, or meaningful work, or even a matter of being a positive person that causes people to push back. Sometimes it's because they believe anything coming out of the sales team is bound to be self-serving. Believe it or not, some people have great disdain for sales.

I didn't understand this early in my career. I was on fire for sales and couldn't imagine any sort of disdain. I remember one incident from my senior year of college. I was at a party, and most of the other people there were older—full-fledged adults in my eyes—and had careers. If you've ever been a college senior yourself, you know there's one question every single person asks you: "Do you have a job yet?"

Thankfully, this time I had a good answer. The day before the party, I had been offered my dream job: I was going to be a sales rep for Procter & Gamble. So when my boyfriend's boss's wife asked me the question, "What are you going to do after graduation?" I proudly said, 'I'm going into sales." She smiled and said, "That's brave of you. I don't think I could ever do that."

At the time, I took it as a compliment. I literally thought she was saying I was cool and courageous—like how you'd tell an astronaut or a firefighter or a race car driver, "Wow, I could never do what you do."

This exact scenario repeated itself many times over the next few years. Every single time someone said, "I could never be in sales," I thought they were complimenting me and my noble, courageous contribution to the world.

Eventually I caught on and realized that's not what they meant at all. When people said "I could never be in sales," they didn't mean my job was astronaut-, firefighter-, or race car driver–level cool. They meant something else entirely. Imagine my dismay when I realized that what people really meant was, "Sales is so icky. I could never lower myself to do something like *that*."

The sad truth is, a lot of people still believe sales is about convincing people to do something they don't want to do. Nothing could be further from the truth. You're reading *Selling with Noble Purpose*, so my guess is you have just as great an affinity for sales as I do. It's the commercial center of a business: without sales, you don't have a business. Sales isn't about coercing people; it's about helping people understand the value of something you're already excited about. Something you know can have a positive impact on them.

Part of the purpose of this book is to restore nobility to the sales profession.

To get the rest of your organization moving in a Noble Purpose direction, you need to take a sales approach. By that I mean, you need to do exactly what a good salesperson does: empathize with the person on the other side of the table, find out their goals, speak their language, figure out how you can you can help them, and make it easy for them to say yes.

Skip the "Aha! I Was Wrong" Moment

After watching and coaching thousands of sales teams and leaders, I've come to understand one thing: people don't need to realize they're doing it wrong in order for them to start doing it right.

As leaders, we often think we need to create the "aha" moment: the moment when the other person says, "I've been doing this all wrong. Wow, thanks. Now I understand, and I'm ready to change."

That moment is completely unnecessary. As much as you may want it, you don't need this kind of self-realization to move forward. I've seen leaders go from someone who couldn't look up from their spreadsheet to someone who stands onstage telling a customer impact story that moves people to tears (see Chapter 8). From where I sit, they've made a 180. But in their mind, they just made a few tweaks. It doesn't matter if they realize how much they've changed; what matters most is that they're doing it. Accurate self assessment is not required in order for people to improve. Don't waste your time helping people see the error of their ways. What's more effective is to extend a friendly invitation to join your movement and position it as something they will enjoy.

Your role as a sales leader is to bring the voices of your customers into the center of your organization. You may encounter naysayers. If, after trying to use the approaches described here, some people are still in the negative camp, move on. You have bigger fish to fry. Now it's time for you to harness the power of your Noble Purpose with customers.

Chapter 9: Why Seemingly Sane People Resist Noble Purpose

Assume good intent. Meet people where they are. To get the CEO, board, boss, and others engaged:

- Explain the financial case for purpose to people who speak that language (CEO, CFO, CRO).
- Discuss forging more meaningful, lasting connections with customers with marketing and sales leadership.
- Reinforce how Noble Purpose helps attract and retain top talent with HR.

If people have a visceral negative response to Noble Purpose, it's often because their mental framework is "I never had fulfillment in my work. Why should others expect it?" It's hard for people when their core beliefs are challenged.

If you encounter negativity like this: play to the top of the room. Top performers quickly get excited and see the value. When you play to the top of the room, the middle catches up. The bottom has a choice: get left behind, ask for help, or act like a jerk.

(continued)

(continued)

Remember the six places where CEO language can dramatically elevate and reinforce your purpose: town halls, earnings calls, executive team meetings, strategy and budget sessions, one-on-one updates, and casual hallway conversations.

Do one thing: Share The Big Six CEO Moments of Purpose with your CEO and other senior leaders.

Activating Your Purpose with Customers

In order to be irreplaceable, one must always be different.

—Coco Channel

In Part 3, you'll learn how to create competitive differentiation where it matters most: in the eyes of your customers. We'll look at how to bring your NSP to life across the table from individual customers and in front of big crowds. You'll read about how a few inventive teams took their sales to the next level by turning a traditional pitch into a transformational engagement, and how you can help your team do the same with your clients.

You'll learn how an NSP approach can help your team gather better customer intelligence and how to use your CRM to create more meaningful customer interactions. We'll provide techniques for leveraging your NSP to create differentiation and emotional engagement in presentations, proposals, and demonstrations, and during negotiations.

We'll talk about how to set your sales team up for success by creating an internal ecosystem that orients them toward customers. And finally, you'll learn why fear has such a chilling effect on a sales team and how you can take fear off the table for your team.

10

Making Your NSP More Than a Tagline

I believe life revolves around our meaningful connections and how we make people feel. That's what your brand should be focused on.
> —Bruce Poon Tip, founder of G Adventures

When you have a compelling purpose, you want to share it. Before you slap your NSP on a white paper and send it out, let's talk about how you can activate live time with your customers.

In this chapter, you'll learn how to help your sales team turn a traditional pitch into a transformational engagement with your clients. The key to bringing your purpose to life with customers is to help them experience it in live time during your sales process.

Creating a Differentiated, Purpose-Fueled Sales Experience

Remember G Adventures from Chapter 2, the sales team whose NSP is *We help people discover more passion, purpose, and happiness*? They're a wildly creative organization. Their employees use their free time to make music videos about their trips. Their marketing materials are gorgeous, and their analytics are laser-focused.

When the sales team adopted their NSP and became the GPS (Global Purpose Specialists), they could have created another killer video showcasing how their trips change lives. They could have done a slick ad campaign to help targeted travel agents see that booking a G trip has a positive impact on the local economies around the world. They did those things.

They also wanted to go further. They challenged themselves. They asked the team, if our NSP is to help people discover more passion, purpose, and happiness, how can we help the travel agents, the people selling to our customers, experience that *during* our sales calls?

First, some background. On a typical sales call in the travel industry, a travel rep describes their offerings to the travel agent. Travel reps have glossy brochures about their trips, hotels, boats, etc. A good rep will ask the agents questions about their client base. A rep will also talk about pricing, specials, etc. He or she is trying to get the agent to send clients on their trips or to their properties. David Green, who ran a large global travel agency at the time G Adventures was implementing their NSP, says, "Most partners come in and try to sell you their product."

G Adventures wanted to differentiate, so they flipped the model. Instead of organizing their sales calls around their product, the GPS team made their calls about the agents. Instead of telling, they started asking. Rather than walking in with a brochure, they walked in with purpose cards.

Purpose cards are a sales tool G Adventures created to engage customers in different kinds of conversations. They're a purple, G-branded deck of cards that asks a provocative question on each card, like:

"What does changing people's lives mean to you?"

"What's the craziest culinary experience you've ever had while traveling?"

"What is the most beautiful sunset you've ever seen?"

The cards were designed to help the agents think more deeply about travel and the impact of their jobs. Green says, "When I was running an agency working with G, their team changed their title to Global Purpose Specialist. This company started using language centered around purpose. We all wanted to know what it meant. And the purpose cards came in, and they said we want to help you around your purpose. There were subtle ways they got the word *purpose* into conversations."

G Adventures channeled their sales team's evangelistic enthusiasm for a product, and pointed it toward their resellers. Sales calls took on a different tone. Agents reconnected with why they got into the business in the first place. Using the questions on the purpose cards, the GPS jumpstarted an entirely different conversation. The agents shared their thoughts about how travel impacted people's lives. The cards directed them with questions like:

"Who is the most inspiring person you've met while traveling?"

"What historical figure would you like to travel with?"

Agents began to look forward to sales calls and even request them. In an environment where other tour reps are turned away, travel offices call people away from their desks to experience sales calls from the GPS team. The cards became a differentiator because of the sales experience they created. Agents loved the experience so much, they started asking for their own set of cards to use in their office. It's not a coincidence that David Green left a high-profile agency leadership position to join G Adventure team as their VP of Commercial. He says, "Coming from an agency background, there was almost an envy. I really wanted to be in the gang."

Imagine you're starting a job as a new travel agent. During your onboarding your boss takes out a deck of G Adventures purpose cards, he pulls out some cards and asks you a few questions. He tells you, "We use these cards at meetings to get to know each other and remind ourselves what a difference our job makes."

As a new agent, you're feeling even more excited about being in the travel business now. You see the big purple G on the cards, and you ask, "What's G Adventures?" Your boss replies, "They're an amazing tour company. Their trips change lives. Their salespeople are called Global Purpose Specialists. They gave us the cards to help us remember our own purpose and passion. Next time the rep comes in, I'll introduce you."

Are you getting what's happening here? A simple sales tool—a deck of purpose cards—has changed the entire customer interaction. G Adventures customers have become their brand ambassadors.

As of this writing, millions of purpose cards are in agent offices all over the world. G Adventures now sells the cards on their website. Travelers from around the world are using the cards on trains and around campfires and dinner tables to discover more passion, purpose, and happiness.

It all started with the question, "How can we activate our NSP during sales calls?"

You may be thinking at this point, "Well, we don't sell adventure travel. Our clients are IT people, bankers, manufacturing firms, plumbers, analysts, etc. They're not going to talk about the most beautiful sunset on sales calls." You're right. G adventures used their tool to jumpstart a conversation about *their* area of expertise.

Let's look at how at someone in a slightly less sexy industry jumpstarted a differentiated conversation with customers. Edmonton-based Servus Credit Union is the largest credit union in the Canadian province of Alberta. They're hardly as flashy as G Adventures, but they're equally committed to their Noble Purpose: *We shape member financial fitness.* Many financial firms use their sales interactions to uncover clients' needs and then pitch them on various products. Servus wanted to engage people in a more meaningful conversation about financial fitness.

Driven by their purpose to shape member financial fitness, Servus created a goal planner to guide financial conversations with prospective members. Using the planner, front-line staff help members identify their *Love to Do's* vs. *Must Do's* vs. *Already Completed* financial priorities. Using a list of choices such as *reduce debt stress, reliable transportation, flexibility in my budget, invest like a guru, personal wellness, educate my kids, travel the world*, and other life-oriented priorities creates a more holistic conversation than the traditional financial discussion. The reps are trained to have an empathetic, caring conversation about what are often sensitive topics. This helps them build a good relationship and understand the member's goals *before* they start talking about personal assets.

This type of conversation is both subtly and dramatically different from the types of conversations most financial institutions have with customers. It's subtle because most firms are more than eager to talk about *your* money. They want to talk about how much money you have and where is it. Clients recognize these questions as a cloak for "How large is your wallet, and how can I get a bigger share of it?"

The Servus process is differentiated. It builds trust that enables their people to ask questions like, "How do you balance saving and spending?" The shift seems subtle, but the results are dramatically different.

Just as G Adventures uses their purpose cards to help clients discover more passion, purpose, and happiness during sales calls, Servus uses their tools to shape member financial fitness in the moment of interaction. It's not "later if you buy from us you might get this kind of benefit"—the sales tools activate the purpose in *live time*. Creating the tool helped Servus ensure consistency in its sales interactions. New associates who might not have the confidence or expertise to jump into a financial fitness conversation now have a tool to help them. It's not a cheat sheet that forces people into a script; it's the opposite. It's an interactive tool that enables their team to demonstrate their sincerity and intent.

As you read about G Adventure and Servus, think about your own NSP and how you can activate it during sales interactions. Notice that both Servus and G Adventures did something very important: they gave their sales teams tools to jumpstart a purpose-oriented interaction. They didn't just tell their teams to focus on the customer and ask better questions; they gave their team a concrete tool to help them engage.

Interaction vs. Infomercial

We often tell sales people to make the call about the customer. But in most cases, the sales collaterals are about the product, and that's why the conversations go in that direction.

For an example of this, let's turn to another field: health care.

Imagine your firm sells a treatment with a clinically proven competitive advantage. Your drug is just as effective as your competitor's for treating the condition, but the big differentiator is that your product has fewer side effects. After researching the target market—physicians and patients—you settle on a core message: *We heal patients with no painful side effects.*

At this point, the temptation is to train the sales team on the messaging. Here's what often happens. The company creates a script with the key elements of the message. You bring the team together for a big sales conference. You have the salespeople practice delivering the same message over and over again until they can all do it the same way every single time. They become so good at it, they sound just like a commercial.

The only problem is ... customers hate commercials!

Sales calls aren't meant to be commercials; they're meant to be interpersonal interactions between two human beings. The minute a salesperson starts sounding like a pre-scripted commercial, customers tune them out.

As the line between marketing and sales becomes more blurred, the challenge for organizations is to create personalized engagement quickly. Buying behavior has changed dramatically, especially business buyers. The majority of the customer journey now takes place online: they've done their homework, they've seen your messaging, and they've compared you against the other options before they meet with you. This is just as true in a B2B setting as it is in consumer sales. The consumer buyer who compares light fixtures online before buying a chandelier mirrors that same behavior at work. They're the IT buyer who compares systems and reads client reviews, the business owner who compares bank rates and reputations, and the physician who looks at drug studies before they meet with a rep.

That's why sales scripts are so ineffective.

With sales calls happening later in the buying process, customers don't need information; the key to differentiation is engagement.

Whatever the length of your sales process, you have to identify the moment when you flip the switch from the collective messaging, which tends to be a marketing function, to interpersonal engagement, which is the heart of sales.

Deep Schemas Drive Engagement

Instead of handing your sales force a scripted message, teach your sales force *why* the message matters. Using NSP-focused tools, you can help your team create a differentiated conversation. If you want them to become true expert advisors, they also need subject matter expertise. You want them to be able to skillfully connect the dots between the individual customer's goals and challenges and your solution.

Let's go back to our health care example. For the drug with fewer side effects, the sales team needs to understand the impact that side effects are having on patients and the practice. Do the side effects cause problems for the nurses or the doctors? How does the issue affect their ability to treat the patient? Do they have to spend extra time? Do side effects prevent the patient from taking the medication?

Schema is your knowledge about the subject: the concepts within it, how they relate to each other, important facts and events pertaining to the subject, etc. For example, I have a deep schema upon which to draw when it comes to sales, and perhaps parenting. I've been deeply involved in both for over two decades and have done extensive study, reading, and practical applications.

But when it comes to chemistry or sky diving, I don't have much knowledge beyond basic information.

If you want your sales force to have compelling conversations and ask insightful questions, they need a deep schema about your subject area.

A salesperson with a deep schema can ask better questions. He or she knows where the pain points *might* be and so knows what to explore. A deep schema also gives the salesperson the confidence to step into a back-and-forth conversation: wherever it goes, he or she knows how to engage. Without a deep schema, the rep is just another generic salesperson reading off a marketing brochure.

It's important to differentiate here. The "spray and pray" model of sales (spray a bunch of stuff out there and pray some of it sticks) is long dead. Improving your sellers' schema doesn't mean you're training them to information dump—quite the opposite. Your team can draw from their knowledge to create robust interactions with customers. Knowing what *most* customers will likely care about can guide a rep to ask better questions. You don't assume you know; instead, you leverage your knowledge to gain faster insights.

Let's look at the differences between a salesperson leading with information vs. a salesperson drawing upon a deep understanding of the issues. Here's how this might play out in our medical example.

- **Statement 1: Leading with information**
  - "Our research reveals that 85% of doctors worry about side effects. Can we talk about how we eliminate these?"

    This may or may not work. If it does work, the conversation will likely be focused on the product, not the physician's practice, and it will not be very engaging or differentiated.

- **Statement 2: Drawing on information**
  - "Side effects have a big impact on patients and physicians. What's been your experience?"

    Now the conversation is about the customer, and they're more likely to engage.

- **Or even better, Statement 3: drawing on customer-specific information**
  - "Your nurse told me that you were having problems with side effects. Can we talk about how side effects are affecting your patients and staff?"

Do you see the difference? Statement 1 assumes this customer is just like every other customer. It leads down a product path. Statement 2 flips it. The rep draws on a common problem to engage the customer in a conversation about how it might be affecting that specific customer. Statement 3 goes even further, addressing an issue that is specific to this customer (that the rep uncovered on a previous call). In this case, the salesperson knew to look for the issue (side effects) because market research and training told the rep it was likely there. The salesperson validated it with someone in the customer's office first and then initiated a conversation about how the issue was affecting this specific client.

The salesperson's understanding of the issues guides discovery. Reread this example and substitute your own product research and insights. This model of using deep schema and research to guide interactive sales conversations applies to any sales interaction.

Let's go back to the two organizations mentioned earlier. The G Adventures team knows a lot about the challenges their agents face because they've done their research. Their white paper "Purpose in the Travel Industry" provides its team with deep information about how travel agents feel about their jobs, and what they're looking for. Servus Credit Union has similar data about their customers. They know what people are saving and spending and how they feel about it.

These firms don't organize their calls around sharing this data. They *draw* upon their data to jump-start meaningful conversations with customers. Their salespeople are trained in two things:

- Deep understanding of the customers' issues and challenges
- Sales skills to get individual customers talking about their issues

To illustrate why it's ineffective to offer information too early, let's look at a subject where lots of people like to tout their wisdom: parenting. Imagine you have a new baby, and you're back at work for the first time.

As someone who well remembers that stage of life, it would be easy for me to give you lots of unsolicited advice. In fact, as I look at you huddled over your coffee, clutching it with both hands as if your very life depends on it, it's obvious to me: you are exhausted. Clearly, you need my help. It's time for me to tell you how to get your baby to sleep better. If you're my friend who trusts me, you may be eager for my advice. If I'm just a random colleague, you may react differently. Perhaps you're doing everything you can and you don't want another person telling you what to do. Or maybe your baby is sleeping great, and you're tired because you stayed up all night working on your novel.

Instead of starting with my point of view, I'm going to draw upon my schema (my knowledge of the subject) and ask you questions like: "How's your baby sleeping? How are *you* sleeping? What's been the most fun part of new parenting for you? How are the mornings going? What's it like to get out the door and get to work?"

The conversation is going to be about you. I'm able to ask you good questions because I have a good understanding of your space. But I'm not making assumptions.

If you tell me that you're bone-crunching tired because no one is sleeping, I can ask you what's going on and express empathy, saying something like, "Wow, I remember that. It's hard. What have you tried?" What will likely happen next is that you will ask me for advice—advice you will perceive as more valuable because it came from someone who has demonstrated they understand your situation.

The same model applies to sales calls. Go back and reread the previous conversation, substitute *customer* for *colleague*, and instead of a baby, imagine we're talking about patients, clients, financial issues, or operational challenges. For a skilled seller, the conversation will follow the same model: draw upon your expertise to ask insightful questions, find out their perspective on the issue, identify where they want to go, and figure out how you can help.

If you want your team members to be perceived as experts and trusted advisors, they need to do more than repeat pre-scripted messages. They need in-depth knowledge about typical customer challenges, and they then need to be able to draw them out of the customer in live time. That's how you ensure that your NSP is more than a tagline.

In our studies of sales team performance, we've looked carefully at the interplay between messages and interactions to determine what works and what doesn't. We discovered three key distinctions between top performers and their average-performing counterparts:

> **Average reps lead with a generic message to get customer interest.** NSP reps begin their calls by discussing specific customer issues and then weave in only the messages that apply to that individual customer's situation.

> **Average salespeople repeat marketing messages exactly as they have been instructed, using the same messages on call after call.**
> Top-performing NSP reps customize their message to help individual customers meet their goals.

> **Average salespeople spend the majority of their customer face time delivering messages.**
> NSP reps spend their face time discussing customer issues. That's why their calls last longer and their customers are more engaged.

Tailoring your approach to the customer is not a new concept. As with many things, it's the depth and consistency of execution that will differentiate your team. You can and should do this at every phase of the sales process.

Avoiding the Data Dump in Demos

Product demos are an area that often goes unaddressed when it comes to tailoring the approach. Whether done by your sales team or another function, the right demo can make or break a sale. The sales enablement team at Fiserv engages with clients and prospective clients throughout the sales process. Two of their most crucial inflection points are discovery and the demo.

Fiserv is a global leader in payments and financial technology; their solutions are complex. They provide account processing and digital banking solutions, card issuer processing and network services, payments, e-commerce, merchant acquiring and processing, and cloud-based point-of-sale solutions. They work with banks and credit unions. Implementing a Fiserv solution can affect every person in the organization.

Not surprisingly, the Fiserv sales process can be lengthy and involve multiple players. Often, someone at one level, typically higher up, drives the decisions, but multiple other levels can stop or push forward the sale. For a sale to stick and have a successful implementation, people at every level need to buy in. A new system or process means change, which requires additional work for the front lines.

When the sales enablement team does a demo, it's crucial they connect to the customer's strategic objectives and also understand the reality of every single person in the room, which can include someone who represents the bank tellers, the IT team, senior leadership, branch operations, and others. The demo is a pivotal point in the sales process; it can create buy-in and urgency to move a sale forward—or, if the demo falls flat, Fiserv can lose the sale.

Fiserv's larger aspiration is to *Move money and information in a way that moves the world.* The sales enablement team got even more specific. They decided their nested purpose (which sits under the larger aspiration or purpose statement) for their team is *We empower success.*

The team started using the game-changing question we talked about in Chapter 5—"How will the client be different as a result of doing business with us?"—as a lens for discovery.

Empowering client success in demos meant the team had to identify what success looks like for *all* of the constituents within their client. This meant the team had to ask more questions in advance and then frame the demo in service of meeting the objectives they had uncovered with the client. It worked. Their demos became more customized and compelling. Because their team knew what success looked like for each person in the room, they could share with each person how the software would improve their function.

Activating their purpose in live time on demos helped the Fiserv team improve buy-in. Clients started to see the sales team enablement team differently—they weren't just there to pitch a product; they were there to empower success. Solution Consultant Kathy Houghtalen says, "This NSP culture is permeating our group, and we are morphing into motivated and enthusiastic success empowerers!"

Fiserv VP of Sales Engagement Lisa St. Germain, who led her team to adopt the approach, says, "This took our demos from product-oriented to client-oriented. With our team aligned around empowering success, we were able to transform what was once a micro-detail run-through of features to a strategic conversation about business results."

St. Germain explains, "A quality implementation is determined by a successful transition from the presales team to the implementation teams. We saw our voice of the client scores improve as we focused on engagement through the lens of our NSP, *We empower success.*"

Activation vs. Proclamation

As you think about the interactions your team has with clients, challenge yourself: How can you go beyond a product pitch? How can you help your clients experience your NSP live time during your sales process? Do you need more differentiated sales aids? Should you use a creative self-assessment tool? Does your team need to ask different questions during discovery?

Announcing your NSP is great. Helping your clients experience it live time is more differentiated. We started this chapter with the G Adventures team of Global Purpose Specialists who use purpose cards to transform their sales process. Now let's look at how they activated their purpose in an even more challenging situation.

The G Adventures team decided to use their new sales approach in a very high-stakes situation: a major industry travel conference. They were one of 20 vendors presenting to an auditorium of the world's highest-volume travel agents. The team had just seven minutes for a presentation, wedged in between 19 other big-name tour operators, cruise lines, and hotel chains: companies with big budgets that would no doubt be pulling out all the stops with impressive dog and pony shows to demonstrate how fabulous they were. The high-end hotel group that went on stage right before G passed out champagne in fluted glasses for everyone in the audience.

In the past, the G Adventures team would have done their own version of the dog and pony show. Their videos are both beautiful and emotionally compelling. If they had just used those, they would have made a great impression. But the GPS team wanted to do more: they wanted to reach into the heart of every agent in the room and help them see how much their work mattered.

When it was time for G Adventures to take the stage, the VP of sales stood up, faced the room full of agents, and asked a simple question: "How many of you have ever booked a trip that changed someone's life?" Almost every single person in the room raised their hand. He then said, "Instead of talking about us, let's spend the next five minutes talking about you. Turn to the person next to you and describe the trip you booked and how it changed the life of your client."

The entire room came alive. The energy soared as agents described booking a golden anniversary trip to the Eiffel Tower, the *I beat cancer* trek through Scotland, and the *I found my true love at 60* honeymoon to Bali. Minutes earlier, this same group of agents had looked bored when a fancy hotel chain served them champagne. Now they were on fire.

That single prompt—asking the agents to describe a life-changing trip they booked—lit up the frontal lobes of almost everyone in the room. Keep in mind, G Adventures had only seven minutes with the audience. They had now spent five of them without even telling people about their trips.

With two minutes left, the VP of Sales called the room back to order. He said, "The way you feel right now is the way we want you to feel every single day. You give people memories that last a lifetime, and we don't ever want you to forget that. Our team of Global Purpose Specialists has been trained to make you feel like this every time you interact with us."

He closed by saying, "Here's a video to remind you why your work matters. If you'd like to talk about discovering more passion, purpose, and happiness, come meet us at our booth." He walked off the stage as the video, showcasing the faces of travelers around the world experiencing happiness, played to the tune of Queen's "Somebody to Love." That, my friends, is the difference between proclaiming your NSP and activating it in live time.

You won't be surprised to learn that, after their mic drop moment, the G Adventures booth was swamped. The team had to run to the van for more brochures. They lined up sales calls for weeks to come.

I confess, when I recount this story, I feel myself getting misty-eyed. I still remember the moment their VP of Marketing called me from the parking deck and exclaimed, "Holy crap, it worked!"

The G Adventures team had the courage to try something different. They weren't content with a traditional "show up and throw up" sales presentation. They wanted to truly engage, and they wanted to do so in a meaningful way. The GPS team and the others described in this chapter went beyond their products: they turned their sales process into a transformational experience for their clients.

Your team can do the same thing. You simply have to decide: "Are we here to talk about us, or are we here to make a difference to the person on the other side of the table?"

Chapter 10: Making Your NSP More Than a Tagline

Activate your NSP in live time with your customers by:

- Creating a differentiated sales experience using impact-focused sales tools like purpose cards.
- Engaging with customers instead of telling customers. Avoid generic pitches, and use time with customers to find out what your NSP means for *them*.
- Deepening the schema of the sales team by helping your team understand typical customer objectives and challenges.

(continued)

(continued)

- Avoiding data dumping. Connect your data to what your customer finds valuable.

Do one thing: Look at your existing sales and marketing materials, and ask yourself, "Are we telling or engaging?" Choose one way you can make your information more engaging when in front of the customer.

CHAPTER

11

The Customer Intelligence You Didn't Know You Needed

As a general rule, the most successful man in life is the man who has the best information.

—Benjamin Disraeli, British politician

If you ask salespeople what their biggest obstacles are, they'll often tell you they're price and competition. Sales leaders tend to have a different perspective. We frequently get inquiries from sales leaders, asking if we can help their team improve their closing skills.

These are real challenges, but in most cases, they're actually symptoms of a larger problem. Issues with price, competition, and closing show up at the end of the sales process, but the real problem occurs much earlier. The root cause is often a lack of customer intelligence.

Telling a salesperson to become a "better closer" is putting the cart before the horse because his or her closing skills aren't usually the root issue. The real problem is the salesperson doesn't know enough about the customer to establish differentiation, value, or urgency.

Selling with Noble Purpose requires you to develop a deeper understanding of your customers. You have to truly know your customers to understand how you can make a difference to them. When your sales team fails to establish a concrete link between your solution and the customer's most compelling goals and challenges, you'll quickly become commoditized.

Lack of customer intelligence is a substantial and largely hidden obstacle. Most salespeople don't even realize what this shortcoming costs them. Rarely will you hear a customer say, "You don't know us well enough to close the deal." More often, they'll tell you they prefer the competition or claim that your price is too high. Or they simply won't take any action at all.

If two salespeople have similar products and pricing, the salesperson who does a better job connecting his or her solution to meaningful customer goals will win the business. The only way to demonstrate real value is to connect the dots. This is how you activate your NSP. You must show, in concrete and meaningful ways, how this specific customer's life and organization will be different—and better—as a result of doing business with you.

To be clear, if you have inferior products, inflated pricing, or a terrible reputation, customer intelligence alone will not make up for those shortfalls. However, if you've met the basic table stakes of your industry, your sales team's ability to understand and connect with high-priority customer goals gives you a huge competitive advantage.

The Five Categories of Critical Customer Information

Most sales organizations gather some level of customer intelligence. The information traditionally deemed important includes things like the customer's buying history, vendor requirements, competitive purchases, financial data, and org charts. These matter, but they don't tell you anything about the customer's high-priority goals and challenges.

You can differentiate yourself and bring your NSP to life by understanding five critical categories of customer information:

- Customer environment
- Customer goals
- Customer challenges
- What success looks like for the customer
- What lack of success looks like for the customer

Think of these five categories as file folders. They provide a system for organizing customer intelligence that will help your sales force do a better job of linking your solution to the issues the customer cares about.

Here are some examples of what salespeople need to know in each area. As you read this list, ask yourself, how well does my sales team understand these about our customers?

Environment

This will help you understand how your contact relates to the organization as a whole and how the organization is positioned within the context of its marketplace. You want to know things such as:

- What's your contact's core function or role?
- What's going on in his or her organization or life?
- Who is the competition, and how do they stack up?
- What is the customer's position in its marketplace?
- What's happening politically inside the organization?

Goals

You want to find out what your contact's objectives are, as well as that of his or her department and the overall organization. The types of things you want to know are:

- What does your contact need to accomplish?
- How is your contact evaluated?
- What does the senior leadership believe is most important?
- What measurements does the customer have in place?
- Where does the customer stand with its goals to date?

Challenges

This area is where you want to find out more about problems and issues that concern both your contact and his or her boss. You want to know things such as:

- What are they worried about?
- What obstacles do they face?
- What are the competitive threats inside and outside the company?
- What resources do they have, and where do they need more?

What Success Looks Like

You'll want to know what an organizational or personal win means for this customer, specifically:

- What is your customer passionate about?
- What does your contact's boss care about most?
- How does your contact define and measure success?
- How will your contact know when he or she has achieved success?
- How does your contact's boss define and measure success?
- How does their organization define and measure success?

What Lack of Success Looks Like

This area is where you want to find out about the potential risks your customer is facing and what the customer's senior leadership is concerned about. You'll want to know:

- What are they afraid of?
- What will happen to the organization if they fail?
- What are the consequences for your contact?

As you scan these lists, you'll notice this information isn't about your product or solution, nor is it about your revenue pipeline or order history. *It's about the customer.* Product- or quota-focused salespeople—the average performers—tend to view customer information through the lens of their products or solutions. NSP-driven salespeople—the top performers—take a more holistic approach.

I cannot emphasize enough how important it is to provide your team with a clear template for the types of information you want them to gather. These five categories of information go beyond purchase requirements. NSP sellers make a concerted effort to understand the customer's complete business environment and the goals and challenges that matter most to their organization. NSP-driven salespeople gather customer information with an eye toward what they're selling; however, they don't limit themselves to the areas that pertain directly to their products.

For example, if they're calling on a technology company, they figure out where that company is in the market and what the firm's long-term plans are. If they're calling on a medical practice, they don't focus on one treatment or disease state; they look at the practice's clinical and financial goals. If they're calling on a bakery, they make a point to understand the bakery's customer base.

Top performers know the difference between purchase requirements and true goals. An average performer will tell you that the customer's goal is to buy a certain type of product. A Noble Purpose seller will give you the full story about a customer or potential customer. The NSP rep knows what the customer does, which markets they compete in, what the most pressing issues are, who the customer's competition is, and what challenges they face. NSP reps understand that buying products or services is never a goal. Customers buy products and services to accomplish the goals they've set forth for their own organizations.

This broader focus enables an NSP salesperson to make strong, concrete recommendations when it's time to close. The five categories of critical customer information are drawn from our study of top performers. These categories represent the body of critical customer intelligence top performers use to differentiate themselves and forge more meaningful connections with their clients.

How Information Improves Your Win Rate

NSP-driven salespeople close bigger deals at higher margins because they connect their solutions to the customer's high-priority goals, challenges, and success factors, rather than narrowly focusing on purchase requirements.

Let's compare the difference between these two sales approaches.

Imagine two salespeople who both sell automated order-processing systems. Both systems have the potential to make the customers 20% more efficient.

The first salesperson has been coached to find out who the buyer is, what the budget is, and who the competition might be. After uncovering this information, the rep gives a presentation. This rep's presentation will most likely be organized around the salesperson's key benefit, which conveys: "Our solution makes you 20% more efficient."

It sounds good. But it's generic. This salesperson is leaving it up to the customer to figure out how a 20% efficiency improvement will affect his or her organization. Average salespeople tend to use the same benefit statements with all their customers.

The second salesperson works for an NSP-driven organization, so the approach differs. They uncover the standard information about the buyer, the buying criteria, and the competition. But this rep's manager also requires the sales rep to uncover information about the customer's environment, goals, challenges, and success factors. The rep knows his or her manager will ask about these things before the presentation. The rep is trained to uncover this information. Uncovering this information early in the process makes calls last longer; the discovery process takes a bit more time and involves a few more players than it did for the first salesperson, who just uncovered basic information.

When it's time to prepare the presentation, the NSP rep has much better customer intelligence. The NSP message connects the dots between the customer information and the salesperson's key benefit.

The NSP rep uses the five categories of critical information to illustrate the impact of a 20% improvement:

Customer environment: "I know you're in a competitive market where customers focus heavily on delivery times."

Customer goals: "Your primary objective is growing market share."

Customer challenge: "Slow turnaround time is costing you customers."

What success looks like: "Improving efficiency will give you a competitive advantage that will help you grow market share."

What lack of success looks like: "If you can't improve efficiency, you're likely to lose customers."

Only then does the NSP rep deliver the message: "Our solution will help you win more customers because your system will be 20% more efficient."

Which one of these sellers created a more compelling case? If you're a buyer, which one of these reps are you more likely to take in to see your CEO or CFO? The first salesperson, who speaks in general terms about efficiency, or the second salesperson, who directly links to your high-priority goals and challenges?

It's worth noting that *the difference between these two presentations is only five sentences.* Good advance intel enabled the NSP rep to create a powerful framing for their solution: it's seen in a totally different context. It now has urgency; it's not just a purchase, it's a way to advance the client's business.

The difference between the preceding two presentations isn't in the product or benefits.

The difference is the customer information.

The first presentation is generic because the salesperson didn't uncover enough relevant customer information to make a compelling case for the proposed solution.

The reason the salesperson is able to give a more compelling message isn't because of better presentation skills. It's because of better information-gathering skills. The second presentation—for the exact same product—describes the impact the solution will have on this specific customer.

The NSP salesperson is able to do this because they did a more thorough job during the fact-finding calls. The NSP rep knows the customer's environment, goals, challenges, and success factors, making it possible to present a more concrete case. You can't make a difference to your customers if you don't understand them.

Without a solid understanding of the customer's environment, goals, challenges, and success factors, salespeople wind up giving generic presentations and proposals. They can't provide concrete descriptions of how the customer will be different because they don't have a thorough understanding of where the customer is today or where the customer wants to go.

Here's the leadership challenge. The reason the NSP salesperson did a better job of fact-finding isn't because a manager said, "Ask better questions" or "Be a better closer." It's because the manager asked very specifically about the five categories of customer information.

Remember Chapter 7, where I talked about how specificity is sexy? Now we're getting even more specific (and, by my definition, even sexier). Generically telling your team to gather more customer intelligence is better than telling them to ignore customer information. But if you want to gain a true competitive advantage, give your team specific direction about the kind of information you want them to gather, give them a place to store it, and give them the skills to uncover it.

The reason the first rep—the average rep—didn't uncover the information isn't because the rep doesn't care about his or her customers. It's because the rep doesn't have a good blueprint.

The questions you ask your salespeople become the questions they ask their customers.

When a manager focuses exclusively on customer order history, contact information, and buying patterns, the salesperson is much less likely to gather the customer intelligence needed to make a compelling presentation.

Go back and look at the questions under the five categories. Imagine asking your reps these questions about their customers during the sales process. What impact would that have on their behavior?

When the manager focuses on true customer intelligence—the customer's environment, goals, challenges, what success looks like, and what lack of success looks like—the salesperson is prompted to look for that information during the discovery stage of the sales process. You don't have to gather information about all of these on every sales call. You can explore these at different levels of depth in different ways for different types of buyers. Much of the information is readily available on the internet.

Some salespeople argue that they don't have time to gather this kind of customer intelligence. The people who make these claims tend to be mid-level performers. Field observation of top-performing salespeople revealed that they spend more time than average performers in the fact-finding stage of the sales cycle. That time reduces objections, generates urgency, strengthens the relationship, and connects to value, which, in turn, increases their close rate and shortens their sales cycle.

Think about one of your upcoming presentations. Look at each of the five categories. How can you and your team do a better job of linking your solution to critical customer information?

You learned in Chapter 5 that asking a salesperson, "How will this customer be different as a result of doing business with us?" ignites a new line of thinking. Asking your sales team about the five critical categories of customer information takes this thinking to the next level and activates it on a behavioral level. It also shows you, the leader, where the gaps are.

Questioning with Purpose

It's easier to identify the information you want to know before you try to come up with specific questions. Once you identify the gaps in the five categories, you can craft questions for your customers to help you get a full picture.

Following are 10 great questions to ask customers. There's space after each question for you to fill in the information you're seeking. For example, say you're calling on a bank. You know a big merger has happened in their market. You want to know: Are they at risk for losing customers? Or are they trying to capitalize on the uncertainty in the market? Once you know what you're looking for, you can use the format, asking something like "What impact does the recent M&A activity have on your strategic plan?" Keep in mind that the word order in the questions is important. These questions are based on our observations about which phrasing gets the best response from customers.

10 Great Questions to Ask Your Customers

Great questions are sincere and well planned, and zero in on the customer's environment, goals, challenges, and success factors:

1. **What impact does this (change, event, challenge, competitive situation) have on your organization?**

   The tendency is to ask, "What do you think about this?" But asking how something affects a person gets you a much deeper, more meaningful response.

   _____

   _____

   _____

   _____

2. **What's the most challenging part of (something about the person's role or function)?**

   This demonstrates that you're genuinely interested in what it's like to live in his or her world.

   _____

   _____

   _____

   _____

3. **If you could change anything about (a current pressing situation), what would it be?**

   This helps you understand your contact's goals and challenges. _Warning:_ You want to be sure to ask this in a nonmanipulative way. You're not fishing; you're interested.

   _____

   _____

   _____

   _____

4. **When you look at X (challenge) and Y (other challenge), how do you prioritize between the two?**

   This prompts inner reflection, which, in turn, gives you clues about the customer's thought process and lets you uncover what's really important to him or her.

   _____

   _____

   _____

   _____

5. **What do you enjoy most about (insert important job activity)?**

   Asking someone to describe the best part of his or her job creates a positive tone and opens a window into that person's world.

   _____

   _____

   _____

   _____

6. **How do you feel about this (key initiative or goal in the customer's organization)?**

   This demonstrates that you're interested in your customer's perspective, not just making the sale.

   _____

   _____

   _____

   _____

7. **What do you think is causing (situation that's on his or her mind)?**

   This prompts your customer to think about root causes, which will enable you to connect the dots—and discover what issues are likely most important to senior leadership.

   _____

   _____

   _____

   _____

8. **How can I best support you on (big project, goal, or challenge)?**

   This enables your contact to define what he or she really wants, and it tees you up to provide specific, requested help.

   _____

   _____

   _____

   _____

9. **What is your deepest fear about (something important to your customer)?**

   This allows your contact to share an area of vulnerability. While counterintuitive, most people actually like to do this, as long as the listener makes it nonjudgmental and safe.

---

10. **What are your highest hopes for (your job, company, or project)?**
When someone shares his or her hopes with you, that person is telling you what really matters to him or her and giving you a chance to join the team.

These questions are designed to jump-start thoughtful, more meaningful conversations. Customers can tell if you're coming from a place of genuine interest. This is not a *check the box, fill it out, get it turned into the boss* questionnaire. If you're just trying to check the box, customers will sense this—and won't reveal as much information.

When you start asking your sales team about the five categories, don't be surprised or frustrated if it's slow going at first. Most salespeople don't think about their customers in this way, and that's why they're not top performers—yet.

If a salesperson answers with product-focused answers (as opposed to true customer information), then push harder. You want your salespeople to take off their product lens and look more holistically at the customer.

When salespeople know that you, the leader, are always going to ask about the customer's environment, goals, and challenges, they will in turn begin seeking that very information on their sales calls. When they're aware that you expect them to understand what success and lack of success look like for each customer, they will come prepared with an answer.

Capturing the right customer information also helps the rest of your organization. When you have accurate information about your customer's goals and challenges, you can share it with your marketing and product development teams. Your salespeople are the conduit to the customer. Sharing the information that salespeople capture about customers broadly gives everyone in your organization better insights into your customers' world.

Understanding customers on a deep level makes your salespeople more empathetic and more assertive at the same time. When you know exactly how the customer will benefit from doing business with you, you have more urgency about closing the deal.

Chapter 11: The Customer Intelligence You Didn't Know You Needed

The questions leaders ask their salespeople become the questions salespeople ask their customers.

You can differentiate yourself and bring your NSP to life by fully understanding five critical categories of customer information:

- *Customer environment*—What's going on inside the organization and in their market?
- *Customer goals*—What are they trying to accomplish in the macro and micro?
- *Customer challenges*—What are the business challenges they face internally and externally?
- *What success looks like for the customer*—How have they defined winning internally and externally and what are their metrics for success?
- *What lack of success looks like for the customer*—What's the risk if the organization fails?

These five "file folders" provide a system for organizing customer intelligence to help your sales force do a better job of linking your solution to the issues the customer cares about.

Do one thing: Before important presentations, ask your salespeople about the customer's environment, goals, and challenges. Have them describe what success and lack of success look like for their customer. If they can't do it, they're not ready to close.

12

Three Places Where Differentiation Goes to Die

When you're the only sane person, you look like the only insane person.
  —Criss Jami, American poet, philosopher, and essayist

There are three high-stakes places in the sales process where sales teams run the greatest risk of becoming commoditized:

- Call openings
- Presentation/proposals
- Negotiations

There's a general unspoken expectation that salespeople will handle these three areas in a traditional way. That's why you want to do the opposite.

These three seemingly self-explanatory moments in the sales process are opportunities for true differentiation. The way your team handles these moments tells customers whether you're unique or just another sales team.

You may be reluctant to get into the weeds of your sales team's talk track. Yet, these moments are where your purpose can come alive most for the customer. Let's look at each one of these moments to see how a traditional approach takes you down a transactional path, and how you can help your team avoid that trap. I'm going to get very specific here because:

- The traditional approach is the exact opposite of what works.
- The differentiation you've worked so hard to create will die here if your team acts like everyone else.

Call Openings

I see a lot of well-intentioned sales calls go south because of the opening—and, oddly enough, it's usually just the last few seconds of the opening that send it south. You probably already know that leading with a one-way product pitch isn't effective. But often, even reps who try to start at a higher level wind up pitching too quickly. Here's how it plays out. A rep will start with some really compelling data about an industry change or a business objective, they'll frame up their expertise, and then they'll ask, "Can we talk more about this?"

It sounds good. But let's look at the result. This will go one of two ways. The prospect says, "No, I don't want to talk about that," in which case, goodbye. Or the customer says "Yes." The rep gets excited because it seems they've jumpstarted a conversation. But what happens after the customer says "Yes, I'm interested in that"? Most reps will go right into a pitch. The opening got the customer interested, but instead of a dialogue, the rep is pitching with no intel about whether they should be pitching at all.

Here's the Noble Purpose version. A better call opening gets a buyer interested in sharing with you, not just listening to you. You want those early conversations to be about your buyer's business, not your pitch.

A Noble Purpose opening does three things:

1. Jumpstarts a conversation about a challenge, goal, or issue of interest to the customer
2. Positions the seller as an expert who can potentially help
3. Prompts the customer to share *their* perspective on the issue

That's where the **you-me-you** technique comes in. Start with a business topic of interest to the customer; that's the "you" part, meaning the other person, your customer. Do your research, and find something relevant. If you're a technology company calling a retailer, and you read an article about online ordering, you might say something about how technology is changing the entire customer experience. Then give a brief statement about your expertise, like, "We help retailers better engage customers." That's the "me" part.

Now here's where most reps get tripped up. It's easy to ask, "Can I talk to you about that?" But then who's talking? The seller. Instead, go back the customer. Ask a question like, "What kind of customer experience are *you* trying to create?" That's where the magic happens, going back to "you" the customer.

Now the conversation is about their business, in an area you can impact.

Let's walk through a couple more examples. Imagine you sell medical devices, and your Noble Purpose is to help patients feel better faster. You're talking to a CIO of a major hospital.

First, a topic interesting to the customer:

You (something of interest to customer): "The 65+ population is projected to increase by 20% in the next five years, which means an increase in heart-related illnesses."

Now, your expertise:

Me (your expertise): "We've helped hundreds of hospitals adapt to the increasing demand for cardiac treatments."

And last, an insightful question, which prompts the customer to talk:

You (back to the customer's perspective): "How is *your* hospital preparing to support the demands?"

You start with something likely of interest to the customer, then a brief statement about your expertise to show them you're someone you're worth speaking to, and then flip it back to the customer.

To illustrate why this technique is so powerful, imagine you work for a financial institution, and your NSP is to help your customers thrive. Here are two different ways to talk to start talking to a client about advisory services.

I just read that 32% of people
would rather go to the DMV than
make a financial plan.

I work with a lot of clients to
make it less painful.

vs.

I'd like to be your trusted
advisor. Can we talk about your
financial plans?

What are the most challenging
aspects of financial planning for
you?

Compare the you-me-you opening to the rep who says: "I'd like to be your trusted advisor. Can we talk about your financial plans?" They may be sincere, yet as someone who has been called on by multiple would-be advisors, I can promise you it's no different than what everyone else is saying.

It's basically, "I'm nice and want to help, so can you spend a bunch of time telling me about yourself?" Insert any other industry or topic, and the result is the same: a well-meaning rep who wants your time but doesn't know much about you.

The "you-me-you" technique cuts through the clutter. The first two sentences create interest and establish your expertise. Remember, this isn't your whole sales call. It's an *opening*: a tool that frames what the conversation will be about. The expertise statement is very short, simply to give credibility. It's not a description of your offering. The ending question is the key. It's what propels you into a meaningful conversation, which is what selling with Noble Purpose is all about.

You might ask, what if the customer doesn't want to talk about the area you bring up? There are two answers to that. First, do your homework beforehand so that your topic is compelling. Second, if for whatever reason it's not compelling to this customer, you haven't damaged yourself. When you demonstrate expertise in your industry along with genuine interest, customers are more likely to see you as a peer. They're likely to say, "That's not the issue, but this is," and start a conversation.

The following page illustrates how a subtle shift in language jumpstarts a much more valuable conversation.

Can you spot the difference? If you specialize in customer engagement software—or, as in our case, you're a consultant who works in the space—both of these opening statements would be pretty good. Yet the second one lays the foundation for true connection.

Traditional Opening

You (customer): A lot of firms in your space have a challenge with differentiation.

Me (expertise): We've helped hundreds of organizations cut through the clutter to win bigger deals and create competitive differentiation that attracts more clients.

More me: Can we talk about that?

The client says yes, and the seller proceeds to pitch without any connection to customer goals.

Results in a transactional conversation.

Noble Purpose – You-Me-You Opening

You (customer): You have some formidable competitors. I imagine establishing differentiation is crucial.

Me (expertise): We've helped several firms cut through the clutter to win bigger deals and create competitive differentiation that attracts more clients.

You (customer): What are your biggest challenges with differentiation?

Jumpstarts a customer-focused, engaging, differentiated conversation that will enable the seller to connect the dots when they're ready to present.

The "you-me-you" technique can be used in person, over the phone, or even in an email. To be clear, you're not trying to manipulate customers into talking about something they're not interested in. Rather, you're being intentional about language.

If you want to add value and be differentiated, you need to know more about your customer's life and business than your competition. You want to establish yourself from the very start as someone with expertise in your subject area and someone who is sincerely interested in the customer.

Presentations and Proposals That Generate Urgency

When you do great work in the discovery process, you should leverage it in your presentation. Sadly, many presentations and proposals wind up being a generic and sometimes flowery description of the seller's product or solution. Ideally, you're so in sync with your buyer that you move seamlessly from discovery to solution, with both of you aligned on the goal.

In the real world, sales can take longer and may involve a lot more than a single highly engaged buyer. Your buyer forgets what you talked about on the last call. Sometimes buyers leave their role or company; sales get delayed. And as much as you may try to engage with all the decision-makers, sometimes your proposal is reviewed by someone you've never even talked to. Anyone who has ever lost a deal you thought you'd already closed, because a higher-up executive or committee you didn't know about declined it, knows the pain I am talking about here.

You want your presentations and proposals to create urgency. You want them to be so compelling and high- impact that the customer can't live without your solution. And you want the value to be clear, even if your materials get passed around to others. The challenge is, most organizations use standard templates for their presentations and proposals, which can make them very generic. Or they let their salespeople wing it, which creates inconsistency. You can do better.

The best model is a hybrid—a customizable template with prompts for your team to spell out how exactly you will deliver on your purpose for each specific customer.

Your presentations and proposals should demonstrate to your customers the impact your solution will have on their organization in very specific terms. For example, if your NSP is to help clients drive revenue and do work that makes them proud (which is ours, at McLeod & More), your proposal should illustrate how you're going to increase the customer's revenue and emotional engagement. If your NSP is to help clients improve their financial wellness, you should know what financial wellness means to them and tell them how you are going to improve it.

In Chapter 11, you read about the five categories of critical customer information: environment, goals, challenges, what success looks like, and what lack of success looks like to this customer. Presentations and proposals are where you leverage these to create urgency. They provide the context that makes your solution more compelling.

To make presentations and proposals compelling, be sure your team does the following:

1. **Recap the intelligence.** Succinctly summarize the client's environment, goals, and challenges.

2. **Describe the endgame.** Clearly state what success and lack of success look like for the client, as they would describe it.

3. **Paint a picture of your impact.** Once you have agreement about where the customer is today, tell the customer how they will be different as a result of doing business with you. This is where you describe how you're going to activate your NSP for this customer. Note that this is not a description of what your NSP is; rather, it's a description of how you're going to help this particular customer experience it. This means that you have to have done your homework prior to the presentation.

4. **Provide proof you can deliver.** You can include a relevant customer impact story (see Chapter 8) to illustrate how you've made a difference to other customers with similar goals.

You'll notice this process follows the "customer first, product second" methodology.

Written proposals can follow the same format. To set your team up for success, create a template that leaves placeholders for the salesperson to fill in the specifics for each individual customer.

This serves several purposes:

- Salespeople can create presentations quickly and easily.
- Salespeople must uncover critical customer information to fill in the placeholders before they give presentations.
- You ensure that salespeople stay pointed to the customers.

Here's how this differentiates your team from traditional reps:

Traditional transactional sellers	Noble Purpose presentation
Our company is wonderful.	Your company environment, challenges, and goals are these.
Our goal is this.	Success for you looks like this; lack of success is that.
Here's our solution.	Here's how you will be different as a result of doing business with us.
Clients benefit in this generic way.	These specific clients changed in these specific ways (vivid client impact stories).

Which solution is going to seem more compelling to the customer? Which seller is going to be taken to senior leadership? Which organization seems more differentiated?

When you expect your team to follow this format, over time, salespeople gather better information during discovery. They know they're going to have to summarize the information in their proposals and presentations. NSP presentations and storytelling become an organizational habit.

Keeping Your Purpose Alive in Negotiations

When you work hard to create real value for your clients, it's painful to watch it erode during negotiations. The best way to avoid this is to solidify your value *before* it comes down to price. The more you differentiate yourself early in the process, the less you'll find deals coming down to price.

You're better off putting your efforts into creating a differentiated experience up front. When sales leaders say, "I want my team to be better negotiators," investigation often reveals that the problem is not at the end of the sales process; it's a failure to create value early in the process.

You already know that sales teams who overemphasize financial targets and underemphasize client impact are the organizations most likely to be commoditized. Having said that, if you're in sales, negotiation is going to happen. The first thing you want to do is make sure your team has clarity about how you deliver on your NSP, so they can hold fast to it during a negotiation.

I used to teach hardball negotiating skills. Here's what I've observed: people who view negotiation skills as a technique to get what *they* want are not as effective as the people who truly believe there can be a win-win solution. Salespeople who merely *act* as if they want the other person to win aren't as successful as the salespeople who truly *want* the other person to win. It's a mindset difference that affects your outcomes.

I don't teach hardball techniques anymore because they're not conducive to creating partnerships with clients. The challenge is, many customers have been trained in the hardball approach. So, it's helpful to understand where they're coming from. Hardball negotiators start by eroding your value story. They'll make it all about price. They'll tell you that the additional services you provide, such as customer service, warranties, and so on, aren't needed. They'll tell you those are of no value to them. They'll strip away everything except price.

Then, *after* you've agreed to the lowest possible price, they'll try to build back in the things they previously said were of no value. They'll say things like, "I can't believe you aren't going to offer any service. What kind of company are you? Don't you support your products?"

Do not be lured into this. There are some buyers who care only about price, but in most cases, the aforementioned behaviors are just a tactic. Many major purchasing organizations split the users from the purchasing people. The users are required to vet vendors to identify which ones meet the standards. After they identify all the vendors who can meet the specs, they turn it over to the purchasing department, which pits the vendors against each other so they can beat them up on price.

In my experience, organizations who employ this model do get better pricing as a result. They also get a lot less service from their suppliers. As suppliers are forced to whittle the price down, they pull back support and resources. They put their lower-priced, less experienced people on the project. They cut costs wherever they can, even if it means eroding client value. They're also resentful of the client. It's a horrible foundation for a relationship, and a downward spiral you want to avoid.

As a Noble Purpose sales team, you want to focus your sellers on activating your Noble Purpose so effectively that you can stand on your value.

Look at the difference between the questions Noble Purpose sellers ask earlier versus the questions transactional sellers wind up asking later:

Noble Purpose sellers ask early:	Transactional sellers ask later:
• What impact will this have on your business?	• What kind of price do you need?
• What role does this play in the larger picture?	• Where can we cut back?
• How does this fit into your overall priorities for your job?	• How are you evaluating this?
• What effect will this have on your boss?	• What will get your boss to agree?

Noble Purpose sellers are proactive about building value in advance of negotiation, while transactional sellers tend to be more reactive. Their questions start after the client brings up price.

Notice, Noble Purpose sellers aren't describing their value: they're asking the client to articulate the value they perceive. They're not manipulating the client; these questions are asked with honest intent. They want to know what value the client places on solving their challenge. This reduces the likelihood of price negotiations, and if they do wind up in a price negotiation, Noble Purpose sellers have a clear value story to lean on. Even if they wind up being sent to a transactional purchasing department, they're more likely to get strong support from their buyer, who has clearly articulated the value for the organization.

Noble Purpose sellers aren't at risk of eroding their competitive differentiation in the negotiation process because they establish their unique value before negotiation starts.

If you want your team to be better negotiators, help them differentiate early in the sales process. Then they can go into negotiations confident of their clearly differentiated value rather than worried the client is going to erode it.

Go Beyond Normal

Keeping competitive differentiation alive during crucial sales inflection points can mean the difference between a team that wins high-margin business and reps who find themselves commoditized. Your team can handle these in the normal way, or you can use them as opportunities to stand out. If you want to create differentiation:

- Open with the intent to engage in a meaningful way.
- Organize proposals around critical client information and how the customer will be different as a result of doing business with you.
- Build on your value when you negotiate.

Your team can do better than the standard transactional sales process. Your NSP is your driving force. Let clients know how they will be different as a result of doing business with you.

Chapter 12: Three Places Where Differentiation Goes to Die

There are three places where standard practices can erode differentiation. Move beyond the traditional transactional approach to make your team more compelling.

Call openings: differentiate by using the "you-me-you" technique.

- You: I understand (compelling business issue) may be a challenge in your industry.
- Me: A brief statement of your expertise
- You: A well-crafted question about an area you can impact

Presentations and proposals:

- Summarize the five categories of critical customer information.
- Spell out exactly how the customer will be different as a result of doing business with you.

(continued)

(continued)

- Provide proof with a customer impact story that will get people talking.

Keeping your purpose alive during tough negotiations:

- Build value before negotiation with deep customer intelligence.
- Prepare your buyer to tell your story to others.
- Don't give away services to lower the price (it will hurt your reputation).

Do one thing: Look at the three critical places, and ask your team to flip the script.

13

The Dirty Little Secret About Sales Training

Nothing contributes so much to tranquilize the mind as a steady purpose—a point on which the soul may fix its intellectual eye.

—Mary Shelley, English novelist

Earlier in my career, I was a sales trainer for several well-known sales training firms. I was quite earnest about my role. As a former VP of sales, I knew the stakes were high: improving seller behavior has a big impact on the company and the reps themselves. I spent hours helping salespeople practice techniques. I worked with them after class or came in early if they wanted extra guidance. I thought I was making a big difference in their lives.

When I moved into the role of field coach, I quickly discovered that the training was not having the impact I had hoped. During ride-alongs, I painfully observed many salespeople who had been stars in the classroom quickly reverting to their old behaviors in the field.

I remember one rep in particular. During the training session, she'd nailed the challenging skill practices with difficult scenarios using true-to-life customer situations. Imagine my disappointment when it became obvious after a few sales calls that she wasn't using any of the skills she'd been taught. The six-step call model? Forget using it; there was no evidence that she even remembered it. The four types of questions? She barely asked even one.

After some frank conversations and a few more painful field ride-alongs with other reps, there was no escaping the truth: the sales call models, questioning techniques, and planning tools we were teaching in the classroom were rarely used in actual customer conversations. Managers were not reinforcing them, and most reps couldn't even remember them.

The question was, why?

I have to admit, this was an agonizing time for me. I'd spent years trying to help salespeople be more effective. Now I was being confronted with hard evidence that my work hadn't made much difference at all. But it wasn't just my programs; it was all the programs. I realized this once I got my own ego out of the way and started digging. I studied a variety of companies who were using a variety of selling skills programs.

The sad truth was almost always the same. It didn't matter whether it was a simple four-step call model or a complex multi-phased strategy program, and whether the questioning technique had a fancy acronym or used basic labels like "open" and "closed." It didn't matter who had run the program—or even which program it was. Time and again, salespeople would learn the skills in the classroom and forget them in front of the customer.

It makes me ill to think about the time and money that had been wasted. How many people had spent time away from their families learning skills they never used? How much time had been lost from the field? How many workbooks, videos, and decks and webinars had been created that were now just gathering dust?

It would have been totally depressing ... if not for the outliers. The only exception to these findings were the top-performing NSP-driven reps. These outlier salespeople—top performers driven by a sense of Noble Purpose—were also outliers when it came to sales training, in that they were the rare group of people who actually used the skills in the field. They attended the same programs as their colleagues, yet whereas others forgot the techniques, the NSP reps applied them.

Here's why: they had a different North Star.

Any good sales training program teaches salespeople to focus on the customer. Salespeople often experience an "Aha!" moment in a classroom setting. They recognize where they've been too focused on their products and how paying more attention to customers' needs and goals will benefit everyone. Since there's no pressure to make the sale in the classroom, salespeople have an open mindset—and the skills stick. But when they get back into real customer conversations, with the pressure to close, the old mindset returns, and they quickly forget the skills they learned.

Skills like deep discovery and customer-focused presentations don't stick with average reps because their orientation is toward themselves, their products, and their quotas. Their leaders then (unintentionally) reinforce this internally focused orientation.

NSP reps are different. They retain higher-level sales skills because what they're learning matches their mindset. It doesn't matter what's going on in the rest of the organization. Their internal frame is, *I'm here to make a difference to my customers*. When they learn a new questioning technique or a planning strategy, they view it through the lens of an NSP.

In the previous chapters, we've covered several sales techniques. These are a great start. However, to make the skills stick and create a truly differentiated organization, you also want to be proactive about teaching your team new mindsets.

Sales Training Addresses the Symptoms, Not the Cause

If you want to elevate your team's behavior, you must elevate their thinking.

As you know, the challenge with any training (sales or any other type) is making it stick. You've probably experienced this: you send your rep to sales training. They come back on fire; they make a few great sales calls. Within a month, it's as if the training never happened.

Organizations try to address this problem in a variety of ways. You can make the training more emotionally and kinesthetically engaging; instead of a lecture, you use self-discovery learning. You can do more live-time practices and use more real-life customer examples.

Training sales managers to reinforce sales training is also crucial. Without reinforcement, even the most effective training fails. According to a 2014 study conducted by Alliance Sales & Marketing, without follow-up, salespeople will *lose 80%–90%* of what they learned in training within a month.

All of these things matter. But there's one thing that has a bigger impact than anything else, and most organizations overlook it. True sales transformation requires a new mindset for the skills training to sit on top of.

We will not solve problems with the same thinking we used when we created them.

—Albert Einstein

When salespeople go to training, they typically learn to be customer-focused. But whatever methodology you use, whether you're challenging customers, spinning them, or trying to use strategic selling, the implied endgame is always the same: the close. *This* is the root problem.

Every technique the salesperson learns winds up being in the service of the close. On the surface, this sounds like the entire point of sales training: to help your reps close more deals. That may be the macro point, but here's how it plays out in the micro. A salesperson learns a new method for asking discovery questions. They use it, it starts working, the customer's answer reveals a surface-level need, and with the first scent of opportunity in the air, the salesperson starts pitching, discovery ends, and it's back to the *let me tell you about our solution* show.

If you're a sales leader, you've probably witnessed this behavior. An inkling of interest causes the seller to jump into telling. Some of the most painful coaching calls of my life have been spent watching a seller jump too early and miss the chance for true engagement.

Your NSP is the linchpin—it's the game-changer that shifts the focus of your sales efforts. When you train your team, you position the skills in service of the customer. The close is what naturally follows. For most teams, this requires a different mental framework. When we teach selling skills, we keep the NSP on the wall, physically and metaphorically. Every skill is positioned to help sellers activate the NSP with customers. Executing this shift requires some counterintuitive thinking.

Two Distinct Mental Abilities of Top Performers

F. Scott Fitzgerald said, "The test of a first-rate intelligence is the ability to hold two opposed ideas in the mind at the same time, and still retain the ability to function." Top performers have a different North Star, and they also have two core mental abilities that enable them to engage customers in a differentiated way. They can:

1. Hold two agendas in their mind at the same time
2. Sit with the uncertainty

Here's how these two play out. While average performers are focused exclusively on the close, top performers are able to focus on the customer *and* keep the close in their mind at the same time. They're able to maintain both agendas. They can do this because they've also mastered a second crucial mental ability: they're comfortable with uncertainty.

These mental models—holding two agendas and being able to sit with uncertainty—are the essential underpinnings for top sales performance. They're also both intimately and directly connected to each other. The only way you can hold two agendas in your mind at the same time is if you're okay with some uncertainty. If you're not able to sit with uncertainty, the two agendas will battle each other inside your mind. And if you're in sales, the agenda called *my quota* will usually win.

The reason average performers struggle to point their full attention toward the customer isn't because they're bad people or don't care about the customer's goals. It's because they're afraid that if they put their own agenda on pause, it will be lost. They might not be fully conscious of their own internal thought process, but it's usually there.

After observing hundreds of reps, this point became obvious: average performers can't hold space for the customer's goals because their brains are too filled with their own objectives. Their fear of not accomplishing their own goals prevents them from stepping into the uncertainty of a back-and-forth interaction. They don't have repeated experiences of sales calls where a more open, customer-focused conversation resulted in a high-impact solution. Because they haven't done it often, they're not confident enough to put their own agenda on pause.

This is particularly evident during times of uncertainty and change. Average reps become even more anxious about their numbers, and they double down on their own agenda.

Compare that with high-performing NSP reps whose mindset is:

- The sales call is about the customer's agenda and my agenda.

- If I put my agenda on pause, to fully explore their agenda, I'm confident I'll find a way to help them, even if I don't know exactly what that looks like yet.

Top performers have complete confidence that they'll ultimately be able to help the customer, but they're not attached to having it play out in a certain way. They are no less focused on making the sale than their counterparts; in fact, they're usually more focused. They're enthusiastic about their offering, but they're not determined to make every single customer interaction play out "just so." Sitting with uncertainty does not mean the absence of a plan. Far from it: top performers have a plan, *and* they're flexible. It's their confidence in their ultimate ability to help that enables them to put their plan on pause. They're not overly attached to a specific talk track or timeline.

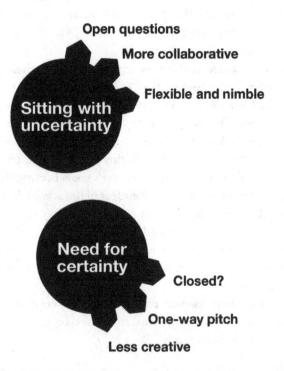

Open questions

More collaborative

Flexible and nimble

Sitting with uncertainty

Need for certainty

Closed?

One-way pitch

Less creative

The ability to hold two ideas simultaneously and sit with uncertainty enables a more sophisticated approach to interpersonal interactions. These are mental abilities you can teach. The first step is to call them out. Tell your team that these two mental abilities are what enables top performers to freely explore new information rather than blowing past it in an attempt to close. This changes the tone of their calls, and it allows customers to feel heard and understood. It improves trust and increases the level of customer intelligence they gather. When it's time to recommend a solution, NSP reps have more concrete information and can make a more compelling case.

Top performers never have the "Am I done asking about you? Can I talk about me now?" moment so typical of transactional sellers. For top performers, the entire sales interaction is about the customer.

Average performers gravitate toward more scripted sales calls because they get anxious in the face of new information. That's why they try to close too early and too often.

If you've ever suffered the gut-wrenching sales manager experience of watching your salesperson ignore customer cues and miss important information because they were so eager to close the sale, you understand the perils of being too attached to a pre-scripted call plan.

How Sitting with Uncertainty Reduces Objections

When we get requests to train salespeople in "overcoming obstacles" or "handling objections," I've learned to look deeper, to the root issues. Average salespeople tend to spend a lot of time dealing with objections and obstacles. This is often because they miss information earlier in the process. This causes their sales cycles to flounder, stall, and take longer to close—because as much as they try to avoid them, obstacles remain. Getting comfortable with uncertainty enables sellers to surface objections earlier, before the customer has locked down their thinking. When there's no proposal on the table, the customer is not defensive; they're simply sharing.

Sellers who are willing to step into the uncertainty of true collaboration create more dynamic solutions.

Shifting your mind from default patterns isn't easy. Trying to tell a Type A sales rep with a quota on the line that he or she should be a better listener and ask more questions is kindof like your mom or a Sunday school teacher telling you to be more kind. You know it's something that you *should* do, but it's hard to remember the advice in the heat of the moment—especially when money, or your ego, is at stake.

Human beings love certainty, and we love our own agendas. That's why, as a leader, you need to ground your team in these three crucial mental frames:

- This is about the customer's agenda *and* my agenda.
- I'm confident enough to sit with uncertainty while we explore.
- I am here to improve life for the customer ... (your NSP).

Put these on the wall during your sales training, and repeat them before every call. These are the mental models you want to embed in your team. When you build client-focused skills on top of these mental frameworks, the skills stick.

Your Customers Are Mind Readers Whether They Realize It or Not

Have you ever gotten a feeling about someone before they even said a word? Of course you have. It's not hard to read someone else's mood. If your boss walks in with a scowl, you know today is not a good day to ask for a raise.

We're constantly reading each other's moods, intentions, and mindsets. Sometimes we do this consciously, but most of the time, it's done subconsciously. Your customers read people, too.

Customers decide very quickly whether someone is authentic and believable.

In a study for his book *Silent Messages*, about the implicit communications of attitude and emotions, Albert Mehrabian, professor emeritus of psychology at UCLA, asked the question, "What makes someone credible?" or "Why do we trust someone?"

The answer is *congruence*. Your words need to match your tone, tempo, and body language. When someone's words disagree with his or her tone and nonverbal behavior, people are more likely to believe the tonality and nonverbal behaviors communicated than the actual words. Mehrabian found that the believability of someone's message was influenced only 7% by content (the words), 38% by voice tone and tempo (the way the words are said), and 55% by body language and facial expressions.

This means when a customer is deciding whether a salesperson is credible, only 7% of their assessment is based on the words the salesperson says. The other 93% is likely to be based on the salesperson's tone, facial expressions, and body language.

When you're building belief with your sales team, you're shaping their mental talk track, which is what they're going to be *unconsciously* communicating to their customers every single day.

For example, imagine a salesperson doing a presentation for a customer. The verbal message is, "We want to help you improve your business." But underneath, they're thinking, *When will this deal close? I gotta hit my number.* Their nonverbal message is more likely to be tense and anxious. Picture a salesperson pushing the contract across the desk, looking like they are about to pounce. It doesn't matter what words they're saying: the message to the customer is *this is about me; buy now.*

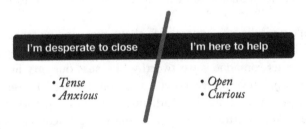

Now let's imagine a salesperson whose manager has built belief in their NSP. The salesperson's internal talk track is *I'm here to help.* What non-verbals will they likely be communicating?

As a sales leader, you can approach this information in one of two ways. You can spend a lot of time and money teaching your salespeople how to intentionally manipulate their tone, tempo, facial expressions, and body language to make them seem credible, or you can address the root cause, which is their mindset: the internal talk that drives their tone, facial expressions, and body language.

The reason this chapter is called "The Dirty Little Secret About Sales Training" is because there's a reason most sales training programs don't stick. It's because they teach skills without addressing mindset and intent. This becomes quickly apparent during times of volatility, when the sales process is disrupted. Reps who don't have the right mindset struggle to adapt. Fortunately, this is an entirely solvable problem.

The mindset salespeople bring into their customer interactions sets the stage for everything else they do. Mindset drives behavior. It's the centerpiece for the actions salespeople take. The way you think about a situation determines your approach and directs your actions. Giving your people a new way to think about their interactions changes everything.

Customers read a salesperson's tone, tempo, facial expressions, and body language because they instinctively know that those things reveal the rep's true intent. Your internal dialogue is constantly leaking out, whether you're aware of it or not. You can try to cover it with clever body language tricks, but it's a lot easier (and more honest) to just think the right thought in the first place.

It's worth noting that authenticity is becoming ever more important these days, especially as buyers trend younger and more female. These demographics are particularly skilled at reading intent. As personal finance expert Dave Ramsey says, "If you're interviewing financial planners, and your wife doesn't like the person, walk out immediately. Women are reading people on a totally different level than most men can understand. Her intuition is probably right."

I don't typically use generalities about men and women, but on this point, I will tell you: women's intuition is real. Centuries of learning how to assess whether someone is trustworthy—because our very lives depended on it—give women a pretty good gauge on motive. Those differences aside, the research tells us that authenticity is more important than ever to all buyers. Your customers are consciously and unconsciously assessing your intent. It's worth nothing that when the COVID crisis hit, transactional "me first" sellers were quickly identified and promptly ignored by customers who turned to people they trusted to have their best interests at heart.

Salespeople who sell with Noble Purpose—the top performers—don't worry too much about their body language or tone because when their internal thoughts leak out, it actually has a positive impact on customers.

The 10-Second Game-Changer

I'll close out this chapter with a model we use to help salespeople align their minds toward their purpose before sales calls. We call it the *10-second game-changer*.

Imagine you're about to walk into a critical customer interaction. Stop, plant your feet, and do this:

10-second game changer

1. **Breathe:**
   This gets oxygen to your brain and more blood flowing through your body.

2. **Think:**
   This is about the customer's agenda and my agenda. I have a plan, and I'm flexible. I'm confident enough to sit with uncertainty.

3. **Believe:**
   I'm here to help this customer … (your NSP).

Use this technique to center yourself and put yourself in the right headspace. It will remind you of your larger purpose and help you bring your best, most creative, fully alive self into any situation. Sales teams who use this mental training technique notice a difference very quickly. You show up more grounded, confident, and open.

I use this technique myself before I go on stage to keynote or have an important client conversation. I find that when I do it, it helps me stay in the moment and be fully present. I feel a difference throughout my entire body. I confess, I don't always remember to do this. When I forget, I'm more likely to get all wrapped in my own thoughts, and I don't fully connect. Some refer to this as *monkey mind*: a Buddhist term meaning unsettled and restless. The 10-second game-changer calms your monkey mind. Improving your internal mental model always improves your external impact.

Your internal dialogue drives your external presentation. As a sales leader, you play a powerful role in shaping your team's mindsets and beliefs. When you establish new mental models for your team, you start to see a shift in their behavior.

Aligning your sales training with your NSP enables your team to bring their hearts and souls to work and do the best for their clients.

Chapter 13: The Dirty Little Secret About Sales Training

Mindset precedes behavior. Most sales training is taught in the service of the close, which creates a transactional mindset. Instead, position all training in the service of your NSP.

The two mental abilities that separate transactional salespeople from top-performing Noble Purpose sellers are the ability to:

- Hold two agendas in their minds at the same time
- Sit with uncertainty

When you teach consultative sales without reframing toward a customer impact mindset:

- The skills do not stick because the daily cadence of *close the deal, hit the number* takes over.
- The skills can be perceived as manipulative by customers because they are reading intent nonverbally.

To make sales training stick, organizations must reorient the North Star of the organization to customer impact and teach sellers the two mental abilities of top performers.

Do one thing: Reframe your sales skills training in the service of your NSP.

14

Using Technology to Humanize Customers

If we continue to develop our technology without wisdom or prudence, our servant may prove to be our executioner.

—General Omar Nelson Bradley

What do you do when you wake up? Are you one of those mindful people who meditates and exercises before you engage with the outer world? Or are you like the rest of us, who wake up and check our phones?

No matter what ritual you practice, the moment you open your first screen of the day, be it your phone, tablet, or laptop, it directs many of your thoughts and actions. In recent years, we have become more mindful about directing our own days, rather than just responding to whatever our devices send our way. But the devices are still an important part of our daily sales cadence.

We've talked about your sales team's mindset and behaviors, and the types of customer intelligence that will make the team more competitive.

We've talked about the techniques to keep them focused. Now let's talk about the technology that directs so much of your team's daily activity.

How Your CRM Affects Sales Calls

Compare and contrast the following two scenarios. Two competing salespeople are calling on the same customer. Salesperson A is making his call at 10:00 a.m., and Salesperson B is making her call at 11:00 a.m. They both do the exact same thing before they hop on their respective calls: glance at their device to review the customer's information. Here's where the differences start.

Salesperson A sees where the customer is in the sales process, some basic intelligence about their organization, their purchase requirements, and their order history.

Salesperson B sees five boxes:

1. Environment
2. Goals
3. Challenges
4. What success looks like
5. What lack of success looks like

Each box contains a succinct summary of the information the salesperson has gathered on previous sales calls.

Which salesperson is going to make the better call? Who is going to open with something of interest to the customer? Who is going to ask better questions? Who is better prepared to discuss the customer's most pertinent business issues? Who is going to do a better job of aligning the solution with the customer's key goals?

Now take it to the next level. If you're the customer, which screen would you rather have a salesperson looking at before making a sales call on you?

The answer is obvious, of course: Salesperson B is going to be better prepared because she's going into the sales call thinking about the customer. If the two salespeople's products and pricing are about the same, Salesperson B will probably have a more insightful, meaningful conversation because her customer relationship management (CRM) system set her up to be thinking deeply about the person in front of her.

Salesperson A's CRM set him up to make a product-focused sales call. The last thing the rep saw before he went into the call was the pipeline report. With no prompting to focus on the customer's goals and challenges, Salesperson A will do what most average-performing salespeople do: pitch his products and services.

Salesperson B's CRM set her up to make a customer-focused sales call because it put information about the customer's environment, goals, challenges, and success factors up front to ensure that they were the last things she thought about before going into her call. And the last thing she thinks about *before* walking in usually determines the first thing she'll say when she gets there.

Play this out with an inside sales team; the model is the same. Whatever they're looking at on their screen is going to drive their conversation.

Why Computer Screens Are More Powerful Than Sales Managers

What percentage of sales calls does a salesperson make with his or her manager? 2%? 10%? For what percentage of those sales calls does a rep get pre-call or post-call coaching from a manager? Half, maybe? It's likely much less.

Now let's look at the technology. What percentage of sales calls requires a rep to interact with your CRM or other data system? Probably just about all of them.

For most reps, the CRM is a more dominant presence in their sales activity than their manager. It's scary to think the technology has a more significant impact on your salespeople than their boss does; it's also reality. Salespeople spend more time interacting with their screens than they do with their managers.

In the previous chapters, you learned why and how to require more robust customer information to compel better sales call behavior. Now I'd like you to consider how to use your technology to take this to the next level.

When you're coaching salespeople to capture more information about customers' environments, goals, challenges, and success factors, you need to give them somewhere to record it. This is a tricky dance; you don't want to overburden your team by requiring that they capture endless information. The information you ask them to capture should drive sales behavior. Your sales team should see the win for doing it.

> *Your technology should be humanizing your customers,*
> *not the opposite.*

If you want your team to focus on customers, make sure your systems and technology are:

- Including personal and emotive information beyond traditional targets and logistics
- Capturing true customer intelligence (the five categories of critical customer information from Chapter 11: environment, goals, challenges, success, and lack of success)
- Pulling that information front and center for your reps
- Prompting your managers to ask about client impact
- Pointing your team toward your NSP

Technology can have a chilling effect on your sales team's emotional engagement with clients. You can't afford to let that happen. Here are some specific ways our clients and others have brought client impact to life:

- Share customer impact stories via Slack or other internal messaging services.
- Include a "How will this customer be different?" field in pipeline reports.
- Insert the five categories of critical customer information (environment, goals, challenges, success, and lack of success) in customer profiles.
- Require salespeople to have the five categories of critical customer information before they can get pricing.
- Create a library of client impact stories to easily pull into presentations.
- Send voice memos and videos instead of text and emails to emotionally engage.
- Make your NSP the default desktop or phone wallpaper.
- Include a clear articulation of "How will this customer be different?" when you pass customers between reps (for example, business development to account exec) or hand them off to support/implementation.

You can be just another sales force who says they want to make a difference to customers, or you can be the rare company that actually does it.

Capturing the right information about your customers helps you put your good intentions into action.

Your endgame is making a difference to customers; your technology should help you do exactly that.

Chapter 14: Using Technology to Humanize Customers

Technology should humanize your customers, not the opposite. CRM systems are the primary drivers of rep behavior. To prompt deeper discovery, use your CRM to capture the five categories of critical customer information: environment, goals, challenges, what success looks like, and what lack of success looks like.

In addition to your CRM, here are other ways to use technology to bring customers to life:

- Share client impact stories via Slack or other internal messaging services.
- Send voice memos and videos instead of text and emails to emotionally engage.
- Include a clear articulation of "How will this customer be different?" when you pass customers between reps (for example, business development to account exec) or hand them off to support/implementation.
- Create a library of client impact stories to easily pull into presentations.

Do one thing: Make sure your CRM has a place to capture information about customers' environments, goals, challenges, and success factors. If it currently doesn't, revamp it so that it does.

15

How Fear Flatlines a Sales Team

We must build dikes of courage to hold back the flood of fear.
—Martin Luther King, Jr.

We've talked about how to activate your NSP with customers. There's another crucial element to making all this work: take fear off the table. Fear has a chilling effect on our ability to engage. When you're afraid, your focus is on yourself, not the person on the other side of the table. If you've ever found yourself staring down the short end of a bad revenue report, you know what it's like to be afraid. It's a cold, clammy finger of dread. It starts in your gut and spreads like ice water through your veins, moving into your arms and legs. Your heart beats faster, your breathing becomes shallow, and you break out in a cold sweat.

This is hardly the right mindset for a successful sales call.

Some old-school leaders consider fear to be a great motivator for salespeople. To be fair, it does work in the short term. Here's what we've observed:

fear of failure can jumpstart sales *activity*, but it has a chilling effect on sales *behavior*.

Fear makes you frantic. You want salespeople who are focused.

Fear ignites the most primal, self-serving part of your brain. When your brain has been hijacked by fear, your personal short-term interests trump everything else.

Why Fear Causes Salespeople to Fail

Salespeople who are afraid don't show up with purpose. They show up with angst. And your clients can read it. Fear-based salespeople aren't effective because they:

- Feel frantic
- Think only of the short term
- Are more likely to product-pitch
- Don't ask insightful questions
- Are less creative
- Think about themselves more than the customer
- Worry about covering mistakes instead of fixing them
- Resist the unknown
- Tell their boss what he or she wants to hear
- Fail to connect in a meaningful way

Salespeople who ground themselves in purpose:

- Stay focused
- Are long-term strategists
- Fix mistakes
- Are customer-oriented
- Tell the boss what he or she needs to hear

- Manage unknowns
- Work harder in the face of adversity

When you're worried about yourself, you go into protection mode. When you know other people are counting on you, you step up and go the extra mile.

As a leader, *your job is to take fear off the table for your team*. Your purpose serves as your dike of courage to hold back the flood of fear.

Here's how a leader at Salesforce described taking fear off the table in a recent session: "When you look at these big revenue targets, it's easy to be afraid. You think, how am I possibly going to get this kind of revenue out of this customer list? Instead, I put my number aside and look at each potential client through the lens of a bigger purpose. I look at each customer and ask: How can I help them? How can I get creative? How can we empower them to connect with their customers in a whole new way? I list all the things we could do for them. By the time I'm through the list, I have my revenue number."

Sales can be scary. You're only as good as your last quarter, and you've got to reinvent all the time. Despite their seemingly confident exteriors, most salespeople are secretly terrified that they'll fail. Customers can feel the same way. Behind many of the toughest-negotiating purchasing managers is a deep-seated fear of getting called on the carpet for making the wrong decision.

Fear can kick-start someone into action—that's why leaders use it. But it's not a sustainable source of motivation. You can do better; there are more effective ways to create urgency.

Don't Take Your Lizard Brain on Sales Calls

You learned how a compelling NSP and customer impact stories ignite your team's brain's frontal lobes, giving them access to higher-level decision-making, creativity, and thought processes. Fear does just the opposite. Fear ignites your amygdala, often referred to as the *lizard brain*. The lizard brain is a holdover from our more prehistoric ancestors. It has two responses: fight or flight.

Daniel Goleman, widely known as the father of emotional intelligence, coined the phrase "amygdala hijack" to describe what happens when fear takes over. Goleman describes it this way: "In the brain's architecture, the amygdala is poised something like an alarm company where operators stand ready to send out emergency calls to the fire department, police, and a neighbor whenever a home security system signals trouble. When it sounds an alarm of, say, fear, it sends out urgent messages to every major part of the brain: it triggers the secretion of the body's fight-or-flight hormones, mobilizes the centers for movement and activates the cardiovascular system, the muscles, and the gut."

The amygdala is the most primitive part of your brain. It doesn't have higher-level decision-making skills. It responds only to perceived threats. The lizard brain isn't very smart. It can't distinguish between a threat to your life and a threat to your ego, so it responds to both in the same way.

When a salesperson is afraid to lose a deal, their body responds as if their very life is at risk. All they think about is trying to alleviate their fear. When bosses use fear, salespeople focus on pleasing the boss, instead of making a difference to the customer. I know—I've been there.

An Eye-Opening Lesson in Fear-Based Leadership

When I was a sales manager for P&G in my mid-20s, I had an experience with fear-based leadership that forever altered my perspective on sales management. By way of background, P&G is one of the most disciplined sales organizations in the world. They have extremely high expectations, and it's a competitive environment.

It's not a coincidence that many P&G managers are ex-military. I often say half-jokingly I grew up in the P&G "Thank you, sir, may I please have another!" school of sales management. There is an esprit de corps that comes from being part of a high-performing team. Your boss is tough, but you know he or she wants you to succeed. Some of my most gratifying experiences at P&G were taking a new college grad and turning him or her into a sales machine within 30 days. The sales leadership skills I learned there laid the foundation for my career. I'm forever grateful for my experiences at P&G—including the one I'm about to tell you about.

Six months into my tenure as a sales manager, we got a new "big boss," and he was coming to town to make sales calls with us. To say I was nervous would be putting it mildly. He was two levels above me; I was up for a promotion, and knew this encounter was critical.

My boss and I picked up Mr. Big Boss at the airport. His flight was late, so he jumped in our car at the curb and we rushed straight to my customer's office, where we were presenting a new product line. I gave what I thought was a good presentation: the customer agreed to buy most of the new items. Mr. Big Boss didn't say much afterward. We then headed straight for my boss's customer, where he gave a similar presentation and the client bought most of the new items.

We drove back to our office and parked. Just as we were about to get out of the car, Mr. Big Boss said, "Don't you want to hear my feedback?" With me sitting in the backseat of my boss's company-issued Ford Taurus, I watched as Mr. Big Boss proceeded to tear my boss apart. He went through the presentation page by page with a scathing critique of every item.

Keep in mind, both of the actual sales calls had gone well. Both customers agreed to take most of the new items. But Mr. Big Boss thought we should have gone for more—more SKUs, more shelf space, more advertising support.

As Mr. Big Boss ripped through my boss, I sat silently in the backseat, watching as my tall, confident, smart, 50-year-old boss slumped lower and lower with every word. By the time Mr. Big Boss got to the last page, my boss was a defeated man. His head was practically on the steering wheel. My first thought was, "I'm about to be fired." My next thought was, "We're both going to be fired." I felt like I wanted to throw up.

My boss took Mr. Big Boss back to the airport. It wasn't a fun ride. The scathing written report came two days later. Mr. Big Boss was disappointed in us on every level. His main criticism was that we should have sold our customers more items. In retrospect, he was right. We should have. We had just gone for the standard. Had we talked in advance about how the extra items might benefit the customers, we could have built a strong case. But Mr. Big Boss never once talked about the customers. Instead, he ripped through town like a tornado, leaving a wake of petrified salespeople behind him. He went on to the next city and did the exact same thing there.

We kept our jobs, and two months later, he came back. Were we afraid? You better believe we were. We were also ready—ready to cram every item down our customers' throats that we possibly could. We had quit thinking about our customer relationships by that point. The only thing on our minds was how we could save face with our boss.

Earlier in the book, we talked about the benefits of vulnerability. If you want to grow, you have to be open. In the spirit of helping us all learn, I'm going to tell you what we did back then. It wasn't pretty or noble.

I prepped every single one of my customers in advance. I flat out told them, "The big boss is coming to town. Please help me out and agree with everything I suggest. We can work the details out later." I had good relationships with my customers, so they went along with the plan. Although I had a knot in my stomach the entire time, the day went well—everything according to the script I had so carefully manufactured. At the end of the day, Mr. Big Boss grunted, "Much better." When the memo came after this trip, he noted the improvement.

Later, when I went back to thank my customers and take them to lunch, they reduced the number of items and bought about the same number of products they usually did. While my reputation wasn't ruined, it wasn't helped either.

What are the lessons from this? If you want to make the case for fear-based leadership, you could say Mr. Big Boss got good results. After all, we did sell more items while he was on the sales call. But when you peel back the layers to look at the actual business results, Mr. Big Boss did more harm than good.

We didn't drive any additional long-term revenue because none of the sales stuck. I found out later the other sales managers in our region had done the same thing. None of the sales were sustainable, because we hadn't really made a sale at all; we'd just jerry-rigged things to please the boss. I wasn't thinking about making a good business case for the products; I was thinking, "I hope I keep my job."

In hindsight, Mr. Big Boss may have actually been a good guy. I have no idea what was going on in his personal or business life. As I said earlier, we don't know what's in people's hearts unless they tell us. Fear makes people do crazy things. Whatever the reason for the way he acted, I'm grateful for the lesson.

The Ripple Effect of Fear

When salespeople are afraid of their boss's critique, they wind up having two conversations in their head. One is about the customer, but the other, more dominant conversation, is about the boss.

Picture a salesperson at the front of a room giving a presentation with both their boss and their customer watching. Prior to the call, the boss had reamed out the salesperson about poor performance so far this month. What do you think is going on inside that salesperson's head?

The detrimental effect of fear-based leadership extends far beyond that. Salespeople who are afraid of the boss wind up coaching their customers and create fake scenarios just to look good (like I did). This ultimately affects the entire organization, setting the following chain of events in motion:

- **Your pipeline is unpredictable.** Salespeople are afraid to admit when sales look shaky.
- **Sales leadership doesn't get an accurate read on the market.** The boss doesn't know what customers really think because salespeople hide all potentially negative information.
- **You waste customer goodwill by creating fake sales calls.** When the inevitable late order or mistake happens, salespeople who have already spent the customers' goodwill faking things for the boss won't have any left when they need it.
- **Customers no longer trust your company.** When customers see that salespeople are "acting" for their boss, they no longer believe that the salespeople will tell them the truth, either.
- **Customers don't take you to senior levels.** When customers see a salesperson who is afraid of his or her boss, they're less likely to introduce that salesperson to their boss.
- **Customers have a lower opinion of your company.** They realize very quickly that you are not an organization that values the truth.
- **You send a message that the boss is more important than the customers.** And unfortunately, this is a fairly common experience.

Senior leaders routinely experience an altered reality when they go out in the field because their salespeople are petrified to tell—and show—them the truth.

This doesn't mean you have to be a softie. You can, and should, demand the best from your team. For example, if Mr. Big Boss had been tough and demanded we do better *for* our customers, it would have taken our brains to a completely different place. Instead of being so self-protective, we would have focused on the customers. People don't take criticism as personally when they know you're working toward a common purpose.

Bosses who demand the best on behalf of customers have a different effect. They remind their salespeople they're all on the same team. Commitment to the team is what gives you the courage to show up as your best self, no matter how scary the situation.

Why Shared Commitment Gives You Courage

Courage isn't the absence of fear. It's the ability to act in the face of fear. In my quest to understand courage and what makes people perform well in adverse circumstances, I've interviewed several combat veterans. Almost all of them acknowledge being afraid. They also tell you that two things help soldiers act in the face of fear:

- They have extensive training.
- They're emotionally invested in their team.

Training helps a soldier remain calm in the face of chaos. He or she knows what to do, so the response is automatic. Commitment to the team is what prompts a soldier to push through and draw on their skills in the toughest situations. Putting yourself in the service of a cause bigger than yourself gives you more courage than if you were just trying to do something for yourself. In the moment of battle, it's not the fear of the drill sergeant that prompts a soldier to charge forward; it's the commitment to the team. History is filled with examples of men and women who overcame their fear and adversity on behalf of something bigger than themselves.

Thankfully, a sales career doesn't carry the same risks as a battle. But it does require courage.

Your job as a leader is to keep the lizard brain at bay. You can't completely eliminate fear, but you can give your people the skills to overcome it. Just like the military, you can help your team conquer fear by:

- Providing extensive training, including mindset training, sales skills, and product expertise
- Building commitment to the team and purpose through shared stories and belief-building exercises

Training enables people to act in the face of uncertainty. Reminding people that they're part of something bigger than themselves increases their commitment to the team.

The best leaders set high standards. However, the standards are aimed at serving an important goal or cause. True believers don't resent high standards; they appreciate them. Fear is a given—in business and in life. There's a big difference between being afraid of your boss and being afraid of letting your team down. When you're afraid of your boss, you go into protection mode. When you're afraid of letting your team down, you give it your all.

How to Conquer Fear When You're Broke

If you work for yourself or you're on straight commission, fear of failure takes on a whole different tone. Not hitting your numbers can mean the difference between keeping your home and being out on the street. People often ask me, "How do you keep your Noble Purpose alive if you're petrified you won't be able to pay the rent?"

The answer is twofold. First, it's harder when you're broke. Second, that's when you need your Noble Purpose the most. I experienced this first-hand. In 2007 my husband Bob and I purchased a small manufacturing company. My husband was coming off a 25-year career with a Fortune 200 manufacturing firm. He'd been a senior executive in finance and sales and had experience in the construction industry. The company we bought—or, I should say, the company we plunked down much of our life savings and took out a huge loan to buy—made large illuminated signs like you'd see outside of Wendy's or The Gap.

If we had a Magic-8 Ball, we couldn't have picked a worse moment to buy a business or a worse industry to get into. Within months, the construction market began to weaken. By 2008, when the economy officially hit the skids, it was like someone turned off a faucet. Our sales evaporated overnight. We went from slow to nothing.

As things started to go south, I tried to help my husband and the team. I was a sales consultant, after all; surely I could solve this. I created new marketing materials, launched a prospecting program, and worked on our sales process. The gains were marginal at best. The truth was, we'd overpaid. We were deeply in debt, in the depths of a recession that showed no signs of abating. The sales weren't there, and we were circling the drain, emotionally and financially.

One Sunday night two years in, when the sign company was looking hopeless, I had a speaking engagement at a local entrepreneur group's year-end holiday celebration. As part of the program, the members were sharing their success stories. Two women stood up to share their business journey:

"For years it's been our dream to open a day spa," they said. "We've had setbacks on financing, we've had two locations fall through, but after much work, last week our dream came true." They became emotional as they described what happened, "Last week, the men came to put up our sign." By this point, they were wiping tears from their eyes as one described the scene: "As we watched the crane lift the sign into place, we started hugging each other." Her voice now breaking, she said, "It wasn't a dream anymore. It was **real!**"

Every single person in the room could envision those two business-women standing there crying and hugging each other as the crane hoisted their sign into the air. In that moment, I realized that our company wasn't some crummy little sign manufacturing business. We were part of the American dream! The day a businessperson's sign goes up is one of the biggest days in that person's life. All of a sudden, our work had meaning.

I raced home to my husband.

By this point, we were out of money, our equipment was breaking down left and right, and Bob was exhausted from the stress. He looked at me like I was a bit crazy when I started spewing the story. When I asked if I could speak to his team the next morning at their Monday morning huddle, he said yes.

So at 7:00 a.m. in a cold manufacturing facility, I told 20 rough-and-tough manufacturing guys the story about the two ladies opening the day spa. I got teary-eyed as I described them crying and hugging each other. I told the team, "We're part of the biggest day in someone's life. We don't just make signs; we validate people's dreams!"

There was dead silence. All the guys looked at the floor. I thought, "Oh, great, they're probably thinking, 'As if things aren't bad enough. We're on the verge of closing this crummy company, and now we have to listen to the boss's nutty wife talk about some emotional mumbo-jumbo.'" Bob shifted uncomfortably and gave me one of those forced smiles you give your kid when they trip going on stage or come in last in a race.

Finally, the foreman spoke. "You know, when we put up that Rita's Frozen Custard sign last week, her whole family came out to watch." One of the install guys said, "When we put up that new Dairy Queen sign, the manager asked me to take his picture beside it." Within moments everyone was telling a story.

I watched their faces light up. One minute they were blue-collar guys punching a clock for a failing sign company. The next minute, they were men who made people's dreams come true. When the office staff came in an hour later, we shared the stories with them. They got similarly excited.

So with no money in the bank, looming debt, and a pile of broken-down equipment, we decided that we would give the business a purpose. We became the company that *validated people's dreams*. Every time we got an order, the salesperson told the manufacturing team the backstory about the business that bought the sign. We started calling jobs by the name of the owner or manager. Instead of saying, "We're making a Dairy Queen sign," the guys started saying, "We're making a sign for Bill, who just bought a Dairy Queen."

When the manufacturing team finished a sign, they all signed the inside of it with Sharpies before it went out. The install guys took pictures of the sign with the proud owners. We sent a copy to the customer and put up another copy next to the front door so that all the employees could see the owners beaming next to their sign.

Bob and the salesmen started introducing themselves as "the guys who validate dreams." Within a month, it was a different organization. People noticed, and we started getting a little more business. The transformation inside the organization was amazing. I watched construction guys who had never felt very emotional about their jobs come to work on fire. One of the guys said, "I've been making signs for 20 years. I've never worked at a place like this before; this is different. This is fun." Keep in mind, these were hourly workers who knew that their company was on the brink of closing and that their entire industry was in the toilet. Yet for many of them, for the first time in their lives, they were excited about work.

This story would be great if it had a happy ending. But it doesn't. The goodwill and enthusiasm we built weren't enough to overcome a mountain of debt and a crumbling economy. The company closed, taking most of our savings with it. We helped the guys find other jobs, sold most of the equipment for scrap, and walked away with a huge bill from the IRS.

So why am I telling you this?

Because we made a mistake. *I* made a mistake. I let my fear get the best of me. I didn't bring purpose into the equation because I was afraid a bunch of blue-collar guys wouldn't go for it. I couldn't have been more wrong. I turned to purpose when we were too broke to try anything else. If we had found our purpose earlier, if we hadn't been afraid to get emotional, things might have gone differently.

Salespeople aren't the only people who succumb to fear. As leaders, many of us are afraid to get real about our emotions. We often hold ourselves back from becoming fully engaged. We want our lives to matter. But it's easier—and safer—to check off the tasks than it is to open our hearts and start talking about something big like purpose.

Leaders frequently confide in me, saying, "I'm afraid this won't work. I'm afraid people will think I'm soft or weird, or not serious about business." I understand; I was afraid, too. We allowed the pressing needs of revenue and our own discomfort with emotions to keep us from bringing purpose into our organization. It's a mistake I won't make again, and it's a mistake I hope you can avoid. I'm no longer embarrassed to talk about touchy-feely stuff at work because I know firsthand how it can transform even a seemingly hopeless situation.

If you told me that we would buy a company and spend the next two years working like dogs only to go broke at the end, I wouldn't have believed you. But that's exactly what happened. On the scale of human suffering, worse tragedies have been endured. But at the time, it felt catastrophic to us. The worst day was when we had to tell our oldest daughter that the money we had saved for her college was gone.

You're reading this book, so you know things eventually got better. What you might not know is how hard it was to focus on my Noble Purpose when we were broke. After the sign business tanked, we had to figure out how to support our family. We were still deep in the recession. My consulting business was floundering because I'd neglected it while trying to help my husband fix the sign company. Executive jobs were being slashed left and right, so we decided my husband should join my business and we would try to rebound.

We set an ambitious goal: quadruple the revenue of the business in 24 months. To say that I was afraid is putting it mildly. I can remember lying awake at night staring at the ceiling with my heart pounding so loudly I could barely breathe.

It wasn't hard to put clients first when we were financially comfortable. When we were desperate for cash, there were days when the idea of Noble Purpose seemed like a luxury- a pie-in-the sky dream that I could pursue when things became more stable. I remember going into my office, staring at the big revenue goal on the whiteboard, and thinking, "Right now, all I care about is the money."

My back was up against the wall—I was going to have to decide if I was really committed to my purpose, or if I would abandon it. Some days, it took everything I had to stay calm. My family needed me to show up as my best self, and so did my clients. I couldn't run around frantically; I had to focus.

When the stress was at its worst, I'd put in my earbuds and go for a run, often late at night. As I ran through the streets of my neighborhood in the dark, I'd think, "Dammit, I am going to make a difference and make money if it kills me. I'm going to behave in a way that I can feel proud of when I look back on my life."

It worked: slowly at first, and then it picked up steam. The more I helped my clients find their purpose, the more I rediscovered my own. As our clients became more successful, so did we.

We generated more revenue in one year than I had in the previous five years. Twenty-four months after my husband joined me in the business, our daughter was accepted to her top college choice, and we had the money to pay for it.

If you're living on commission, or your commission has evaporated and you're totally broke, I've been there. I know it's hard; in fact, it's terrifyingly awful. But if you can marshal the courage to lean into a Noble Purpose approach, things will start to change for the better. Put your fear on pause, and focus on what matters: your customers. Find someone you can help. The world responds to a generous heart. Consider this council from Jeff Weiner, former LinkedIn CEO: "Imagine a world where a global economic downturn doesn't limit our ability to execute, but reinforces the essential quality of our purpose and actually strengthens our resolve when people need us most."

We're all afraid at times. Maybe you're afraid you'll lose your job or fail. Maybe you're afraid that you're be "found out"—or, worst of all, maybe you're afraid your life doesn't matter. But the truth is, it does. Your actions and beliefs have power. Don't underestimate the power of one person to change the trajectory of an organization—or your own power to change the trajectory of your life. You are here to do more than simply show up for work. If you want to make a difference, take fear off the table and help yourself and your team step into a bigger, bolder way of doing business. They deserve it, and so do you.

Chapter 15: How Fear Flatlines a Sales Team

The leader's job is to take fear off the table. Fear has a chilling effect on our ability to engage. When you're afraid, your focus is on yourself, not the person on the other side of the table.

When salespeople are afraid, they:

- Don't listen well
- Get defensive when they hear objections
- Think in the short term and care more about making the number today than building a sustainable business in the future
- Are less likely to ask deeper questions

Fear makes you frantic. You want salespeople who are focused. Take fear off the table by focusing your team on the impact they have on customers.

(continued)

(*continued*)

When you help your team step into a bigger, bolder way of doing business, the market notices.

Do one thing: Make a pact with your team that you are not going to let fear stand in your way.

Creating a Tribe of True Believers

Once the stage is set, the presence of an outstanding leader is indispensable. With-out him (or her) there will be no movement.
— Eric Hoffer, author of *The True Believer*

S elling with Noble Purpose is not just a technique; it's a new way of life for a sales team. It's a distinctive orientation toward sales—one that creates more differentiation and more emotional engagement.

In some ways, the NSP approach is easier to maintain than other sales methodologies, because it's oriented around one simple point: customer impact. A sales team focused on making a difference to customers will outsell a sales team focused on internal targets and quotas. That single, galvanizing idea creates a force field of energy. In other ways, NSP is more challenging because it requires a mindset shift that runs counter to the prevailing culture of most organizations.

In Part 4, we'll look at the critical moments where integrating your NSP into the daily cadence of sales gives you the biggest wins. You'll learn how to leverage your NSP in sales meetings, ride-alongs, coaching, recruiting, interviews, and even budget meetings. You'll also learn how to use your NSP to make faster decisions and how to keep low-value distractions from sucking the soul out of your sales efforts.

As a sales leader, you're the linchpin. You're the one who decides whether your team is just another average sales force or you're really going to make a difference in the lives of your customers. There are a few key places where bringing customer impact to the fore has an outsize impact on your team. Leading a tribe of true believers is more challenging than running an average organization. It's also infinitely more rewarding and a hell of a lot more fun.

16

Sustaining the "High" of the Close

What is love when it's not for dopamine?
—Saurabh Sharma, Indian author and lyricist

We all know what it feels like. The contract comes through. The payment hits the bank account. You get the PO. It's the moment of the close, and it's positively terrific. It's when everything you've worked for pays off. It's a high. Literally. When you score a win, your brain releases endorphins, dopamine, oxytocin, and serotonin, a cocktail of feel-good chemicals that activate your brain's pleasure center and makes your whole body feel better.

This is not a bad thing. For most salespeople, it's a visceral whole-body experience. That's why sales teams ring bells and high-five each other.

The challenge is, that feeling can be fleeting. The high of winning a deal evaporates when the pipeline report looks bad, or a customer backs out. Your brain can easily tumble back to a lower-confidence, less-engaged version of yourself.

Hardly the right mindset for a sales call.

You don't want your sales team to be always grasping for that high. You want a sales team who can *bring* that high. You want a Noble Purpose sales team who can reverse negativity, who can stay confident in the face of setbacks, and who can lift each other up when things go wrong.

You want a team that is resilient.

Grasping for the feel-good of a close might sound like a great motivation for a team, but in my experience, it doesn't promote the most engaging sales behavior. If you've ever been on the receiving end of a salesperson desperate to close, you know exactly what I'm talking about.

In Chapter 15, we talked about the lizard brain and how fear has a chilling effect on sales calls. Now let's talk about the flip side: the feel-good chemicals that create emotional engagement for your team and customers, and how you as a leader can create an environment that ignites them.

Dopamine, endorphins, oxytocin, and serotonin are commonly referred to as the *feel-good quartet* of chemicals responsible for happiness. But they're not all the same. Dopamine is the neurotransmitter that controls your brain's reward and pleasure center. It's associated with chasing a desired object. The quick satisfaction you get from a like on social media or winning the annual sales contest quickly fades. You're left wanting more, and more, and more.

The other feel-good brain chemical is serotonin. Unlike dopamine, serotonin is associated with alignment to a larger purpose and long-term accomplishments. If you want a resilient team, you need to be proactive about going beyond the short term (dopamine) and creating a culture that also emphasizes longer-term fulfillment (serotonin).

Much has been written about our society's addiction to dopamine. The ping of the tweet pulls away from the present moment. These quick hits often keep us from long-term strategic thinking. It's disconcerting.

We don't have to give up those dopamine hits entirely. The foundation of purpose-driven sales leadership is to point people in the direction of the long-term, deep connection (versus immediate, short-term hits). You want to create feedback loops that add in longer-term, serotonin-based thinking, while still giving your team the quick wins that stimulate dopamine.

Before we talk more about how to make the feel-good of the close last longer than a nanosecond, we need to address one more danger area. It's a dopamine-driven path many leaders take when they're trying to ignite sales energy. Perhaps you've experienced this yourself.

"Kill the Competition" Is Not a Rallying Cry

When the senior leadership team took the stage at the sales kick-off, they wanted to rally the troops. Their new product was going to hit the competition where it hurt: in their wallets. Their aim was to take the competitor's most profitable deals.

"We're going to obliterate them!"

"We're going to make those guys worry about their mortgages!"

The sales force was pumped. Fists were raised. They were poised to attack. They were practically frothing at the mouth. There was only one problem: this short-term dopamine conversation was creating energy, but was it going to create the right sales behaviors?

Probably not.

The entire sales narrative was about obliterating the competition, not winning the customers. There's a big difference. Focusing on beating the competition, rather than winning customers, is a strategic error that often goes unnoticed in the heat of the battle. Yet over time, this classic mistake erodes growth, stifles innovation, and ultimately creates a price-driven, commoditized business.

Have you ever observed a salesperson who spent most of his or her customer face time trashing the competition? It's hardly engaging.

I'm going to risk the ire of traditional sales experts here, to say that sales is not like hand-to-hand combat or football or baseball or boxing or any of the other frequently used sports analogies. You don't get in the ring with your competition and beat them about the head until they give up.

Sales is more like figure skating or a cooking competition. You perform, the competition performs, and the customer is the judge who decides which one is best. It's not all measurable: some of it is substance, some of it is style; it's one part fact, one part opinion; and the judging can be very subjective. But in the end, it's not what the two teams think about each other that counts; it's the judge's opinion that counts.

To be clear, you want to study the other team, identify their weak points, and craft your performance to show why you're better. But a team overly focused on killing the competition will not win. This is a short-term, dopamine-fueled way of thinking that puts your team on a very non-differentiated path. When leaders emphasize short-term payoff—*Kill the competition and get a dopamine hit*—over longer-lasting purpose and impact—*Make a difference to clients and let the serotonin flow*—poor results follow.

It produces three predictable problems:

1. **Transactional relationships.** Craving a dopamine hit causes salespeople to turn away from customers in pursuit of self-gain. They're likely to make shortsighted deals, damage relationships, and cut margins in order to win.
2. **Lack of strategic thinking.** When you're addicted to quick hits, next year is irrelevant. A team on dopamine does not think deeply about the future; they're less likely to innovate or spot potential threats.
3. **Ethical lapses.** When the incentive is to win at all costs, employees will go to any length to avoid perceived failure. Addiction to dopamine creates environments ripe for cheating and stealing.

As a Noble Purpose team, you can do better. Rather than relying on the quick hit, you can give your team a feel-good that lasts longer.

How to Keep the Serotonin Flowing

You want a resilient team of people who know how to reset themselves when the market changes or things go wrong. You want a team who carry so much serotonin in their back pockets that they spread it around to customers.

Here are some things you can do to keep the high of the close alive:

1. **When you win a deal:**

    After the fist bumps, ask the team the game-changing question: "How will this customer be different as a result of doing business with us?" Write it down, or better yet, make a video on your phone. Every single time you discuss that client, bring it up. Show the video to the support and implementation teams.

    Reliving the experience is crucial. Here's why: chemically, your brain doesn't differentiate between an actual moment and reliving that moment. When you tell the story of the close and, most importantly, how it impacted the customer, you get another hit of dopamine, and you also reinforce the longer-lasting serotonin high of making a difference.

2. **When you lose a deal:**

    It's okay to feel bad for a while. A loss is a loss. In fact, giving yourself and your team permission to sit with sadness is what enables you to work through it. Pretending a loss didn't happen and you're not upset only prolongs it. Wallow in it, roll on the floor, and scream if you need to. Once you've cleared out the negative emotions, reset. Ask yourself and the team: What's the most impactful sale we've ever made? Why did that matter to the customer? How can we do it again? Re-experiencing past successes reverses a downward brain spiral. It stimulates the serotonin required to rebound.

Gratitude: The Gateway Drug to Happiness

Let's talk about one more way to keep your team alive and excited: gratitude. Like dopamine, once you feel gratitude, you want more. But unlike a Facebook or Instagram ping, gratitude is the gift that keeps on giving. It points you out into the world, and it can be more readily shared.

Gratitude is one of the cheapest, easiest, highest-impact things you can bring to your sales team. It has helped transform our business and several of our clients' businesses during tough times.

Think about your work, your team, and your customers. What are you grateful for? Can you feel the mental shift? Share this with your team. It will strengthen your connection with them and help them see your human side. After you've done this a time or two, ask your team, "What are you grateful for?" Trust me, even on a bad day, there's still something to be grateful about.

Closing deals is a glorious high. Making a difference and creating a team that changes your industry is even more exciting. That in itself is something to be grateful for.

Chapter 16: Sustaining the "High" of the Close

Closing a deal is great; you want a team who can carry that feeling beyond that single moment.

Narratives like "kill the competition" and "close the deal at all costs" feel energizing in the moment, but they're not sustainable sources of deep connection. These short-term rallying cries result in transactional relationships, lack of strategic thinking, and ethical lapses.

(continued)

(*continued*)

After you win a deal, ask the game-changing question: "How will this customer be different as a result of doing business with us?" This ignites long-term, serotonin-driven emotions. Your team forms a stronger, more personal connection that will take them far beyond that closing.

During moments of challenge, use gratitude to reset yourself and your team.

Do one thing: Next time you win a big deal, ask the game-changing question (after you fist-bump, of course).

17

Sales Meetings That Inspire Action (from Everyone)

The tribe is hyper-aware of what's being celebrated, and when you celebrate those that are moving in the right direction, you create a powerful push in that direction.

—Seth Godin, author, entrepreneur, and teacher

Sales meetings are a chance for celebration and sharing. The question is, what are you celebrating, and what are you sharing?

Sometimes people think Noble Purpose means ignoring sales numbers or, even worse, getting rid of sales targets. I say "even worse" because if you're serious about your Noble Sales Purpose, you need to measure it. Your numbers reflect how well you serve your customers, so you want to celebrate that every chance you get.

You also want to connect the dots for your team to show them what the numbers represent, which is customer impact. A few small tweaks can dramatically improve the impact of your sales meeting effectiveness and create a deeper emotional connection to customers for your team.

Let's look at the traditional approach versus what happens when you frame things through the lens of your NSP.

	Traditional	Noble purpose
Sales results	We added 100 million dollars in revenue. Here's a look at our stock price.	We helped a million new customers. Here's the impact we're having on these real live humans.
Reward and recognition	Jane closed a million-dollar sale. She's our best salesperson.	Jane had a huge impact on clients. Here's what the million-dollar solutions did for her biggest client.
Product intros	Here are the new products and all of their features.	Our clients have a pressing challenge. Here are the solutions we created to help them.
Sales team hears	We sold a bunch of products this year, and next year we need to sell a bunch more.	We made a difference for our customers, and next year we're going to change their world in an even bigger way.
Results in...	**Transactional sellers**	**Tribe of true believers**

What strikes you about the difference in approaches? Look closely; the facts about sales results, rewards, and products are actually the same. It's the framing that changes. This is how you as a sales leader can point your team toward customers. This approach can be used in a small weekly huddle or your big Sales Kick-off. I cannot emphasize enough how these seemingly simple reframes can impact your team's beliefs and behavior. It jolts them out of the traditional *ho-hum, here are the numbers, here's the pipeline, rinse and repeat* meetings that so many salespeople are used to.

Kurt Shreiner, president of corporate financial services for Atlantic Capital Bank (see Chapter 2), once told me, "I've been going to the same sales meeting since June 20, 1985." How many salespeople feel the same way? Each meeting can be summed up with "Here's how much money we made.

How can we make more?" As Shreiner says, "I lived through the Gordon Gekko era."

Shreiner changed his weekly sales meetings to recalibrate his team. "Now we start with our Noble Purpose (*We fuel prosperity*) and then drive the rest of the meetings toward client impact." He adds, "You have to be clear: you're doing this for the client."

After the shift, Shreiner's meetings became more engaging. Instead of the traditional internal focus, the sales team is pointed toward customer impact. They're more creative and innovative. They review opportunities and sales from the client's perspective. When they have a win, they describe the impact on the client. This builds belief and reinforces that *we are here to fuel prosperity*.

Why Traditional Meetings Can Unintentionally Erode Morale

Let's take a closer look at the two different approaches for celebrating sales success and how they impact your team.

Traditional Sales Celebration

Imagine you're a sales rep, sitting with your peers at your annual sales conference. It's time for the awards. You had a good year, but you know you're not going to be the top rep. The VP of sales starts the awards. She announces everyone who went above quota. You stand with the rest of the group over quota and get a round of applause. Like we said, it was a good year for you.

Now it's time for the big winner. With a drum roll and a bit of fanfare, the VP announces, "Stan is our top rep!" She brings Stan onstage, and everyone cheers. The VP recounts some of Stan's big deals. Stan is beaming. He gets a trophy and a big bonus check. Stan is the rainmaker.

How do you feel? Maybe you're a super-generous human being and you're really excited for Stan. Maybe you don't care much one way or the other; you're just wondering when they're going to open the bar. Or maybe you're the more competitive type, and you're looking at Stan on that stage and thinking, "That should be *me*." Your face is smiling, but inside, your thoughts are, "Stan, I hope you enjoy it this year, buddy boy, because next year you're going to be sitting in my seat, and *I'm* going to be onstage."

Or maybe it's a little bit of all these. Maybe you're happy for Stan, you want a drink, and you're also plotting to annihilate him next year. The meeting breaks, you head to the bar, and you buy Stan a drink and congratulate him with as much graciousness as you can muster.

I've seen it hundreds of times. Watching Stan get his award *will* motivate your most competitive salespeople. The fiercely competitive will want to beat Stan, and several of them will go to great lengths to do so. But most of the team will stay in the middle of the pack.

A 2017 study from Fred Miao of the University of Portland, published in the *Journal of Personal Selling and Sales Management*, revealed that "top-performer rewards have a double-edged sword effect on fellow salespeople's selling skills, opportunism and sales performance. The issue is not the rewards, it's the way we handle them."

There's a way to evolve this scenario. You can frame Stan's award in a way that will inspire everyone, propel your top-end people, build pride and belief, and have an even more dramatic impact on Stan. It starts by including the voice that was missing from Stan's celebration: the customers themselves. Let's look at a different approach.

The Noble Purpose Flip

It's the same sales meeting. You're sitting there with your peers as the award ceremony begins. The VP of sales starts by putting up a big number on the screen: 1,000,000. "Do you see that number?" she asks the team. "That's how many customers we helped this year. Every single one of you played a role. Let's stand up and cheer! Look around the room; you are looking at a team who made a difference."

While everyone is standing and clapping, photos and client logos are flashing across the screen. The VP says, "These people are why we're here."

When that cheering is over and everyone is reseated, she starts calling out the top-tier performers, including you. When she calls your name, she announces the number of customers you helped this year. She flashes all their names on the screen. She says, "Congratulations! You are a change-maker." Your friend takes a picture of you with the customer logos on the screen behind you. You text it to your kids.

Now it's time for the top rep award. Before she announces Stan's name, the VP says, "I want to show you a video." It's one of Stan's customers. The customer says, "I want to tell you how much we appreciate our relationship."

The customer goes on to describe the impact your firm's solution had on their organization. Then the VP calls Stan onstage and hands him the big check, saying, "This is because you made a difference to your customers. You enabled their success, and when they're successful, we're successful. I'm giving you this award on behalf of the team and on behalf of all the customers you helped. Congratulations."

How do you feel now? This framing shifts the focus from Stan to the impact Stan has on customers. Stan is still singled out. He still gets his big check. But the whole tone of the room has changed. Now we're in this together; we're celebrating the fact that our entire company is changing our industry. We're making a difference, and we're lifting up the person who had the biggest impact of all.

You might still wish you were Stan, but it's unlikely you're plotting his demise. You're probably thinking, "Wow, did you hear what that customer said about him? I want my customers to say that about me." You no longer want to *beat* Stan—you want to *be* Stan.

Do you see the difference in the thought patterns? Now every single person in the room is thinking about customer impact. This isn't fantasy land. This is exactly how G Adventures, Supportworks, Atlantic Capital Bank, and other companies you're read about in this book run their sales conferences.

Small Shift, Big Impact

Here's how making a shift from an internal self-focus to an external client impacts the sales team:

- **Lower- and mid-level performers** get the message loud and clear: this is what success looks like here. Hearing a customer describe Stan's impact gives them a story they can repeat to their own customers. This drives engagement and performance.

- **Top-tier performers** have more pride in their own contributions. Instead of being embarrassed about not winning, they are thinking about the customers they did help and how they can do more of it. This helps retention; they're not going to leave because they lost. It also drives behavior: they know what it takes to win.

- **The big winner** is still going to text his wife a picture of the check. But now when he calls her, he's also going to tell her the customer impact story. They will probably share a moment of pride together, and it's something Stan's going to repeat to his kids and his parents. He goes home knowing he made a difference, his work matters, and he matters.

You want people to leave your meetings inspired and excited about making a difference to customers.

This kind of meeting also impacts two other groups of people:

- **Home office staff.** People who don't have regular contact with customers think, "Wow, we really make a difference." They're going to be more likely to help out your sales team when they know it matters to someone.
- **Senior leaders.** If you're the CEO, this helps you get your other functions dialed into client impact. If you're a sales leader, you want everyone on the senior team to see your Noble Purpose in action.

Noble Purpose does not eliminate sales targets; it puts them in context. They are the result of the impact you have on customers.

The financial recaps, new initiatives, product rollouts, decision-making, recognition, rewards, and everything else you do in meetings should be framed to point your team toward the impact you have on customers. Meetings are about advancing, brainstorming, celebrating, explaining, measuring, and rewarding how well you're achieving your NSP.

Here are some things you can do in any meeting—large or small—to point your team toward your purpose, build belief, and align your actions around the impact you have on clients:

- **Start each meeting with a customer impact story.** This ignites everyone's frontal lobes and reminds them why they're here and resets their brains toward your Noble Purpose. If you do nothing else, this one simple thing shifts belief.
- **Frame sales figures in terms of the number of clients helped.** Instead of "We sold this many widgets," say, "We helped this many clients."
- **Introduce products and initiatives in the context of client goals.** Instead of "Here is our new product," say, "Here's the client challenge or goal, and here's our solution to address it."

- **Celebrate customer success.** If one of your clients wins an award or closes a major sale, showcase it. Tell your team, "We're part of that. When they win big, it's a win for us, too."
- **Ask: "How will the customer be different as a result of this deal?"** When you're discussing opportunities and initiatives, ask the game-changing question. This provokes your seller to think that way, and they all benefit from hearing other team members respond.
- **Lose the deathly dull slides.** Instead of simply presenting information to your team, ask them what that information will mean to clients. This enables them to assimilate the information more thoroughly and use it more effectively in the field.
- **Bring the client into the room, physically and metaphorically.** Bring in a client, or put a photo of a client up on the screen. Tell the team, "Everything we do in this meeting is about improving life for this person." You'll be surprised at just how much your conversations change.
- **Leverage the senior team for client impact.** If your CEO or senior team members are present, ask them to share their vision for the clients. Prep them in advance to make sure they focus on client impact. Ask them the game-changing question: "How are clients different as a result of doing business with us?"
- **Brief all your speakers.** If someone is going to speak at your meeting, they should know your NSP and be able to connect the dots. Set speakers up for success in advance by saying, "Our purpose is to (fuel prosperity, redefine, etc.). Before you share your information, let's talk about how it will help us do that."
- **Share your own story.** People want authentic leaders; share your own story about why your NSP matters to you. Be real: What's your personal experience with the topic? Did you grow up poor, and you don't want others to experience that? Or maybe you grew up well off, and you want everyone to have that. Whatever personal connection you have, share it.

These are all things you can do within the context of your usual meetings. They do not require any extra money, and none of them takes more than five minutes.

Sales meetings are a chance to inspire your team and build belief in your NSP. They can be ho-hum, or you can use them to tell your team, "Our work matters, and so do you."

Chapter 17: Sales Meetings That Inspire Action (from Everyone)

Sales meetings are a crucial time to build belief. The traditional approach creates transactional teams. Shift your approach to build belief and create a differentiated sales team.

Try implementing these actions at your next meeting:

- Start each meeting with a customer impact story.
- Frame sales figures in terms of the number of clients helped.
- Introduce products and initiatives in the context of client goals.
- Celebrate customer success.
- Ask: "How will the customer be different as a result of this deal?"
- Lose the deathly dull slides.
- Bring the client into the room, physically and metaphorically.
- Leverage the senior team for client impact.
- Brief all your speakers.
- Share your own story.

Sharing customer impact stories, introducing products in the context of customer goals, and celebrating *customer* success rallies everyone around your NSP.

Do one thing: Choose one thing from the preceding list to implement at your next meeting.

18

Noble Purpose Sales Coaching

I'm a coach, so I take the issue of control personally.
—Pat Summitt, the all-time winningest coach in NCAA basketball

Coaching is a force multiplier. A manager's words echo in salespeople's heads when they're with customers. One manager with 10 reps can create a differentiated experience for hundreds of customers.

When you send your team out the door or onto the phones with "Go get 'em, tiger" or "Let's close this deal," it's certainly more inspiring than saying nothing. But as a Noble Purpose organization, you can do even better. Your coaching can mean the difference between a successful sales call and an unsuccessful one.

Here are some specific Noble Purpose coaching techniques to help you help your team created a differentiated sales experience.

Before the Sales Call

Ideally, you want to coach your team well in advance of their critical sales calls. But the reality of the field is you might be on the phone the night before or trying to squeeze in a few tips before they jump on a call. Here's how to make the most of the time you have.

If you have 10 hours before the sales call:

- Ask the rep about the five categories of critical customer information (see Chapter 11).
- Ask the rep to put into writing, "How will this customer be different as a result of doing business with us?"
- Share a customer impact story from a similar customer.

If you have 10 minutes before the sales call:

- Ask the game-changing question: "How will this customer be different as a result of doing business with us?"
- If the rep doesn't know, provide one or two suggestions.

If you have 10 seconds before the sales call:

- Do the 10-second game changer activity with the rep (see Chapter 13).
- Breathe.
- Remind the rep that they have a plan and are flexible.
- Say with the rep, "I'm here to (your NSP)."

You want your rep calm, focused, and thinking about their highest aspirations for the customer.

During the Sales Call

When you do a call with your rep, resist the temptation to take over. Your goal as a coach is to prepare your players to succeed when you're not there. That means when you *are* there, you need to be mostly observing, not selling. Make a plan with your rep in advance for you (the manager) to play one of these more minor parts of the call:

- Share some of the positive things the rep has told you about the customer and his or her organization. No fawning: be authentic, and thank the customer for the business.
- Ask the customer about a strategic organizational goal (one of five categories of critical customer information). Customers are often more open with the boss and more likely to share top-level information.
- Tell a customer impact story when the rep cues you. You've probably met with customers in other parts of the country or world; your stories have a high value.
- Handle an obstacle you and the rep have agreed on in advance. Maybe it's something about your company's reliability or performance that you have inside information about. Have the rep cue you when they want you to jump in.
- Describe your Noble Purpose and why your organization is committed to it.

After the Sales Call

When the call is complete, ask the rep to give you their assessment first. Ask:

- What did you do well?
- What would you do differently next time?
- What are the most important things going on in this customer's environment?
- What do you think the customer's key goals and challenges are?
- What does success look like for this customer?
- What does lack of success look like for this customer?
- What are your next steps?

After the rep gives you feedback, provide your own assessment.

Then finish with the game-changing question: "How will this customer be different as a result of doing business with us?"

This process keeps the rep focused on the NSP for their next call with that customer. The internal conversation becomes the external conversation: the more you focus on customers, the more your team will focus on customers.

Patrick Hodges, president and general manager for Blackbaud, the SaaS firm you read about in Chapter 2, says, "People tend to pull me into a deal when things are going wrong or the sale has stalled." As the leader of a large team of salespeople and sales managers, Hodges says his role is often to reset the sales process. He makes it a practice to ask, "What is the customer going to get out of this?" He pushes his team to go beyond operational improvements; he wants the team to go two or three layers deep. How will this help the customer with their mission? What will they be able to do differently? What impact will this have on their constituents? What's the long-term impact?

He says, "When a deal is going south is when salespeople start to panic and think smaller." Instead, Hodges coaches his team to think bigger: he points them toward customer impact and their North Star of purpose. He says, "When I get involved in a deal, I have to take them back to the purpose. When sales stall, it's usually because we need a better story." He uses questions to draw out the story. He says, "When you ask these questions and work through the process with people several times, they learn how to do it on their own."

Noble Purpose coaching ensures that your salespeople internalize the NSP-driven mindset and skills and use them when it matters most—with customers.

Chapter 18: Noble Purpose Sales Coaching

Sales coaching is a crucial tool to shift a team from transactional to client impact. To bring your NSP to life in coaching interactions:
Before the call:

- Ask the game-changing question, "How will this customer be different as a result of doing business with us?"
- If the rep doesn't know, provide one or two suggestions.
- Ask the rep to take a deep breath and repeat your NSP.

During the call, don't take over. Instead, leaders can:

- Describe your Noble Purpose and why your organization is committed to it.

- Tell a customer impact story when the rep cues you. You've probably met with customers in other parts of the country or world; your stories have a high value.

After the call:

- Ask the rep to recap the five categories of critical customer information (environment, goals, challenges, success, lack of success).

Do one thing: Use the outline in this chapter the next time you make calls with a rep.

19

Training Your Frontline to Be Noble Purpose Sellers

Learning is not attained by chance, it must be sought for with ardor and attended to with diligence.

—Abigail Adams, former first lady of the United States

When leaders want to change the behavior of the sales team, training is usually the first solution. As you've seen, though, seller behavior is often the result of the system surrounding the sellers.

There's a reason this chapter is toward the back of the book. The ecosystem surrounding your sellers has a far bigger impact on them than anything you can do in a training program. Having said that, if you want your frontline sellers to adopt new behaviors, training is crucial.

In Chapter 13, you learned the dirty little secret about sales training—the dismal stats about how much well-intentioned training is forgotten in the field. This chapter is about how you can avoid that trap and make your training stick. We've talked about the mindset shift your team needs to make. Now let's look at some specific techniques to get them there.

I'd like to introduce you to a new world of sales training, one that doesn't involve PowerPoint from the front of the room. We're going to take a dive into directed self-discovery learning. To help you experience why this is so different from traditional training, I'm going to ask you to place yourself in this scenario and answer the questions as if you're a participant in the room. Are you ready?

Learning vs. Lecturing

Imagine you're a sales manager. You show up for a sales training program. You're expecting a traditional workshop. Yet as you sit down at the round table (or join the virtual room) with your peers, you notice some things are different. For starters, there's a poster with empty thought bubbles all over it. The instructor tells you, "This is a learning map, and you're about to take part in a simulation. This morning, you're going to have the opportunity to run two very different companies.

Without even a warm-up, the facilitator puts you on a team with 5 other people. He announces, "Congratulations! You're now the leadership team of a fast-growth company whose primary goal is to make money. Based on that purpose, how are you going to run your company?"

Your team looks around at each other as you realize, "Oh, he's serious. It's only 9:05, and we're already supposed to do something." You start to discuss the questions posed to your team on the learning map.

You're a senior leader at a firm whose North Star is money ...

- What are your key priorities?
- How would you measure success?
- What kinds of sales behavior would you expect and reward?
- How would you market the firm?
- How would you approach HR, hiring, incentives, and rewards?
- What would your rallying cry be?

You and your teammates discuss these questions, and you write your answers on your learning map. Here are the kinds of things we usually see.

North Star: money	
Key priorities:	**Drive profit, reduce expenses**
Metrics:	**Revenue, share price margin, deal size**
Marketing:	**Fill the funnel, emphasize features/function**
Sales behavior:	**Close deals, shorten sales cycle**
HR actions:	**Incentives for earnings, eliminate bottom 10%**
Rallying cry:	**Show me the money, coffee is for closers**

Next, your facilitator shifts to a new section of the learning map. He says, "Now you're the senior leadership team of a different kind of company. This company wants to be profitable, but their primary purpose is to make a difference to their customers. It's their North Star. It's how they measure their success."

If your Noble Purpose is to make a difference to customers …

- What are your key priorities?
- How would you measure success?
- What kinds of sales behavior would you expect and reward?
- How would you market the firm?
- How would you approach HR, hiring, incentives, and rewards?
- What would your rallying cry be?

As you and your teammates start discussing this scenario, you notice something. All of a sudden, you're more creative. You start thinking about customers, and you find yourself getting excited. The innovative ideas start to flow.

Your answers this time look very different than last time.

North Star: Noble Purpose	
Key priorities:	Client success, market impact
Metrics:	Net promoter score, client retention, referrals
Marketing:	Emotional engagement, emphasize customer impact
Sales behavior:	Deep discovery, client trust
HR actions:	Build belief, attract purposeful team
Rallying cry:	Make a difference, change the industry

You look at the learning map and see this side by side comparison.

	North Star: money	North Star: Noble Purpose
Key priorities:	Drive profit, reduce expenses	Client success, market impact
Metrics:	Revenue, share price margin, deal size	Net promoter score, client retention, referrals
Marketing:	Fill the funnel, emphasize features/function	Emotional engagement, emphasize customer impact
Sales behavior:	Close deals, shorten sales cycle	Deep discovery, client trust
HR actions:	Incentives for earnings, eliminate bottom 10%	Build belief, attract purposeful team
Rallying cry:	Show me the money, coffee is for closers	Make a difference, change the industry

The facilitator asks, which company is going to be more successful? Which company would you rather work for? Which company would you rather have calling on you? Which company will make more money over time?

What's happening to your brain at this point? Instead of being told information, you're being asked a series of questions, causing you to think.

In their book *Made to Stick*, Chip and Dan Heath say, "The most basic way to get someone's attention is this: Break a pattern." You came in expecting a normal seminar. By jumping you into a learning map, the facilitator has broken a pattern. *You're no longer receiving information: you're creating information.*

Let's go back to our workshop. You're a sales manager, and when your company introduced the concept of Noble Purpose, you heard the stats about what happens when organizations shift to this approach. Now you're actually experiencing it in live time. You're asking yourself and your team, "What happens to us, what happens to our customers, and what happens to our organization when *we* move into this space?"

You and your team created two strategies – a money strategy and a Noble Purpose strategy – and you've played out how the market will respond. You took a single idea and cascaded it all the way through an organization. Looking at the two sides of your learning map, the two companies are as different as night and day.

The facilitator points out something: "As you look at the left side and the right side of the map, both of those lists represent your team's best thinking at the time. You created these two wildly different strategies within 15 minutes of each other. Why do you think they're so different?"

As you and your team discuss it, you realize that only one thing changed: you had a different mental North Star. The first time, when you created the money strategy, your team members were thinking about themselves. The second time, using the Noble Purpose strategy, you were thinking about customers. In less than 20 minutes, your entire team went from a transactional organization to a team laser-focused on customers.

Now the facilitator says something that gives you pause: "You created a more powerful differentiated strategy because the leader (me, the facilitator) pointed you in a different direction using the power of words. In the real world, you're the leader, and your words are the ones pointing your team."

We're one hour into the training. Your entire worldview has shifted, and you recognize that your words are more powerful than you ever imagined. No PowerPoint required.

Self-Discovery Experiential Training Is Stickier

The previous scenario isn't fictional: it's a method we use with teams to jump-start new thinking and help people internalize the shift toward Noble Purpose. And it's an exercise you can run with your team. We do it in workshops, and we also do it virtually. The reason it works is because the exercise is based on principles of directed self-discovery learning.

We talked about why trying to layer new skills on an old mindset doesn't work. When you get back to reality, the old mindset takes over.

You can make your training sticky and get it to take hold of people by creating emotionally engaging experiences that shift people's hearts and minds. The next step is to help them apply their new mental frameworks to real-world activities. It's a method preschool teachers have been using for decades.

Why Maria Montessori Would Have Been a Great Sales Trainer

Years ago, when my children were young, I discovered the work of Dr. Maria Montessori. She believed children learn best in the context of the real world, with materials designed to help them reach their own conclusions. According to Dr. Montessori, "Children acquire knowledge through experience in the environment."

Guess what? It's not just children.

We've all attended the "death by PowerPoint" training programs; we know they don't work. And they're even worse on a Zoom call. To be clear, great speakers are inspiring. I've watched research professor and speaker Brené Brown over and over again. She seeps into my soul. Yet as she and anyone else trying to make real change will tell you, if you want your team to become *fluent* in a new approach, they need to experience it for themselves.

When you watch children using creative materials to learn math or geography at their own pace, you see how quickly they internalize it. The knowledge becomes part of them instead of something they're simply memorizing to regurgitate. And when they work with peers, you can see the learning become more animated as they all contribute.

I always laugh when someone in the training department says, "We need to treat people like adults." I agree with the sentiment; give people credit for being intelligent. It doesn't matter whether the learners are 5 or 45: materials that direct and engage with immediate application make your learning stick.

Here's another example of a self-discovery experience to help a good frontline team get even better. In Chapter 10, you read about the Fiserv sales enablement team, whose NSP is *We empower client success.* As you recall, they made the shift from a standard demo team to a client impact–driven Noble Purpose team.

Their clients were more engaged, and the implementations were stickier and more successful. The next step was to go for best-in-class differentiation. We created a simulation to work through the key inflection points in their sales process. Imagine a hotel ballroom with four lanes—much like swim lanes, only twisting,—taped on the floor, going from one side of the ballroom to the other. The group is divided into four teams; each team has their own lane, running parallel to the other lanes. The lanes represent the customer journey through the sales process. As the teams travel the journey, they stop and practice skills at the crucial pivot points.

Working in teams, they work their way through Discovery, uncovering the five categories of critical customer information (see Chapter 11). They do "you-me-you" call openings to bring their NSP to life (see Chapter 12). They ask meaningful questions. They plan their product demos to answer the question "How will the customer be different as a result of doing business with us?" They create compelling customer impact stories to illustrate their expertise (see Chapter 8). There are chance cards—unexpected twists and turns that they have to respond to in live time.

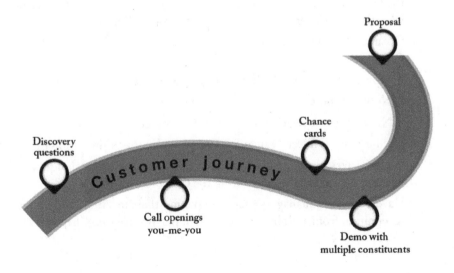

The experience is high-energy and competitive; and, most importantly, it builds skills and belief. By the end of the day, every single person has practiced bringing their NSP—*We empower success*—to life in every phase of the sales process, and they've heard their peers do it as well. They've been actively engaged all day, and they have great examples of what their NSP looks like in action. Plus they had fun.

Compare that to the usual *sit in a darkened conference room with slides* style of meeting we've all seen too many of. Instead of listening, the team is doing. When people have the opportunity to self-discover, leverage peer learning, and apply it to live-time situations, the learning sticks.

Here are some other ideas to make your current sales training more effective:

- Do the transaction-driven versus purpose-driven exercise at the beginning of this chapter.
- Help your team forge a stronger functional and personal connection with your purpose by asking:
    ○ How does your job connect to our Noble Purpose?
    ○ What does our Noble Purpose mean to you?
- Create a customer journey map to practice skills at pivotal areas of your sales process. You can go all out and map it across a ballroom or just use a simple flip chart.
- Pick three target customers, and have your team research them using the five categories of critical customer information. Ask them to present what they believe are the customers' most compelling issues.
- Create customer scenarios for your team to practice the skills in Chapter 12:
    ○ "You-me-you" call openings to improve engagement
    ○ Noble Purpose proposals to increase the win rate
    ○ Noble Purpose negotiation to maintain margins
- Hold a Story-Off (see "Engaging Clients with Stories" in Chapter 8).
- Create a coaching circle where managers practice the techniques in Chapter 18 (before the call, during the call, and after the call).
- Have your sales managers practice opening their meetings and giving recognition from a Noble Purpose client perspective (see Chapter 17).

When we certify trainers in our Noble Purpose programs, we tell them, "You're not only teaching techniques, you're moving hearts and minds." As you think about your own sales training, ask yourself, "Are we lecturing? Or are we creating an environment where people can truly learn?"

The purpose of training is to create a team of people who can succeed when you're not there. When your Noble Purpose is etched into the hearts and minds of your team and they have the skills to activate it, your job as a leader becomes much easier.

Chapter 19: Training Your Frontline to Be Noble Purpose Sellers

When training is pointed in service of the close, instead of in service of the customer, it doesn't stick. To train NSP-driven reps, help them discover for themselves the impact that shifting to a purpose-driven approach has on customers.

Do the transaction-driven vs. purpose-driven exercise at the beginning of this chapter to jumpstart a mindset shift.

Make sure your team is practicing live-time skills during training. Define winning from the customer's perspective.

Do one thing: Pick one thing from the list at the end of this chapter to bring your NSP into your next sales training program.

CHAPTER

20

Incentivizing Purpose

There are two things people want more than sex and money—recognition and praise.

—Mary Kay Ash, founder of Mary Kay Cosmetics, Inc.

There aren't many jobs where they publicly publish the performance reviews. But sales is one of them. In sales, there's nowhere to hide: everyone knows how you're doing.

We've all seen sales teams scramble to make year-end bonuses, pulling forward every bit of revenue they can. They hit the target, yet it's often at the expense of customer relationships and future business. You can do better. You want to do more than hit your revenue targets. You're trying to create *sticky* revenue: revenue that comes back to you again and again. You want to create such a differentiated sales experience that your customers don't look elsewhere.

There have been lots of studies about sales incentives, but for the most part, the research focuses on driving short-term revenue. It's as if salespeople are cash registers—push this button, hit that key, and bang! Out comes the money. You already know that's not true. Incentivizing *long-term* success means rewarding the right behaviors and galvanizing your team to create differentiation.

Most sales teams already have a commission plan, a president's club, and other financial incentives to reward top sellers. There are plenty of simple models to illustrate how to do that. You want to do more. A Noble Purpose leader creates rewards, recognition, and incentives that get the team so emotionally invested that they create emotionally engaged clients who become your best ambassadors.

To be clear, I'm all for monetary rewards for sales performance. The people who generate revenue should get a share of it. I've been a commissioned salesperson, P&L leader, and business owner whose income was dependent on sales for most of my career. My principle is always that as your sellers make you more profitable, you should make them more profitable.

Having said that, let's look at some additional creative ways you can point your team toward your purpose and create a tribe of true believers who are in it for the long haul.

What the Marshmallow Experiment Tells Us About Sales Incentives

Perhaps you're familiar with the famous Stanford *marshmallow experiment*. The 1972 experiment conducted by Professor Walter Mischel was a study in delayed gratification.

In the study, a child (usually about age 4 or 5) was offered a choice between one marshmallow immediately or two marshmallows if they could wait for several minutes. The researcher left the room, leaving the child alone with the single marshmallow for 15 minutes. Most of the children ate the marshmallow.

The children who were able to delay gratification and sit there for a solid 15 minutes with a marshmallow in front of them, and not eat it, were rewarded with two marshmallows. If you know anything about 4- and 5-year-olds, you can imagine how difficult it is for a young child to not eat a marshmallow. Some kids ate it the moment the researcher closed the door. Others tried jumping up and down, closing their eyes, walking to the other side of the room, and using a multitude of other self-imposed distraction techniques to avoid eating the marshmallow. One child even took a little nibble of the back of the marshmallow and turned it around, hoping the researcher wouldn't notice. Only a few children managed to wait the entire time.

Here's where it gets interesting and has direct ramifications for business. The researchers followed the children as they grew up. Over time, the children who were able to delay gratification scored better on a variety of life measures, including a better ability to handle stress, better social skills, lower substance abuse, and even better test scores.

Using the marshmallow study of 5-year-olds as our jumping-off point for incentives is not meant to imply that your people are children. It's the opposite; it's simply that we're all human. Given the choice, especially when we're tired and frustrated, we don't want to take the time to strategize how to get two marshmallows; we just want to eat one marshmallow right now.

The marshmallow experiment illustrates the challenges and rewards for delayed gratification. Your job is to help your team see that when you delay the gratification of trying to make a short-term grab for the customer's money (one marshmallow), you can get a bigger, more meaningful sale later (two marshmallows).

When researchers reran the marshmallow experiment years later and controlled for social and economic background, they discovered, not surprisingly, that the children who were able to delay gratification were more likely to come from stable environments where there was food in the pantry and adults kept their promises.

It wasn't that they were more strategic kids; it was that their environment made them more confident. Remember the earlier chapter about sitting with uncertainty? When your environment teaches you *it's okay to wait, you get better things in the end, you don't have to worry, we'll support you*, you're more likely to play for the second marshmallow.

As a leader, you create the environment. Paint a picture for your team of what two marshmallows looks like, and *also* reward them for the behaviors that will get them there. Year-end bonuses are great, but incremental rewards, which don't always have to be monetary, will keep the momentum going.

Hit Your Goals with Momentum

Kyle Porter, founder and CEO of Atlanta-based startup SalesLoft, says, "Our goal is to hit our revenue numbers with momentum." SalesLoft, a SaaS firm that provides a sales engagement platform, was founded on "a shared belief that modern sales should be more about authentic, sincere interactions than insincere mass outreach programs and other less-personal sales strategies."

Porter conceptualized the momentum concept after signing up for a bike race. At 78 miles, it was much longer than any other race he had done. He says, "I was riding it by myself. I saw all these people with the same jersey. I asked, 'Hey, what are you doing?' They said, 'Come hang out with us.'" He stayed with their pack for miles. He says, "By mile 58, I was huffing and puffing. The leader said, 'Hey, do you want to help? Pull up front.'"

Porter, who was already exhausted, says, "I was dreading it, but you can't say no." Yet he found when he pulled to the front of the team, "It was so much easier. I had the whole group behind me, pulling for me." He says, "When I hit the finish line, I had more momentum, more energy, more capabilities than ever before, and that is exactly how we want to hit our revenue milestones."

SalesLoft has driven dramatic revenue growth in a short period of time. Named a top 10 fast-growth firm, their series D fundraising round raised $70 million. Many startups push for fast revenue growth. SalesLoft has made a point to reward client engagement. SalesLoft knows that rewarding and recognizing team members who embody their purpose creates stickier revenue. Instead of merely hitting their goals, they want to incentivize their team to hit the goals with momentum.

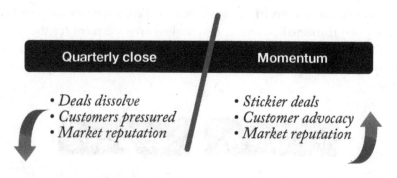

Quarterly close	Momentum
• Deals dissolve	• Stickier deals
• Customers pressured	• Customer advocacy
• Market reputation	• Market reputation

A leader who tells his or her team, "I want to hit our numbers with power, influence, and trajectory" has a big advantage over a leader who simply says, "Hit the number." It's an entirely different set of marching orders.

SalesLoft consistently wins Best Place to Work awards, and they attract top talent. Their solution is considered a top-tier sales engagement platform, and they're constantly innovating. Their team morale is off the chart, and being in their meetings is like swimming in a sea of positive energy.

Rewarding your sales team for things like being the seller with the most engaged customers, best display of strategic thinking, and longest-lasting customer contract reinforces: "This is a two-marshmallow game here, people." You want everyone to know, "We're more than transactional cash registers. We're Noble Purpose sellers."

Why the Winner-Takes-All Model Fails Midyear

One of the challenges with many sales incentive programs is that they only reward the top tier. Imagine you're a top performer; you're on track to deliver $2 million for the year. You'll make the bonus club and go on the incentive trip. Your morale is high, but then you lose a big account in October. Now you'll never make $2 million. Do you quit trying? Do you throw all your sales into next year?

If your only incentive is to hit the top tier, you'll likely give up on this year and start loading up next year. Let's be honest: people find a way to game the system. Look at your comp plan and ask yourself, what's the incentive for people who aren't top performers? Make no mistake, the cache and cash for being a top performer is a good thing—a very good thing. The pride that comes from making the President's Club or the Inner Circle is real. People should strive for that. Top performers look forward to it.

But you also want to ensure that the people who aren't going to make the top end keep their head in the game.

Reward the Right Behaviors

Patrick Hodges, general manager for Blackbaud, whom you first read about in Chapter 2, runs a big team, many of whom are in their first sales job. They have a long sales cycle, so it's unlikely new people are going to be bringing in big numbers quickly. It would be easy for them to get discouraged. To keep his team motivated and focused on the right behaviors with customers, Hodges provides tiered incentives. He says, "As sales changes, customer relationships become even more important. You want your people to develop those skills and you want to reward them for it." He also notes it's very costly to replace people. He says instead, "You need to help your 50% and 70%ers to get better."

People who may not qualify for Blackbaud's President's Club can still be successful and earn rewards. Sellers who meet preset criteria that include completion of training, validated comprehension pre-set with testing and role-plays, and baseline sales performance can earn additional money. They also get interim promotions within their role. Hodges says, "It gives people forward career momentum."

Notice that Hodges is purposeful about rewarding people for learning. They have to pass tests and do customer-focused role-plays to demonstrate they're fluent in the right behaviors to qualify. By doing this, he's reinforcing, "We're learners, we're always improving, and we want to become experts in the right sales behaviors." It's also important to note that Hodge's program includes a level of sales performance; he's not handing out meaningless participation trophies.

At SalesLoft, Porter and his team reward and recognize "Lofters" who embody their purpose and values. They make a big deal of it at weekly meetings and publicize it on LinkedIn and Instagram. Imagine your boss sharing a photo of you describing how you "put customers first" and "have a bias toward action" (two of SalesLoft's values). Your friends see it in your Instagram feed—there you are with the CEO, getting an award for the way you treat customers.

Giving Everyone a Trophy Is Not the Answer

Now is a good time to discuss a group we get a lot of questions about: millennials. You can't address recognition and incentives without talking about young people. Millennials and Generation Z behind them have a reputation for wanting instant rewards. When they do good work, they want someone to notice.

I'm going to state my premise right up front: the things younger generations are asking for in terms of rewards, recognition, and incentives benefit everyone, including the business overall.

Many think the "everybody gets a trophy" or "snowflake generation," as some refer to them, are adverse to hard work. This has not been my experience; quite the opposite, in fact. Some of our most successful clients are filled with young people who are on fire for their work.

Blackbaud and SalesLoft are excellent examples. Patrick Hodges crafted Blackbaud's interim rewards program because he knew the young people on his team wanted something immediate. By giving out tiered promotions and interim rewards, Hodges is building his tribe of true believers.

When you tell your parents and announce on LinkedIn, "I just became a Level II Account Exec," it fuels pride: pride in yourself, and pride in your organization. Hodges is incentivizing his team for living their purpose. His people could easily give up when they don't get success right away; or if they are successful, they could job-hop for more money. Instead, he's giving them interim wins and helping them forge a stronger bond with the organization and their customers.

Social validation ▶ Stronger affinity

While generations are not monolithic and people are obviously unique, generations do share common cultural expectations. One reason the purpose movement has taken off is that younger people have demanded it. As a leader, this is very good news; it means you have lots of tools beyond money to incentivize your team. After working with a number of younger teams, here are some observations about incentives. The data tells us they apply to younger people; personally, I think they apply to most of us:

- **Participation trophies are meaningless.** When young people move out of their parents' homes, they generally don't take their participation trophies with them. You may still have your third-place ribbon for track (that you actually won), but young people know they didn't win that plastic junk. The joke is on the parents who spent the time and money to ensure everyone felt special. Young people see these for what they are: souvenirs.

- **People want a real win and to be unique while they're doing it.** Yes, younger people were all told they're "special" by their parents. Now they want to prove it. They need to see that your company is reshaping the market, or whatever your version of differentiation is. Give out recognition and rewards that spotlight their contribution *and* broadcast why your firm is unique. It builds pride.

- **Consistent meaningful feedback *is* a reward.** People want to know how they're doing *now*; it shouldn't wait for review time. Quick hits of feedback are like rocket fuel. It doesn't all have to come from you. Create self-reinforcing feedback loops involving customers and other team members. Live-time "how am I doing" feedback like scoring customer intelligence for robustness or assessing call quality gives people recognition and boosts confidence.

- **Salespeople aren't fragile, but they (sometimes) need help with resilience.** You want a team who can deal with setbacks. It's especially important for young people, who don't have the life experience to realize that "this too shall pass." To build resilience, reward it. Publically recognize people who rebound after a bad call or tough quarter. Create a Rebounder Award or a "you got this" incentive for someone who can win a deal after losing one.

If you find yourself thinking, "I did it with no fluffy incentives or nicey-nice feedback! Their paycheck should be enough," here's a quick reminder: if you create a transactional relationship with your employees, they'll create a transactional relationship with your customers. Both your customers and your team will quickly jump ship for a better price.

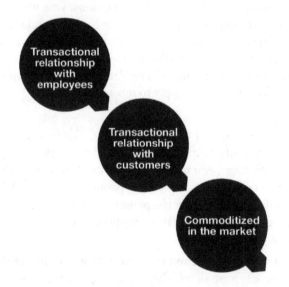

You want your rewards and incentives to build long-term pride in your team that will translate over to customers. Money matters, and so do lots of other things.

Why Public Recognition Is Powerful

Zach Selch, principal of Global Sales Mentor, describes one of his most memorable sales awards; it's something he still remembers even though it happened over 20 years ago.

At the time, Selch was the director of international sales for South Asia for a Fortune 100 company. He says, "I closed the single biggest deal ever for the corporation, which included the single biggest PO in the history of one of the product divisions." The product division was so excited about the sale, Selch says, "They made a golf shirt for the specific deal—the only time in the corporation a shirt was made for one deal. About a hundred were printed up. I got three; the rest went to people who worked on the deal and the top management of the company. Everybody knew the people wearing the shirt were in on the deal, and the whole company knew it was my deal. I was a freakin' rock star for a day. The best feeling ever!"

There were 250 people in the company with responsibilities similar to Selch. But only he had "the shirt." It was a unique wearable "trophy." He says it instilled fantastic pride in himself and his support team.

It's worth noting that Selch made a big commission on that sale. Again, you should pay your people for bringing in business. He said the commission on that single sale was double his previous year's salary. But 20 years later, what he remembers most is the way he felt when he was wearing "the shirt." To this day, the two most important things Selch has displayed in his office are his paratrooper beret (30 years old) and that golf shirt (20 years old) in shadow boxes, for all the world to see.

You want incentives that make your people feeling like freakin' rock stars.

Nine Ways to Incentivize Your Purpose

Here are nine things you can do (some monetary, some not) to reward long-term focus, drive the right behaviors, and build pride with your team:

- **Reward customer results.** Does your organization improve customer efficiency? Do you help your customers sell more to their customers? How do you help your clients improve their organizations? Find a way to measure your customers' results and provide awards to salespeople who excel at getting the best results for customers.

- **Recognize and reward interim behavior.** Can you create a Best Discovery award for someone who really rocks the five categories of critical customer information (see Chapter 11)? What about the best call opening of the week? Or the most customer-focused presentation? Get creative. You don't have to give out cash; the winner can get their name on the leader board and choose lunch on Friday.

- **Reward customer retention.** Who has the longest-running customer contract? Whose deals never go out to bid? Which service team helps you keep business? Reward and recognize the behaviors that keep your customers engaged.

- **Give out NSP exemplar awards.** Did you have a rep sleep in his or her car, in the snow, like the Graham-White rep in Chapter 8? Did one of your salespeople do the right thing in a tough ethical dilemma? Did your support staff catch an error before it went out the door? Take a page from SalesLoft, and share your awards publically. Look for ways to recognize and reward the people who exemplify your Noble Purpose in action.

- **Give incremental promotions.** Flatter organizations mean fewer regular promotions. Use Blackbaud's tiered system, where salespeople move into graduating positions of responsibility and salary, earning bonuses and upward mobility within the sales role.

- **Crowdsource and reward best in class.** Hold a contest for creating the best presentation or sales engagement tool. Give a cash prize and bragging rights to the winner. You'll access your team's best thinking and wind up with useful tools. Name the winning presentation after the winner. Sally's killer proposal should become legendary.

- **Showcase the shiny objects.** If you're going to give away something, bring it into the office and put it right up front. You want to create a tangible talisman. If you're giving away tickets, put them at the front of your bullpen, along with a photo of the venue and souvenir hat. You want people to see them every day. If it's a bragging rights contest, create a wrestler-style belt or a jacket or hat the winner can wear for the week. It might seem silly, but you'd be surprised how fun it makes it for people.

- **Memorialize wins.** Make sure the wins are public. Remember, you want people to feel like freakin' rock stars. Print golf shirts for the winning team; put a banner over their cubes. You want everyone to see "here's what we did."

- **Bring in customers and support staff to make awards more impactful.** Blackbaud regularly brings in customers when they give out sales awards. Having the customer talk about the impact the solution had on their organization makes the award more special and builds pride in the whole team. Include the support team. The customer and the backstage team will appreciate the recognition: it reinforces why your company cares more than your competition, and it differentiates you in a powerful way.

There are lots of ways to provide incentives. Get creative with your team. Your incentives should create a high today that drives the right behaviors for tomorrow. You're building a tribe of true believers; you want them focused and excited.

Chapter 20: Incentivizing Purpose

You want to do more than hit revenue numbers: you want to hit them with momentum. To create sticky revenue, teach your team that *it's a two-marshmallow game.*

Teach your team the art of delayed gratification by rewarding and recognizing the right behaviors. The winner-takes-all model has a chilling effect on mid-level performers and can cause people to unnecessarily pull forward or hold back revenue, which negatively affects customers.

Nine ways to incentivize your purpose:

- Reward customer results.
- Recognize and reward interim behavior (like rocking discovery with the five categories of critical customer information).
- Reward customer retention.
- Give out NSP exemplar awards (like SalesLoft on social media).
- Create incremental promotions (like Blackbaud's tiered system).
- Crowdsource and reward the best ideas.
- Showcase your shiny objects.
- Memorialize wins with tangible artifacts like shirts and banners.
- Bring in customers and support staff to make awards more impactful.

Do one thing: Pick one thing from the list and do it.

21

Winning Top Talent

A noble person attracts noble people and knows how to hold onto them.
—Johann Wolfgang von Goethe, German writer and statesman

Imagine you're looking for a sales job and you come across two postings. The first one says, "We strive to be the preferred provider for our customers by offering a unique value-added solution. We're looking for a highly motivated salesperson who can drive revenue and be compensated accordingly." The second posting says, "Would you like to help us change the world?"

Which one are you going to click?

Most people don't start looking for a new position because they want more money. They start looking because they're unhappy at work. And that unhappiness often springs from a lack of appreciation, meaning, and purpose. Ideally, you're able to offer a competitive salary, benefits, and above-average perks. But there's one thing people want even more than that: they want to feel like they matter. They want to make a difference.

Join Us If You Want Make a Difference

Here are a few examples of compelling recruiting messages, pulled directly off our clients' websites:

G Adventures: We look for individuals who are passionate and purpose-driven. Be part of something greater than yourself. We are more than just a travel company. We combine innovative business ideas and social responsibility to transcend travel and ultimately change people's lives, including yours.

SalesLoft: You're smart, talented, and driven. You could work anywhere you want. You choose SalesLoft because at SalesLoft, we want to help you become the best version of yourself through your service to others: our Customers and your Team Members.

Blackbaud: Come change the world with us. Our team of over 3,300 employees is passionate about helping customers use innovative technology to make a difference in the world. Working here means making an impact in the lives of others every day. At Blackbaud, it is possible to change the world and grow your career at the same time. Come find out how.

Supportworks: We're redefining home contracting. Through that process, we've become more than a manufacturer of products. We are a provider of radical business supports that are redefining our industry. We're also redefining the workplace, creating a space where people feel welcomed, free, and encouraged.

Atlantic Capital Bank: Join a team with purpose. We believe that banking is a noble profession and that, at Atlantic Capital, we are part of something much larger than ourselves. If this sounds like you, then consider joining our team.

As you read these, what goes through your head? Despite being in industries where other firms struggle to get good people, these organizations have their choice of top talent. To be clear, they're all great places to work. But their leaders will tell you, they didn't always have great packages to offer people. The way these firms *became* great places to work was by leading with their purpose and attracting people who were excited about it.

Sales job #1	Sales job #2
Value added end-to-end solutions	*Change the world*

Which job are you more excited about?

Leading with your purpose enables you to attract the best people—remember, purpose-driven employees outperform transactional employees. It also enables you to weed out the wrong people.

Let's look at how purpose can help you during the interview process.

If you're recruiting and interviewing at a standard company, like the generic end-to-end value-added solution firm, you're going to have to tease out from the interviewee how that person will connect with customers. And how many times has a person shown you his or her best face in an interview and not lived up to that on the job? The generic description of your offering doesn't provide a good jumping-off point to assess their motivation, engagement, or resilience.

When you have a clear purpose, whether it's fueling prosperity or redefining your industry, you have a different, better filter. When the person comes in, you can ask, "What about our purpose is interesting to you?" Describe how you make a difference to customers, and then assess the candidate's response. Does the candidate light up and get excited? Does the candidate have an emotional pull to your NSP, or does it fall flat with him or her?

Top performers who will go the extra mile for customers will get excited about your NSP in the interview. They'll immediately personalize it. The best people will have researched it online and thought about it beforehand, and they'll come in prepared to tell you why they're ready to tell everyone about your purpose. Remember, top performers are the people with passion and purpose—that's who you're looking for.

Your NSP serves as a litmus test in interviews. If a candidate doesn't get excited about your NSP in the interview, that tells you everything you need to know. He or she doesn't need to jump up and down; you simply want to see evidence that the candidate is enthused and engaged about the idea of making a difference.

In Chapter 20, we talked about millennials and Generation Z in terms of incentives. Now let's talk about younger generations from a hiring perspective. There are two crucial things you need to know:

1. **Purpose is essential for younger generations.** Previous generations crave meaning and purpose, but we've been conditioned (by the world) to accept money as a substitute. Younger generations aren't having it. They were raised to believe they could change the world, and they're not going to do a job that doesn't matter. They're not only evaluating your purpose, they're also assessing whether you're authentic about it.

2. **They're articulating the unspoken dreams of their parents.** The generation who watched their parents put work first for decades only to be laid off during the recession learned a thing or two. They're not shy about letting people know what they want from work. While many find it unsettling, like generations before them, they are creating a better situation for themselves and those who follow.

Again, every person is unique. But the research about millennials and Z's tells us loud and clear that when it comes to recruiting, purpose is a deciding factor. Younger people are not content with the traditional transactional work model. Working for decades to make partner or hoping your boss will dole out a bonus is not enough for them. They're reshaping the world of work in powerful ways that make work better for everyone.

Many of us grew our careers in a time when purpose and meaning were rarely discussed at work. How might your early jobs have been different if your firm had talked to you about Noble Purpose? When you bring purpose to the fore, you attract the highest performers of every generation.

Onboarding Should Get People More Excited, Not Less Excited

Once you've hired the right people, you want to keep their enthusiasm alive during onboarding. Leaders are often surprised to learn how seemingly small things that happen in the early days have a big impact on morale. Purpose-driven leaders make a point to assess onboarding from the employee perspective.

In his book *Trailblazer*, Marc Benioff, founder of Salesforce, says, "As a leader, you need to be a lot more concerned about what people aren't saying that what they are saying." New employees aren't likely to tell the boss the onboarding is disengaging or boring. But they will tell each other.

Reading comments on Salesforce's internal Chatter helps Benioff keep abreast of things that might go unnoticed to a typical CEO. He writes, "One of the first significant grievances had to do with the company's onboarding process. Apparently, new hires were less than thrilled with it. The thread was flooded with complaints from new hires about laptops that hadn't arrived, phones that weren't connected, missing ID badges, and so on. The tipping point was when a new employee quit on her first day. A consensus emerged that our onboarding process was akin to 'hazing,' and we knew we had to fix the problem immediately."

Benioff understood the impact. He says, "For a company that had added 10,000 employees in a single two-year stretch, onboarding was mission critical."

As you think about your own onboarding, ask yourself, would you be proud to have your customers go through it? If your best friend or spouse went through it, would they be more excited about your firm or less excited?

Salesforce took action. Benioff says, "We revamped the entire process to make it less erratic and more consistent, while also increasing the amount of personalized one-on-one attention for every individual employee."

Theresa Ludvigson is a senior director of global onboarding at Salesforce. She describes their intent in a Salesforce blog post: "Their (employees') first experience with us should be a reflection of our brand. That's why we revamped our Day 1 program to be memorable, engaging, and fun. No 'death by PowerPoint' here, even for our remote employees. We place a huge emphasis on our high-touch programs because we know they foster the sense of belonging and community that makes new hires want to stick around."

Ludvigson says, "Onboarding is as much about technology as it is about the human connection. It's about letting new hires know they're part of something special—but that doesn't happen by accident."

In their book *The Power of Moments*, Chip and Dan Heath noted that in most firms, the first day of work is frequently an underwhelming experience. The receptionist doesn't know who you are, you have to fill out a bunch of forms, you can't find your desk, and if you do, there's no computer. You get a big manual to read. They write, "The lack of attention paid to an employee's first day is mind-boggling."

The Heaths describe how John Deere transformed the way employees experience that crucial first day. Lani Lorenz Fry, who worked in global brand strategy and marketing for John Deere, discovered that leaders in Asia were struggling with employee engagement and retention. Unlike the Midwest, where your grandfather may have owned a John Deere tractor, employees in other markets didn't have an emotional connection to the brand.

Fry and her colleagues wanted to change that. Collaborating with customer experience consultant Lew Carbone, they designed an innovative first-day experience. Here's an abbreviated version of the magic they created for that first day, as described beautifully by Chip and Dan Heath in *The Power of Moments*:

As you get settled (into your desk for the first time) you notice the background image on your monitor: it's a gorgeous shot of John Deere equipment on a farm at sunset, and the copy says, "welcome to the most important work you'll ever do."

You notice you've already received your first email. It's from Sam Allen, the CEO of John Deere. In a short video he talks about the company's mission: "to provide the food, shelter, and infrastructure that will be needed by the world's growing population." He closes by saying, "Enjoy the rest of your first day, and I hope you'll enjoy a long and successful, fulfilling career as part of the John Deere team."

Now you notice there's a gift on your desk. It's a stainless steel replica of John Deere's original "self-polishing plow" created in 1837. An accompanying card explains why farmers loved it.

At midday (your host) collects you for a lunch off-site with a small group. They ask about your background and tell you about some of the projects they're working on. Later in the day, the department manager

*(your boss's boss) comes over and makes plans to have
lunch with you the next week.
You leave the office that day thinking, I belong here.
The work we're doing matters. And I matter to them.*

The two big human needs are belonging and significance. In that first-day experience, John Deere tells new team members, You're going to get both of those here. Compare that to when most new salespeople walk in, and the first thing you hand them is a quota. They get the message really fast: here you're just a number. Instead of starting with a job description or target list, think about how you can welcome people into your tribe of true believers. From the first time they click on your website to the moment they walk through your doors, you want people to know that this work matters, and so do they.

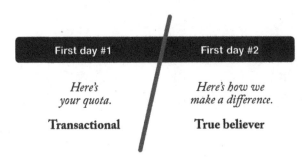

As you look at your own hiring and onboarding experiences, ask yourself: Are we selling this as just another job? Or are we inviting people into a world of purpose where they can make a real difference?

Chapter 21: Winning Top Talent

A Noble Purpose helps you recruit top talent. Be proactive about sharing your NSP publically to attract like minds: people who also want to make a difference in the world.

(continued)

(continued)

Share your NSP in interviews, and watch how candidates respond. Purpose allows you to demonstrate and observe an authentic connection in the pursuit of something greater.

Showcase your NSP on the crucial first day, and keep it alive through onboarding by helping your new hires feel the connection to your team and the meaning behind your NSP.

Do one thing: Bring up your NSP in the interview. Pay careful attention to the candidate's response.

How to Keep Your NSP from Dying in Accounting

It is difficult to get a man to understand something, when his salary depends on his not understanding it.

—Upton Sinclair, writer

The true test of your Noble Purpose is how well you can keep it alive in the face of adversity. Every organization experiences financial ups and downs, market issues, operational issues, and other challenges. Sometimes they come with no warning. When times get tough, there are two things people will defend: their budget and their functional area. It can get ugly. Recently, I was an eyewitness to a scene like this; it wasn't pretty. I call it *The Tale of Two Budgets*.

Our story begins in a conference room.

The two men glared at each other from opposite sides of the conference table, looking like mortal enemies—and in some ways, they were. Steve, the younger of the two, had his hands perched on the arms of his chair, clenching his fingers on the edges as if he were ready to leap into battle. Bill looked like a war-weary soldier. He'd been through this type of fight before, and he knew it wouldn't end well. He loosened his collar, let out a sigh, and leaned back in his chair, crossing his arms and looking over his glasses, as if daring Steve to speak first.

It worked. Steve took the bait.

"My team can't survive on this budget!" Steve shouted. "Are you trying to kill us?"

Bill looked at Steve with the dismissive disdain one might have for a chubby toddler stomping his feet for more cake. Steve was always whining about not getting enough. Didn't he understand? Bill had bigger issues to contend with; he reported to the top. Steve's petty demands revealed what Bill had long suspected: Steve cared only about his own department. He wasn't seeing the big picture. He thought to himself, "He just doesn't get it."

How many times have you found yourself saying exactly that about a colleague? He or she just doesn't *get it*. It's the ultimate corporate insult.

The case of Bill and Steve was an actual interchange I observed between a chief financial officer, Bill, and a division sales manager, Steve. (Names have been changed to protect the well-intentioned.)

The point of contention was the trade show budget. Bill had cut the budget, and Steve, the sales manager, wanted the money back. Bill's argument was, "We need to hit the profit numbers, or we won't be in business next year." Steve's counterargument was, "We need to be at these trade shows, or we won't have any customers next year." Who's right? It's hard to say. They're both doing the very best they can to meet the goals they've been assigned. And therein lies the problem.

When your livelihood depends on hitting your departmental targets, your alliance is always toward your own function. Without belief in a shared purpose, departmental goals will always be the priority.

Business is filled with competing agendas. Salespeople have different goals than finance people. Marketing has different goals than HR. Manufacturing and product development have different objectives. The list goes on and on. Everyone believes that his or her agenda is the most important. In a way, each person is right; each personal agenda is the most important thing—to that person.

People on one side of the company don't understand what people on the other side are doing. Groups pull back and forth against each other in a daily tug-of-war that's ineffective at best and destructive at worst. Whoever has the strongest voice wins. The result is rework, misalignment, and missed opportunities. Over time, you wind up with disengagement, which can turn into silos and, ultimately, result in turf wars.

It's a ridiculous waste of time and mental energy; it's also a fact in many organizations. As a leader who is connected to customers, you can use your NSP to break through the clutter, bring silos together, and help your entire team make better decisions.

In Chapter 3, I introduced you to the 6P model. It's a framework for strategy, and it also works for bringing silos together, reframing inter-departmental battles, and making well-informed operational decisions.

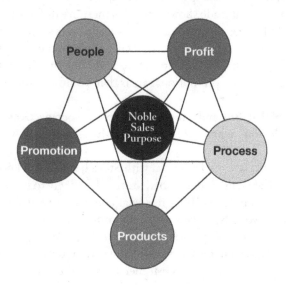

How Overattachment Costs You Money

The story of Bill and Steve fighting about the budget is an all-too-common corporate occurrence. Bill, the CFO, was focused on his P—*profit*. He has to deliver the quarterly earnings. Steve, the sales manager, was focused on his P—*promotion*. He had to get new customers in the pipeline for next year. Bill and Steve's conversation would have played out differently if they had been pointed toward a shared purpose, at least from an emotional perspective. They might still fight about promotional trade show spending, but it wouldn't become so personal.

When you know the person on the other side is working toward the same endgame, you're more likely to assume they have good intent.

The Six-P model reframes these kinds of conversations. Looking through the lens of NSP doesn't change each person's expertise; it changes each person's perspective. The question is not, "Should we or should we not do trade shows?" The question now becomes, "How do the sales promotions rank against other ways of accomplishing our NSP?" Instead of arguing about a single line item, they're now both focused on the big picture: their NSP.

Framing the conversation through the lens of an NSP takes Bill and Steve in a new direction. It's more likely to lead them to discuss a wider variety of options. They'll start asking questions like, "How do our customers benefit from our attendance at trade shows? Perhaps there are different ways of doing trade shows. What has the past payout on trade shows been? What impact do they have on new customers, existing customers, and prospects? How can we improve that? What can we do before and after the shows to maximize returns? Are there other promotional areas that would be more effective than trade shows?"

The fact that Bill and Steve have different perspectives is no longer a negative. It's now a positive, because both perspectives will be serving their NSP.

Bill is less likely to be frustrated with Steve because Bill knows that promotion is a critical element in the mix. Steve is less likely to be angry with Bill because he understands that Bill's financial controls are important. After all, you can't achieve your NSP without a solid profit. Now, they both *get it*. And most importantly, *they believe their colleague gets it as well*.

The Six-P model helps you manage the natural tension between departments. It keeps the voice of the customer front and center and ensures that you have all the other areas covered as well.

Why Silos Turn Into Turf Wars

Most turf wars start as silos. Well-intentioned people create goals and objectives that pertain to their area of expertise. They build out their department using the lens that they understand most fully: their own function. They become attached to their goals and plans. It can turn into a battle when one silo bumps up against another group whose goals seem like they conflict.

Many attribute silos and turf wars to ego. I have a different, more empathetic lens on this. Fighting means you care. Have you ever been part of an apathetic team or seen an apathetic organization? They don't bother to fight with each other over what's best for the organization, because they don't give two flips.

You want a team who cares enough to argue about the best way to spend your money, time, and resources.

Creative tension is a good thing for an organization. For example, consider Disney. Two of Disney's legendary Four Keys are Safety and Show. The other two Keys are Courtesy and Efficiency, but for the purposes of this example, let's stick with Safety and Show. Disney takes safety very seriously. They set standards that are higher than required. They also create magic. As they say, "Show breathes life into the stories we tell our guests."

Imagine you work for Disney, and you're in a meeting. The topic is, how does Tinker Bell kick off the fireworks show? The Show people probably want her to fly over the entire park holding a real fire-lit wand in her hand, with her dizzyingly high flight fueled by an invisible jetpack. If the Safety people had their way, Tinker Bell would probably be standing on solid ground, waving a flashlight. But they don't do either of these things. Instead, they pursue Safety and Show simultaneously. Every night, night after night, Tinker Bell flies safely down on an invisible wire, lights the castle, and starts the fireworks show. The people at Disney hold two seemingly competing ideas in their mind at the same time, and they pursue both Safety and Show with excellence.

One of our clients likes this example so much that in moments of conflict he often says, "We need to do the Tinker Bell thing" to remind his team that they can work out a creative solution.

At Disney, the teams push and pull against each other in a collaborative way because both teams are trying to create a place Where Dreams Come True. The secret is making sure you're focused on the right endgame.

The Cost of Overemphasis

You already know from Chapter 3 what happens when you overemphasize profit: you create a transactional relationship with your team and customers. Overemphasizing other areas can be detrimental as well.

Have you ever observed any of these?

- Finance creates a new budgeting model, but no one uses the new forms or gets their numbers in on time.
- The IT department launches a new process, but employees work around it so that they can continue using the old system.
- Product development creates a flanker brand, but no one sells the new items to the customer.
- Promotions start with hype but don't gain traction because other employees view them as a distraction from the daily routine.
- The HR department creates an extensive curriculum, but business leaders don't want to take people out of the field for training.

When people don't understand how an initiative fits in with the bigger picture, they view it as irrelevant. The problem isn't conflicting agendas; the problem is lack of integration. In a healthy organization, *you want people to have different agendas*:

- You want the finance people to have rigorous controls for profit.
- You want manufacturing and operations focused on continual improvement of internal processes.
- You want research and development to dream up crazy new products.
- You want sales and marketing to push the envelope on promotion.
- You want HR to be passionate about people.

These different departments exist because each of their roles is crucial. It's when one department dominates that you start to run into problems.

Here are some common signs of overemphasis, followed by suggestions for dealing with it.

Signs that you may be overemphasizing profit:

- People try to game the comp plan.
- You discuss customers only as numbers.
- Meetings start and end with financial reports.
- You discuss stock price more than you discuss customers.
- People resent senior leaders.

Signs that you may be overemphasizing process:

- Teams get bogged down in minutiae about efficiency at the expense of outcomes.
- Task forces grow in number and size.
- Internal studies take precedence over customer feedback.
- You begin to use a lot of acronyms.
- Internal metrics become more important than external metrics.
- You spend more time on reports than meeting with customers.
- Manufacturing doesn't meet with customers.
- Salespeople become skeptical of the home office.

Signs you may be overemphasizing products:

- Product development cycles take longer than the industry average.
- Salespeople aren't excited about new products.
- Product launches don't focus on customer goals.
- Product updates don't include customer feedback.
- Your catalogue contains lots of products that have very small sales.
- New products divert from core competencies.

Signs you may be overemphasizing promotion:

- You talk about industry leadership rather than customer impact.
- Beating the competition becomes more important than helping customers.
- You copy the competitor instead of innovating for customers.
- You attend the same trade shows every year with no benefit analysis.
- Your advertising mix never changes.

Signs you may be overemphasizing people (yes, this is possible):

- You conduct training for the sake of checking boxes.
- Vacation schedules are a frequent topic of discussion.
- Employees develop an entitlement mentality.
- Development plans are written without business goals.

How to Bring the Customer's Voice into the Room

If you spotted your company in these examples, don't despair. You're hardly alone. Most organizations struggle to keep the customer front and center. As a sales leader, you can play a powerful role in bringing the customer's voice into your organization. Here are some things you can do to get alignment:

- Post the Six-P model on the wall of your conference room.
- Use your NSP as a decision-making filter. Ask, "How will this help us achieve our purpose?"
- Tell customer impact stories (see Chapter 8) on a regular basis.
- Record customers sharing their stories, and show the video at meetings to get the rest of the team aligned toward customers.
- Create a "day in the life of a customer" experience for your sales team and senior leaders.
- Ask each team to provide examples of how they're delivering on your NSP.

As you look at these, notice that you don't have to be in charge to execute on them. If you sit on a multifunctional team, you can implement these as part of your role. It's important to note that some departments and some leaders may be farther away from customers than others. Before you assume bad intent or try to go after a single department, try the previous suggestions to get everyone on the same page.

If, after you do this, you still see overemphasis in key areas, here are some specific ways to address it.

To avoid overemphasizing profit at the expense of customers:

- Make a practice of taking senior leaders, including the CFO, to meet your customers. (Most executives meet only with other executives; distinguish yourself by exposing your leadership to actual users.)
- Put your NSP in your annual report, right beside your financials.
- Discuss your NSP at board meetings.
- Include purpose metrics in your scorecard.

To avoid creating process-improvement silos:

- Take cross-departmental leaders to customer meetings.
- Get customer feedback before you make system changes.
- Pair your internal process team with their counterparts in the customer's world.

To avoid creating products that don't matter to customers:

- Have product development teams spend a day in the life of your customers.
- List concrete ways that products will impact the customer before you approve them.
- Include customer impact stories in all product launches.

To avoid engaging in promotional activities that don't positively affect customers:

- Create customer advisory groups (in person and/or virtual).
- Spend more time talking about customers than talking about competitors.
- Choose customer events over industry events.

To avoid ineffective people development:

- Announce your NSP at the start of every training meeting or session.
- Ask each person to identify how improving his or her skills will help them activate your NSP and have an impact on customers.
- Make NSP stories part of new hire training and executive onboarding.

As you look at these lists, think about the priorities and initiatives inside your organization. How do they stack up when you run them through the filter of your purpose? Are they advancing your purpose? Are they the best ways to spend your time, money, and mental effort? Asking these questions may cull or shift your list of projects. The Atlantic Capital Bank team you read about in Chapter 21 uses their NSP—*We fuel prosperity*—as a litmus test for projects. Asking how projects will fuel their client's prosperity helped them cull lower-value projects and put their resources into projects that would deliver a high impact to their customers and brand.

Pointing people toward a shared purpose helps your team calm down about the minor things and get excited about the major things. When people understand the big picture, the natural tension between roles becomes creative energy. It's a force that enables you to make good financial decisions and point your entire organization in the direction of customers.

Nobody feels proud of building a fiefdom; people would rather be part of something more meaningful. As a sales leader, you have the opportunity to remind your peers in other departments about the impact they have on customers. Your colleagues want their work to matter just as much as you do. You can be the one who shows them why it does.

The internal conversation will always become the external conversation. Your NSP need not be confined to sales; it's a powerful tool that you can use to get your entire organization pointed in the right direction.

Chapter 22: How to Keep Your NSP from Dying in Accounting

Purpose binds the team together in service of making a difference to customers. Without purpose, functional areas default to their own metrics. Finance defaults to money, HR to people, Sales to promotion, Ops to process, and Product to features and function.

This is not the best endgame. Each of these should be viewed through the lens of client impact.

Silos can turn into turf wars, with the loudest voice prevailing. The Six-P model ensures that customer impact is at the fore of every conversation.

Use the lens of customer impact to assess, prioritize, and evaluate projects.

Do one thing: Think about a looming process renovation project, identify the impact it will have on customers, and make that message the centerpiece of the project.

23

Build a Noble Purpose Culture (and Have More Fun at Work)

Culture eats strategy for breakfast.
—Peter Drucker, management consultant, educator, and author

Every tribe has a culture. Whether it's CrossFit, *Game of Thrones*, Scientology, or your family, there's a lingo, a set of shared beliefs, and governing principles, both spoken and unspoken.

Peter Drucker's original truism—"Culture eats strategy for breakfast"—is even more true today than it was 20 years ago. As increasingly autonomous employees work in increasingly matrixed organizations, your culture becomes the binding element: the glue that makes it all stick together.

This is a book about one thing—*getting your organization aligned, empowered, and laser-focused on making a difference to customers*—so I'll leave the conversations about foosball tables, parental leave, and org structures to other experts. Free lunches, nap pods, and flextime are great. The trend toward more a humane, transparent, inclusive, and supportive work world is long overdue.

But all the free smoothies and ping-pong tables in the world won't create competitive differentiation if your culture isn't pointed toward customer impact. Many of the culture-building programs we see today focus on the circumstances and peripherals of work rather than the work itself. It's as if by making the conditions better, somehow soul-sucking work can become more palatable.

The data tells us that over half the workforce is disengaged. *Harvard Business Review* also reports that 9 out of 10 people are willing to earn less money to do more meaningful work. In tough times, people are grateful for a paycheck. But that doesn't mean they're fully engaged. People want more than security: they want to be part of something bigger than themselves.

It's not work itself that erodes our spirit; it's meaningless work.

At the end of the day, your culture should stand for *something*. If you want to win the market and create a shared belief that your team can rally around, your *something* should be the impact you're having on customers and, in turn, the larger world.

We've talked about strategy and sales behavior; culture is the third part of the purpose trinity that drives differentiation and engagement. Your NSP is the binding agent that brings it all together.

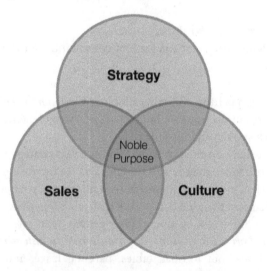

STRATEGY points your organization toward your Noble Purpose.

The **SALES** ecosystem and behaviors activate your NSP with customers.

CULTURE builds belief and reinforces your Noble Purpose with your team.

The reason I save culture for the end of the book is that every single thing we've done so far contributes to your culture. Naming and claiming your Noble Sales Purpose, aligning your sales ecosystem, activating your purpose with customers, and teaching your sales team the right behaviors create a force field of energy. These culture-builders give your team something concrete to attach themselves to.

Your culture is both visible and invisible, consisting of the seen and the unseen. The actions I've described so far are highly visible. They also have an impact on the less visible beliefs and emotional undercurrents swirling around your organization.

Here are some truths about culture:

- If you don't create your culture by design, you will get one by default.
- An organization's culture becomes more visible and obvious during times of change and volatility.
- A traditional business ecosystem and metrics are defaults that point your team inward toward your own financial targets.
- These traditional defaults create a transactional culture that is more likely to:
  - Be less emotionally engaging
  - Create silos
  - Be undercut by the competition for customers and talent
  - Stifle innovation
  - Be self-protective and unprepared to handle disruption
- If you want to create a Noble Purpose culture—where customer impact is prioritized—*you must be intentional about cascading belief and meaning.*

Cascading Meaning

You'll notice I don't mention goals here. Leaders have long been told that clear, cascading goals are the secret of high performance. Yet we're seeing increasing evidence to the contrary.

In their compelling book *Nine Lies About Work*, thought-leader Marcus Buckingham and Cisco Senior Vice President of Leadership and Team Development Ashley Goodall write, "Goals and cascading goals in particular appeal to many leaders who find themselves in search of ways to ensure efficient and aligned execution in their organizations. And, at the same time, it also remains true that for those of us in the trenches, our experience with goals feels non-intuitive, mechanical, fake, and even demeaning."

Corporate goals are rarely a grand vision about what's possible. They're usually just a smaller version of your boss's goals. Sales goals, in particular, are simply your portion of the company target. As Buckingham and Goodall say, "They can make you feel like a cog in a machine."

I'm not suggesting you abandon goals. If you're serious about your purpose, you have sales targets. I am suggesting you need more than traditional goals to build a culture of purpose.

Here are some places where you can be intentional about shaping your culture:

- **Language.** The CrossFit tribe likes to train in "boxes" (versus standard gyms) and knows "Ass to the Grass" means full-depth squats. The words you use on a daily basis are the centerpiece of your culture. A unique and intentional lingo makes your tribe feel special and differentiated. See Appendix B to start crafting your lexicon.

- **Artifacts.** Walk into a Starbucks, and then walk into a McDonald's. Do they feel different? How about your parents' home versus their neighbor's home? If you've ever sorted through a deceased family member's belongings, you know that what we choose to display and save tells others what we value. Be intentional about showcasing your Noble Purpose and your client impact in your space and with your artifacts.

- **Beliefs.** From "We the People" to the 10 Commandments to the counterculture values that bind together generations of Grateful Dead fans, being proactive about proclaiming and discussing your beliefs strengthens your culture and attracts more like minds to your tribe.

- **Daily practices.** Do your meetings start at 9 or 9ish? Is conflict okay, or should it always be avoided? The clearer and more specific you are about "how we do it here," the more your culture sticks.

- **Metrics.** What you measure and how you measure tells people what you value. For example, the Iroquois Nation's uses the seventh-generation metric saying, "In every deliberation, we must consider the impact on the seventh generation ... even if it requires having skin as thick as the bark of a pine." That tells the tribe, "This is our lens for success."

As you look at this list, notice that you don't have to be the CEO to start moving your culture in the right direction. If you're reading this as an HR person, you can tackle any or all of these within the scope of your role. And if you're a sales manager with a team of five, you can create your team's culture.

One of the most successful implementations of Noble Purpose in the world began with a small team. They were intentional about their language and behavior. They started to get results, and within 18 months, the Noble Purpose philosophy spread to include 18,000 people worldwide. You don't have to have formal authority to lead. You simply need to decide that you're going to start speaking and acting differently.

As Liz Wiseman, author of the book *Multipliers*, writes, "Building a culture is neither a one-time injection nor a sheep deep; it requires connection to the deep layers of the culture—it necessitates going from surface level cultural elements (such as shared language and behavior) to affect the deeper cultural elements such as (ritual and norms)."

Noble Purpose Culture-Builders

We've talked about the substantial things that will point your team toward your Noble Purpose. Here are some smaller things you can do immediately.

Noble Purpose culture-builders	
Language	• Host a book talk. • Share the Noble Purpose terms in Appendix B with your team. • Tell customer impact stories to start your meetings.
Artifacts	• Put pictures of your clients on the walls. • Create a belief book to share with your team and clients (ask them to help).
Belief	• Put your Noble Purpose on screensavers and stationery. • Discuss the questions in Appendix C, and ask your team how they impact clients.
Daily practices	• Write *How will the client be different as a result of doing business with us?* on the wall in your meeting room, and ask that question at critical points.
Metrics	• Measure and talk about client success, both formally and informally.

Good intentions are a great start, but you must go further. You want to build a culture of true believers. To do that, you need to be intentional about giving them something to stand for and reinforcing it every single day. Think about how many causes, charities, and churches start out with grand aspirations and wind up becoming a grind of infighting and turf wars. As Wiseman notes, "There is a short shelf life on inspiration without action."

It's not the lack of nobility in the purpose that causes organizations to get derailed; it's a lack of alignment around how to accomplish it and a slow erosion of good intentions. You want your culture to reflect the best intentions of your people.

Work is where people spend most of their waking hours. That work ought to mean something.

Making a difference to your customers might not seem like changing the world. But let me ask you:

- If you make your team's work more meaningful, how does that affect the way they show up for everything else in their lives?
- When you make your customers more successful, what might they be able to accomplish?
- If you set a new standard for your industry, how does that impact the world?

The way we work affects the way we live, and the way we live affects everything else in the world. Being a Noble Purpose leader is about getting better business results. It's also about creating a workplace that's worth showing up for.

Chapter 23: Build a Noble Purpose Culture (and Have More Fun at Work)

If you do not create your culture by design, you will end up with a culture by default.

Things like asking the game-changing question, bringing client impact to the fore of your meetings, and recruiting with an eye to purpose-driven talent lay the groundwork for a culture of Noble Purpose.

To sustain your culture, build Noble Purpose into your

- Language
- Artifacts
- Beliefs
- Daily practices
- Metrics

Do one thing: Your language is the easiest thing to adjust. Start telling a customer impact story on a regular basis to teammates who do not work with clients.

Conclusion:

Life on Purpose

Regret for the things we did can be tempered over time; it is regret for things we did not do that is inconsolable.

—Sydney J. Harris, journalist and author

After a recent speech, a man came up to me and said, "I like my job, but my wife is the one who has the real Noble Purpose. She's a preschool teacher." "What do you do?" I asked. He said, "I run a logistics team." He was the leader of more than 100 people.

Now, I love a good preschool teacher. If you've read most or even part of this book, you know that I frequently draw from parenting and family examples to illustrate human dynamics.

But let's do a little math here. A preschool teacher has 10 or 20 students a year. Their little minds are quite malleable, and toddlers are (mostly) a delight to engage with. However, this man was managing more than 100 people! His words, his moods, and his actions were affecting how 100 human beings spent their days. And every one of those people was taking their day home to their family and friends.

We often underestimate the power of our presence because we feel so pressed to deliver tangible results. Sometimes it's all you can do to make it through the day and get at least a few concrete tasks off your plate.

One of the key principles of this book is how the intangible becomes tangible. The qualitative things you do as a leader impact the quantitative results of your organization. But the truth is, the impact of your actions extends well beyond your business results. The way you show up as a leader at work impacts the way your team shows up for almost every single aspect of their lives.

The Second-Most-Important Person in the World

When I first became a manager, at the ripe age of 25, I called my dad to tell him I had finally gotten promoted. The backstory is, I'd been passed over for a previous promotion and was beginning to question whether company leadership thought I was management material. I wanted the promotion with every fiber of my being. I'd watched other people pass me by, and couldn't bear to have it happen again. Back then, when you got promoted to manager, you even got an *all-leather* company-issued briefcase. It was a public signal: "I'm in charge of something." I'd watched the people who carried briefcases ride up and down in the elevator, and oh, how I longed to become one of them.

The day I finally got the promotion and the briefcase, I called my dad, who gave me an insightful and somewhat scary reframe on my new accomplishment. He said, "Congratulations—you've just become the second-most important person in the lives of your team."

What?

He went on to say, "Beyond your spouse, your boss has the power to make your life miserable or make your life wonderful."

It scared me to death because I knew he was right. Part of me wanted to run into my boss's office, throw the briefcase at him, and leave the building forever. But I stayed, and I tried to hold up my end of the bargain. At 25, my leadership skills left much to be desired. But my dad certainly gave me a sobering and effective frame for starting the journey.

When you lead people, your voice is in their ears, whether you like it or not. Think about how often your parents talked about their bosses. You probably know about your friends' bosses. You likely remember your own first boss vividly. How often do you think about your current boss? Probably a lot. Much of the way we experience our job is a direct result of the way we experience our leader.

As I reflect on my own early experiences as a leader, I remember thinking, "Two of the people on my team don't have spouses or partners. Does that make me the *most* important person in their lives?" Oh good lord, it was almost too weighty to contemplate. Ideally, your people are grounded in rich lives that aren't entirely dependent on work for self-esteem or happiness. But let's be honest here. Work is where we spend most of our time, and we're socialized to believe work status equals life status.

I've given you all the business reasons why having a Noble Purpose bigger than money makes you more successful. Now let's talk about the personal reason. *Your life is more than a revenue number, and that applies to everyone else as well. The more deeply you understand this, the more impactful your life will be.*

We often forget one simple human truth: you weren't put on this earth simply to make and produce money. No one is. Yes, you need money to live your life. Financially prosperous people and organizations can create more peace and happiness for the world than organizations without resources.

But when your work life becomes transactional, it's easy for the rest of your life to become transactional as well. You coarsen yourself, and it has a ripple effect on the people around you. We've been schooled to believe that our work should produce results for us. But when we flip it and say instead *our work should have an impact on others*, we transform the way we experience ourselves and our organizations.

I've often used the phrase *you can do better* in this book. I'd like to clarify what I mean by *better*. You can almost always get better financial results, and those are beneficial. But *better* is also about the way you experience your life and the story you carry in your heart about why you're here. Reframing yourself in the service of a larger purpose has a profound impact on every endeavor. It makes you a better leader and a more resilient person. Living your life with more purpose calls for deeper reflection, and it creates deeper connections to yourself and others.

Making the Mundane Meaningful

When you decide you have a larger purpose, you're more likely to show up as your best self. Doing better becomes an imperative. I've come to understand that *our mental frame is everything*. The way we look at the world becomes how we experience the world. Our mental frame is the driving force for much of our happiness and also much of our despair. When you change your mental frame, you point yourself in a different direction. You're no longer at the whim of the systems around you; instead, you become an agent of change.

Your mental frame is how you bring meaning to the mundane.

Let's face it: life is not always going to be peak moments. The moments when you win the big deal, when your customer says you changed their world, or when you look across the table and realize you have created a happy family—those are peak, memorable moments of your life.

A full life is also built around the smaller moments. When you find yourself in everyday moments and see *those* moments in the context of a larger purpose, when you see the impact that you can have, then everything becomes bigger and brighter.

Whether it's imagining that your new hires are future CEOs or envisioning your clients creating the next technology breakthrough, when you frame your efforts in the context of a bigger Noble Purpose, your work and life have more meaning.

Your Self-Story Becomes Your Life Story

I'd like to put forth a bold idea for you. When we change the way our work works, we change the way the world works. Business is crossing international borders, race lines, political parties, class distinctions, and all the other ways we have been divided. When we come together in a work setting, it enables us to see how we can come together in other settings as well. Unlocking the power of empathy at work has a transcendent effect on other areas. When we decide that our role is to step into caring about outcomes for other people, we change ourselves, we change our organizations, and we change the cultural landscape that impacts us all.

This conclusion is called *Life on Purpose* because that is my hope for you—that you see the purpose of your larger life, and you experience more meaning in your daily interactions.

The core of living a life on purpose is about the story you tell yourself about why you're here and what you're worth. Your self-story is the central guiding belief of your life. You *are* the belief-builder, and the most important belief to build is your own. You get to decide what you believe about yourself and your place in this world. When you decide that your life is going to be more than just some transactional "going through the motions" event, your soul takes notice.

You're only getting one turn at this life. You deserve to know that your work and your life count for something. You owe it to yourself and the people around you to bring your best self to your most important endeavors.

Your life is a wild and precious gift. And you have complete choice about how you manage it.

So find your purpose, and start living your life like it counts for something, because it does. It counts for something big. When you decide to show up with your heart and soul for the things that matter to you, your whole world expands. When you decide that you matter and you are here to make a difference, you step into living your real life—one that may be bigger than you can ever possibly dream.

Techniques and Tools

The Noble Purpose Shift

Traditional sellers	Noble Purpose sellers
Focus on quota	Focus on customer
Think product first, customer second	Think customer first, product second
How can I sell my product to this customer?	How would this customer be helped by my product?
Stress product features	Stress customer impact
Repeat generic pitch	Tailor presentation to customers
Quickly jump to price	Articulate impact on customers
Annoyingly aggressive	Assertive for customer benefit
View customer as an object to achieve quota	View customer as an opportunity to make a difference

Implementing Noble Purpose in Your Organization

Ready to get started implementing selling with Noble Purpose? Try approaching your game plan in four steps:

1. **Name and claim your Noble Sales Purpose.** Give yourself and your team a rallying cry that points your organization toward customer impact.

2. **Align your ecosystem.** Identify and adjust the pivotal processes and systems, making sure the ecosystem around your team points them toward the customer. This includes things like adding the five categories of critical customer information (listed shortly) in your CRM system; incentivizing long-term, deep customer relationships; and telling client impact stories in town halls.

3. **Arm your belief builders.** Train your managers in telling customer impact stories, coaching with a purpose-driven mindset, and asking the game-changing question—"How will this customer be different as a result of doing business with us?"—in deal reviews.

4. **Train your sales team.** Give your sellers the tools to be successful with customers in purpose-driven conversations, such as interactive sales aids, the "you-me-you" technique (described in a moment), and questions that uncover their buyers' biggest goals and challenges.

Need help? Check out the tools on our website: www.mcleodandmore .com. We also work directly with sales-driven organizations to activate a culture of purpose in the cadence of daily business. Give us a shout!

The Three Discovery Questions

To tap into your own sense of Noble Purpose, answer the three discovery questions and discuss them with your team:

1. How do you make a difference to your customers?
2. How are you different from your competitors?
3. On your best day, what do you love about your job?

Customer Impact Stories

You can tell customer impact stories internally to ignite emotional engagement. You can also tell customer impact stories to prospects and customers. Here are some guidelines for creating a customer impact story:

- It's true.
- It's short. You should be able to tell the story in less than two minutes, which is about 300 words or less.

- It describes the impact on the customer. A good NSP story doesn't stop at the event; it describes the impact. The twins came home; the parents felt safe. You want your team to think about whom the events affected and the implications for their businesses and lives.

- It includes vivid details. Descriptions such as "six inches of water in the basement, mold, and mildew" add energy and drama to the story.

- It touches emotions. A good NSP story is about human beings whose lives were changed in some way. Emotional words such as *frustrated, angry, delighted,* and *thrilled* add energy to the story.

- It supports your NSP. The story's value and purpose is not to merely entertain; it is to authenticate your NSP.

The Five Categories of Critical Customer Information

Environment

This will help you understand how your contact relates to the organization as a whole and how the organization is positioned within the context of its marketplace. You want to know things such as:

- What's your contact's core function or role?
- What's going on in his or her organization or life?
- Who is the competition, and how do they stack up?
- What is the customer's position in their marketplace?
- What's happening politically inside the organization?

Goals

You want to find out what your contact's objectives are, as well as those of his or her department and the overall organization. The types of things you want to know are:

- What does your contact need to accomplish?
- How is your contact evaluated?

- What does senior leadership believe is most important?
- What measurements does the customer have in place?
- Where does the customer stand with their goals to date?

Challenges

This area is where you want to find out more about problems and issues that concern both your contact and his or her boss. You want to know things such as:

- What are they worried about?
- What obstacles do they face?
- What are the competitive threats inside and outside the company?
- What resources do they have, and where do they need more?

What Success Looks Like

You'll want to know what an organizational or personal win means for this customer, specifically:

- What is your customer passionate about?
- What does your contact's boss care about most?
- How does your contact define and measure success?
- How will your contact know when he or she has achieved success?
- How does your contact's boss define and measure success?
- How does their organization define and measure success?

What Lack of Success Looks Like

This area is where you want to find out about the potential risks your customer is facing and what their senior leadership is concerned about. You'll want to know:

- What are they afraid of?
- What will happen to the organization if they fail?
- What are the consequences for your contact?

The You-Me-You Call Opening

To engage with customers as a Noble Purpose seller, you need to demonstrate your expertise *and* get the customer talking. Try this opening technique in your next customer conversation:

- Start with a business topic of interest to the customer—that's the "you" part. Do your research, and find something relevant. For example, if you're a technology company calling a retailer and you've read an article about online ordering, you might say something about how technology has changed the entire customer experience.
- Give a brief statement about your expertise, such as "We help retailers better engage customers."
- Ask a question such as "What kind of customer experiences are you trying to create?" Now the conversation is about their business, in an area you can impact.

The 10-Second Game-Changer

To reset yourself before or after a customer conversation, try this three-part technique:

1. **Breathe.** This gets oxygen to your brain and more blood flowing through your body.
2. **Think.** "This is about the customer's agenda and my agenda. I have a plan, and I'm flexible. I'm confident enough to sit with uncertainty."
3. **Believe.** I'm here to help this customer ... (your NSP).

The Game-Changing Question

There is a single question a sales leader can ask to increase the emotional engagement of the rep and build a competitively differentiated story: "How will this customer be different as a result of doing business with us?"

The Six CEO Moments of Purpose

1. **Town halls.** Nothing is more powerful than the CEO standing onstage, telling a customer impact story. If he or she doesn't have one, find one, and brief them on it. When the CEO says, "Here's how we make a difference to our customers: this is why we exist," it speaks volumes.

2. **Earnings calls.** CEOs who frame their financial results around the organization's purpose signal to investors, "We're a purpose-driven firm focused on customers." When the CEO says, "Our Noble Purpose is X," it creates a public record. This is very good for your brand.

3. **Executive team meetings.** One CEO we know reads her company's NSP at the start of the monthly executive team meeting. She says, "It's like the bell at school or the gong at church, it calls people into the space and reminds us why we're here."

4. **Strategy and budget sessions.** When the boss asks how this choice will impact our purpose, you change the frame. New initiatives should further your purpose, and budgeting should be done with an eye toward customer impact.

5. **One-on-one updates.** When the CEO asks, "How is your team delivering on our purpose?" it helps non-customer-facing teams connect the dots.

6. **Casual hallway conversations.** It's awkward to run into the CEO. People get nervous. Make it easy and fun. One of our CEO clients loves to say, "Another day of changing lives! Got any good stories for me?" His team may roll their eyes in jest, but they sure know what's important to him.

Glossary

The words of the leader shape your culture. If you're trying to shift your organization from transactional to Noble Purpose, start using the following terms liberally. These words will animate your Noble Purpose and shift the organizational conversation. While these terms are not unique to Noble Purpose, we'll provide some guidance on how to apply them to this philosophy.

Belief-builder: The role of team leaders (formal and informal) who remind everyone of the nobility of the work and the impact you have on customers. Belief is central to creating a high-performance organization.

Company culture: The internal beliefs, norms, rituals, and daily practices that make your organization what it is. If you don't have a culture by design, you'll get one by default. Make sure you're building a culture of purpose by keeping customer impact front and center.

Competitive differentiation: The factual and emotional ways you set yourself apart from the competition. Most people think of competitive differentiation as an extra feature: slightly lower pricing, more flexible terms, etc. But true competitive differentiation goes beyond the spec sheet. To help your organization stand out, be declarative, internally and externally, about the impact you're having and your purpose for being.

Customer advocate: Customers who are emotionally engaged in supporting you. Customer advocate takes customer satisfaction one step further. When you have customer advocates, your customers can't wait to publically sing your praises. More customer advocates results in stickier deals, more referrals, and increasing competitive differentiation.

Customer churn: When paying customers leave. Organizations who are commoditized experience high customer churn, meaning their customers frequently leave them. You want to avoid this costly trap by creating competitive differentiation and emotional engagement with your team and customers. That's the sticky sauce that makes your organization *irresistible*.

Customer impact: The factual and emotive ways you make a difference to customers. This is the North Star of an organization with a Noble Purpose; the root of your NSP. Customer impact is the reason your organization exists.

Customer impact story: A short, emotionally engaging story about how your product/solution or service made a difference to a customer. It includes vivid details and specificity about how the customer was impacted by your work. These stories are used in meetings and coaching sessions to build belief, with customers as proof points.

Customer intelligence: The information you know about your customer. This should go deeper than purchase requirements. NSP customer intelligence means you've clearly articulated the impact you will have on a person or business.

Disengagement: People who show up at work with their bodies but leave their minds and hearts at homes. While this is often blamed on the employees, people are often disengaged because leadership has not given them anything meaningful to believe in.

Emotional engagement: People who believe in a cause bigger than themselves and are internally driven. When teammates and customers are emotionally engaged in their work, their frontal lobes light up, commitment increases, and they become physically stronger and more creative.

External conversation: The conversation you're having with your industry, the market, and your customers. Remember, the internal conversation (the conversation inside your company) always becomes the external conversation. The best place to start changing the external conversation is inside, with your team.

Framing: The mental model you apply to something. Think about a picture frame: framing is what surrounds a task, a fact, or an opinion. For example, a mental framing on customer impact can make a task like filling out paperwork move from tedious to crucial for customer success.

Incentive: Monetary, nonmonetary, and social motivators. Remember, sales incentives don't always have to be monetary. You should pay your team fairly for their contribution, but more qualitative incentives, like public recognition and customer impact, can dramatically up your level of engagement.

Internal conversation: The conversation you have inside your company. Remember, the internal conversation *always* becomes the external conversation. If numbers and deliverables are all you talk about internally (forgetting impact), that's all your team will talk about externally.

Mindset: The mental model you show up with. Our mindsets are what guide our behavior. We all have our own mindsets, but they're malleable. In your team, you want to work toward creating a mindset that is focused on the nobility of customer impact.

Mission: How you execute your Noble Purpose.

Naysayer: A person who wants nothing to do with the new philosophy you're bringing. In fact, this person might be outright negative. Don't assume bad intent. Purpose is new to a lot of people. Meet them where they are, and don't let them take away your mojo.

Noble Sales Purpose (NSP): A definitive statement about how you make a difference in the lives of your customers. It speaks to why you're in business in the first place. Used correctly, your NSP drives every decision you make and every action you take. It becomes the foundation for all your sales activities.

Onboarding: The critical moments when new employees are learning, "What does it mean to work here?" When you animate these moments with purpose, you jump-start emotional engagement and frame the entire employee experience going forward.

Passion: The feeling of excitement you have for a project or organization. Passion is great, but purpose has a greater ability to sustain momentum because it is shared and more steadfast than passion.

Sales tools: The tools you arm your sellers with, to engage with customers. Push yourself to be more creative than brochures or slick sheets. Sales tools should start a conversation, not be a one-way pitch.

Shareholder primacy: An ineffective model that puts shareholders at the core of business strategies and operations. Shareholder results are a lagging indicator. Instead, put purpose at the center of your organization. This leading indicator generates engagement, differentiation, and customer advocacy.

Sticky ideas: Concepts, skills, and stories that your team internalizes. They "stick" to the team's frontal lobes, and reps are able to carry them from one situation to the next.

Sticky revenue: Revenue that comes to you easily because of your reputation. It requires very little work or marketing investment. Deals that renew every year, customers who give referrals, and single-source contracts are evidence that you are living your Noble Purpose.

True believers: The people in your organization who have absolute clarity about how you make a difference to customers and who know deep in their hearts that your work matters. Hold on to these people for dear life and put them in front of the team whenever you can.

Vision: How you see the world when you've fulfilled your purpose.

APPENDIX

C

Frequently Asked Questions

After working in this space for a decade, we find that many leaders have similar questions. Here are the questions we encounter most frequently.

Q: If we don't sell something exciting, do we still have a Noble Sales Purpose?

A: If customers are buying from you, they're getting some value. It may be a matter of connecting the dots to the impact of your solution. For example:

- Air compressors for trains "keep people safe."
- IT services "Make businesses more successful."
- Financial services "Safeguard money and fuel prosperity."

Or maybe the way you do business is changing their perceptions of an entire profession, like Supportworks, who are redefining their industry. If you're not sure, ask your customers why they keep buying from you.

Q: Should I even try to hand this book to my transactional boss?

A: Yes—drop it and run. Don't over-explain. Simply say, "I think this can help us be more competitive," and leave. Let the book work for you; it's written to help people self-discover. As I often say, we don't know what's in people's hearts unless they tell us. You might be surprised. Some of the leaders people thought were the most transactional have wound up being the biggest champions of NSP.

Q: How long does it take to get results?

A: One day and 12 months. Here's what we've observed after implementing Noble Purpose with over 200 firms. When you announce your Noble Purpose, it creates new energy on Day 1. If you're a large organization, it typically it takes about 12 months to shift your culture. In the organizations we work with, we see early wins when people start asking different questions in deal reviews and framing customer presentations differently: they close more business. These wins create momentum: when leaders lift up these bright spots, the culture moves faster. The secret to fast results is to focus on the early wins and not get trapped in the slog. Do the easiest things first, and use them to create momentum.

Q: My team is mired in price wars. How do we get out of them?

A: The answer is probably slowly at first and then faster. The first thing you want to do is name and claim your Noble Sales Purpose. Then, create the stories that prove your purpose. Now you have something new to tell the market. Start new prospects using the Noble Purpose model. Then go back to existing customers, share your new story, and ask, "Have you experienced this?" Get existing customers to spell out the value they're getting from you *before* it's time to renew. This puts you in a stronger position.

Q: Do I need to get higher-ups on board to get started?

A: The short answer is no. One of our most successful clients, a global firm of 18,000 employees, started on their Noble Purpose journey when one manager had a book discussion with her team. They embraced the philosophy and started implementing the models, and they began to get results. Their team became more enthused, and customers became more engaged. Eventually, the results spoke for themselves.

We've observed that when the words in your Noble Purpose are "sticky," people grab them and quickly start talking about them. Although the process takes time, people usually get a few early wins to fuel them for the next step. Don't wait until senior leadership is on board. Start within the realm of your own influence.

Q: How do I introduce this to my team?

A: Give them this book, and show them some of the videos on our website (www.mcleodandmore.com). Our goal is to scale this movement, so we've worked to make it easy for people to spread the word. The language in our articles, the way this book is written, and all the specific tips are designed to help you scale quickly. Walk your team through this book, do one chapter each week, and implement the "Do one thing" tips in the summary boxes at the end of each chapter.

Q: What if my competition has already announced their Noble Purpose?

A: Be different, and be better. A lot of firms are starting to proclaim their Noble Purpose. A few decades ago, organizations began using mission and vision. Some organizations leveraged these concepts to build breakthrough results; for others, they were meaningless words. The same thing is happening with Noble Purpose. The organizations who win will be the ones who successfully activate their Noble Purpose with customers. Look at where your competition is missing the mark. Does it provide an opening? Read Chapter 7 about the Mars versus Purina purpose battle. Winning your space is about the decisions you make and your ability to implement.

Q: What if we already have a mission, vision, or purpose statement? Do I need to redo it?

A: If it's good, keep it. If it's long and boring, look within it to see if there is any client impact–oriented language you can pull from. Read Chapter 6 for examples of powerful, clear language. If nothing in your current statements speaks to client impact, you can create a nested NSP to sit underneath it.

Q: Can everyone become a Noble Purpose seller, or are some people naturally transactional?

A: Yes, some people are naturally transactional; in fact, *most* people are naturally transactional. In our experience, it's not because people want to be that way, it's because traditionally run organizations point them that way, and they haven't learned a different model. Don't assume the worst. If you share the content, name and claim your purpose, follow the tips and models, and train your team, the majority of people will make the shift. Having said that, you may have some people who can't step into the new model. Being clear about your intentions and expectations will help these people self-select out earlier in the process. This is a good thing. It's cheaper and easier than fighting against them. As we say, play to the top of the room, and challenge the rest of the team to get there.

Q: I have a churn-and-burn call center. Can I still do Noble Purpose?

A: Yes. You need to make it simple and easy. Be crystal clear about the impact your solution has on the ultimate customers. Follow Adam Grant's call center example described in Chapter 4. Tell the team stories about whom the sales will impact before they get on the phones, and put pictures of customers up around your space. One of our clients, G Adventures (profiled in Chapter 2), has a big screen that flashes clients' stories and faces in the middle of their call centers. Tell weekly or daily customer impact stories. And help your team deal with rejection by showcasing wins every single day.

Q: This is great for top performers, but what about the lower tier?

A: This is a model to help the rest of your team think and act like top-tier salespeople. When you share it with your team, make that clear. Share the mindsets of top performers, and ask, "How can we all cultivate this?" You can do this without shame or blame. Remember, people do not need to accurately self-assess in order to improve. Meet people where they are, and start by implementing the first section. Change the leadership language and coaching, and lower-level performers will shift. The caveat is, don't overinvest in the problem people. Your best time is spent helping the top get better and the middle move toward the top.

Q: What if all this talk about Noble Purpose makes me hate where I work?

A: Candidly, if you don't think you can change the work situation, and you have honestly tried your best, you need to leave. Find somewhere that speaks to your sense of purpose. As my father always said, "If you're unhappy with them, you need to go, because it's only a matter of time before they're unhappy with you."

Q: What if I'm not sure I can do this?

A: Just start; you don't have to be perfect. The language is sticky, and the concepts work. If you get 50% of it right, things will start to move. Your authenticity as a leader is the most important thing.

Q: Is there a workshop I can do to help my team adopt selling with Noble Purpose?

A: Yes. We offer leadership, coaching, and sales workshops for all levels, both onsite and virtually. We have a team of trainers, and we also certify internal trainers. Go to our website (www.mcleodandmore.com) for more information. We're creating a movement, and we mean it when we say we would love to help you.

Acknowledgments

In this book, we've written about how Noble Purpose is empowering and puts you into a space of gratitude. We offer our heartfelt gratitude to the people who empowered us. First and foremost, we thank our clients, those wonderful people who joined us on this journey and who decided their organizations were going to stand for something bigger than just a cash register. We are truly blessed to be able to work with some of the most amazing high-performing teams on the planet.

I (Lisa) want to thank three important men who were backstage during the original creation of this book. My husband and business partner, Bob McLeod, did background research and handled daily operations so I could write. You are truly a partner in every sense of the word. And positioning expert Mark Levy was instrumental in the first edition of *Selling with Noble Purpose* by helping bring my highest aspirations into sharp focus, and also gave great counsel for this current version.

Finally, I want to thank my dad, Jay Earle, whose voice I still hear in my head whenever I face a professional challenge. I dedicated this book to my father because he gave me a unique gift: he set the expectation that work can, and should, be fun and that it should matter.

Together, we want to thank:

The clients who graciously agreed to share their stories, quotes, and examples in this book: Atlantic Capital Bank, Blackbaud, CMIT, Dave & Buster's, Fiserv, G Adventures, Graham-White, Hootsuite, LinkedIn, Orange County Courts, Roche, Salesforce, SalesLoft,

Servus Credit Union, and Supportworks.

The thought leaders whose work provided valuable insights: Marc Benioff, Dr. Brené Brown, Marcus Buckingham, Jim Collins, Dr. Valerie Good, Nancy Duarte, Ashley Goodall, Adam Grant, Professor Morten Hansen, Chip and Dan Heath, Dr. Yuval Noah Harari, Steve Johnson, Dan Pink, Jim Stengel, Roy Spence, Jeff Stier, and Liz Wiseman.

Our creative team: Drew Lamont for the graphics that punch up the book, Jon Rizzo for our photos and videos, and Dave Whitlock for his unfailing web support.

The team at John Wiley & Sons, Inc.: Matt Holt, who loved the concept from the start; and Peter Knox, Lynn Northrup, Tiffany Taylor, Zach Schisgal, and Shannon Vargo, who helped bring this book to life.

Our always-supportive band of coaches and colleagues: Robbie Kellman Baxter, Chip Bell, Dorie Clark, Scott Edinger, Steven Gaffney, Seth Kahan, Amanda Setili, Libby Wagner, and Alan Weiss, who have all helped shape and support this work.

About the Authors

Lisa Earle McLeod is a bestselling author and executive advisor who teaches leaders around the world. Her work has been featured in *The Wall Street Journal*, *Forbes*, and *Fortune*. She is widely credited with bringing the concept of Noble Purpose into business vernacular. Lisa is the author of five books and a popular keynote speaker who has spoken in over 25 countries. Her firm, McLeod & More, Inc., is dedicated to helping leaders drive revenue and do work that makes them proud.

Elizabeth Lotardo is a researcher and consultant who helps leaders translate purpose and strategy into training, processes, and a compelling organizational narrative. She is a popular LinkedIn Learning author, and her work has been featured in *The Wall Street Journal* and on NPR. She has an undergraduate education in advertising from Boston University and a master's degree in industrial and organizational psychology.

McLeod & More, Inc. is a sales strategy and leadership firm that provides live and virtual consulting, coaching, keynotes, and workshops. Learn more at www.mcleodandmore.com.

Index